WITHDRAWN FROM LIBRARY

Rebel Writer ~

Rebel Writer

Mary Wollstonecraft and Enlightenment Politics

WENDY GUNTHER-CANADA

NORTHERN ILLINOIS UNIVERSITY PRESS   DeKalb

© 2001 by Northern Illinois University Press

Published by the Northern Illinois University Press, DeKalb, Illinois 60115

Manufactured in the United States using acid-free paper

All Rights Reserved

Design by Julia Fauci

Library of Congress Cataloging-in-Publication Data

Gunther-Canada, Wendy

Rebel writer : Mary Wollstonecraft and Enlightenment politics / Wendy Gunther-Canada.

p. cm.

Includes bibliographical references and index.

ISBN 0-87580-280-X (alk. paper)

1. Wollstonecraft, Mary, 1759–1797—Contributions in political science.

2. Wollstonecraft, Mary, 1759–1797—Contributions in feminism.

3. Wollstonecraft, Mary, 1759–1797—Contributions in women's rights. I. Title.

JC176.W65 G86 2001

323.3'4'092--dc21

2001018319

For Milly and Lily Cate

"Sweet Joy Befall Thee"

Contents

Acknowledgments ix

Introduction: At War with the Words 3

1 Political Theory and the Female Reader 13

2 A Voice from the Void 40

3 The Rebel Writer and the Rights of Men 71

4 The Feminist Author and Women's Rights 97

5 Writing the Wrongs of Politics 126

Conclusion: Reading Wollstonecraft 155

Notes 173

Bibliography 191

Index 197

Acknowledgments

Mary Wollstonecraft wrote both *A Vindication of the Rights of Men* and *A Vindication of the Rights of Woman* within a matter of weeks. This study of her feminist political theory has taken me considerably longer than that. In the process I have incurred a number of intellectual debts, which it is my pleasure to acknowledge in full.

As a student of intellectual history I have been gifted with many fine teachers who became models of the academic life for me. Even now I can see Harold Bauman surveying the expansive library in his office at the University of Utah and remarking that among his books he was surrounded by friends. In graduate school I had the good fortune to be befriended by a number of remarkable scholars who inspired me as I completed my graduate studies at Rutgers University. First among them was Benjamin R. Barber, who encouraged me to focus my doctoral research on Mary Wollstonecraft. I remember one late lunch at the student center when this democratic theorist dramatically threw down the introductory chapter to my dissertation and said "this is a book." It took a while, but today those ideas, carefully nurtured, have bloomed into the present study. I would never have finished my doctoral program without the strong support of Linda Zerilli and Susan Carroll. These women introduced me to the world of feminist scholarship, past and present, and helped me feel at home in the sometimes chilly halls of academe. They opened doors for me and their other graduate students at Rutgers, inviting us into both their classrooms and their homes. It was through these doorways that I began to envision myself as a colleague within the field of political science. Finally, I must thank Gordon Schochet, whose work on political rights in the seventeenth century helped me clarify what issues were at stake in the rights debates of the late eighteenth century. His love of the American West created a unique bond between us that did wonders toward dispelling my homesickness. I experienced a special type of grace in being able to work so closely with these energetic teachers. Their images are before me when I enter my classroom, as well as when I leave a research library.

This project owes much to the steady support of my colleagues at the University of Alabama at Birmingham. In the Department of Government and Public Service I have appreciated the collegiality of Steven Haeberle, Bobby Wilson, Mary Ellen Guy, Steven Daniels, Beverly Hawk, and the late Voytek Zubek. Earlier drafts of the following chapters were the subject of healthy criticism and spirited discussion among faculty members within the School of Social and Behavioral Sciences. My gratitude goes to Carolyn Conley, George Liber, Eileen VanSchaik, Colin Davis, Tom McKenna, and Mike McConnell. I have also relied upon Laura van Assendelft of Mary Baldwin College, Francis Moran of New Jersey City University, and Theresa Kemp of the University of Wisconsin–Eau Claire for friendship and footnotes. Weekly interaction with my students has been a constant stimulus that has kept ideas alive and kicking. I am grateful to Linda Patterson, Cecelia Womack, Gene McCall, Laura Peers Barnes, Mark Melanson, Catina Passmore, and Mary Connor.

Over the years my primary research has been supported by generous grants from the Graduate School of the University of Alabama at Birmingham, which have enabled me to travel to archives in the United States and England. While engaged in research, I have been aided by some devoted archivists, especially Doucet Devin Fischer and Daniel Dibbern of the Carl H. Pforzheimer Collection of Shelley and His Circle at the New York Public Library. On my intellectual journey I have not been a solitary walker like Jean-Jacques Rousseau; rather, following in the footsteps of Mary Wollstonecraft, my ideas have benefited from being shared with a vibrant intellectual community. Along the way I have been motivated by the Wollstonecraft scholars who have gone before me. Chief among them is Carol Poston, whose Norton Critical Edition of *A Vindication of the Rights of Woman* brought Wollstonecraft's words to a popular audience of female readers like myself. I could not have engaged in this extended project of tracing the historical development of Wollstonecraft's ideas without the seven-volume scholarly collection *The Works of Mary Wollstonecraft,* edited by Marilyn Butler and Janet Todd. I hope that my efforts extend the pioneering research of Virginia Sapiro, who first challenged political theorists to examine Wollstonecraft's contribution to the conversation of political thought. Lastly, I acknowledge the importance of Gary Kelly's analysis of Wollstonecraft and other women writers on politics to my exploration of gender and political rights. I am truly grateful for the critical insight and the good humor of my fellow travelers.

My current scholarship owes much to the senior scholars who helped me to develop, polish, and publish earlier versions of my analysis of Wollstonecraft's political theory. Some of the ideas that form the basis of chapter 3 first appeared in print as "The Politics of Sense and Sensibility: Mary Wollstonecraft and Catharine Macaulay on Edmund Burke's *Reflections on the Revolution in France*," within Hilda Smith's edited volume, *Women Writers and the Early Modern British Political Tradition*, published by Cambridge University Press (1998). An early version of chapter 4 appeared as "Mary Wollstonecraft's 'Wild Wish': Confounding Sex in the Discourse on Political Rights," in *Feminist Interpretations of Mary Wollstonecraft*, edited by Maria Falco and published by Penn State University Press (University Park, Penn.): 61–83, copyright 1996 Penn State University Press. I am grateful for permission to use this material here.

I want to acknowledge the enthusiastic support of Martin Johnson, acquisitions editor at the Northern Illinois University Press. His cheerful stewardship assisted me as the manuscript made its way through the review process within the press. In the spirit of thanksgiving, let me express my appreciation to the two anonymous readers who reviewed an earlier draft of the manuscript. Their careful reading and cogent comments helped me to craft a stronger argument and deliver a better book to the press. I am humbled by their generous remarks and their thoughtful criticism. With such gracious and gentle readers I admit that any errors that remain within the text are solely my own.

The last word of thanks goes to my family. I am grateful to my parents, Donald and Milly Gunther, for encouraging my scholarship in every way possible. My sister, Janiel Gunther, and I have had many a laugh about teaching, publishing, and our family. Shelley Hill Worthen has long been a sister in spirit, and her good spirits have sustained my own on difficult days. I owe to my partner, K---- C-----, a debt that I can never repay—a cherished shared life of intellectual inquiry. It is my greatest joy that we can share this life with our daughter, Lily Cate, who comes into a world made more just by the efforts of Mary Wollstonecraft to vindicate her sex.

Rebel Writer ~

Alas! A woman that attempts the pen,
Such an intruder on the rights of men.

—Anne Finch,
Countess of Winchilsea

INTRODUCTION

At War with the Words

> The preponderance of inconsistencies, when weighed with precedents, should lessen the most bigoted veneration for antiquity, and force men of the eighteenth century to acknowledge, that our canonized forefathers were unable, or afraid, to revert to reason, without resting on the crutch of authority; and should not be brought as a proof that their children are never to be allowed to walk alone.
>
> —Mary Wollstonecraft,
> *A Vindication of the Rights of Men*

Was Mary Wollstonecraft a political theorist? If we answer yes, then the question becomes whether we should include her writings alongside Jean-Jacques Rousseau and Edmund Burke within the canon of political thought. Much of the current Wollstonecraft scholarship seeks to prove she was a woman worthy of canonical placement.[1] I argue that Wollstonecraft, the author of two controversial tracts on political rights, would not have wanted to be a member of the canonical club. She repeatedly defined her political project as a war of words with the male authors whom she identified as the "canonized forefathers," and she rejected the theoretical tradition as falsely universal and inherently patriarchal.[2] Wollstonecraft targeted her critique at the "male aristocracy" in philosophy, who by categorizing women as lesser beings had "confined the rights of humanity to the male line from Adam downwards."[3] Thus, it is no simple task to add her voice to the conversation of political thought, because her words represent a forceful challenge to the androcentric discourse created by the fathers of the canon.

Mary Wollstonecraft is recognized by modern readers as a pioneering feminist author. Her writing is important to political theory because it adds theoretical complexity to the canonical discussions of sexual difference and political equality. Yet Wollstonecraft came to the text as an outsider, marginalized by both her sex and her rank, as a female born into a middle-class family in financial decline. As an eighteenth-century woman she could not "rest on the crutch of authority" provided by ancient precedent. Rebelling rather than relying on tradition, Wollstonecraft gained her authority through a critical analytical process that transformed her from a female reader into a feminist author. Her feminism arose from a political analysis of her personal experience that radicalized her reading and revolutionized her writing. She brought to her reading a desire for knowledge and a determination to form her own opinions independent of outside authority figures. In her writing she attacked the venerated bigotry of a past that treated women as perpetual children, denying females personal autonomy and political subjectivity. The corpus of Wollstonecraft's work demonstrates the development of feminist political theory as an oppositional discourse.

Mary Wollstonecraft's words interrupt the canonical conversation of political thought. Her writing invites to the theoretical table girls and women whose stories form an alternative tale of subjectivity that is at odds with much of the history of political theory. To read Wollstonecraft is to ask how the story of political founding would be different if told by the daughters of a republic. In an age of democratic revolution she suggested that the neat division between the public and the private spheres in social contract theory could not contain politics. Wollstonecraft dismissed the "absurd unit of husband and wife," claiming that wives had identities and interests separate from their husbands, which required representation beyond the household.[4] She dared to envision an autonomous political identity for women and to articulate a theory of women's rights at a time when the customs of society and the codes of coverture that made wives dependent upon their husbands for legal and political representation denied even the possibility of female independence. Her writing in both treatise and novel represented a fundamental challenge to the political world constituted by the canonical texts.

So why is it that the subversive nature of Wollstonecraft's writing has not been widely recognized? In order to have her say and to reach a female audience she found it necessary to employ multiple literary genres over the course of her career. This strategy has contributed to the current problem of classifying her work. Her use of different literary forms represented a systematic attack on the discursive boundaries of gender and genre that historically have denied women a political voice. In both didactic novels and polemical tracts she contested the categorical distinctions of sex that excluded women from the exercise of political rights while she confounded the genre boundaries of political theory that denied women the authority to write about politics.

Mary Wollstonecraft began her literary career as an educational writer and lady novelist, following many other eighteenth-century women into a discursive space that gave them a public platform but limited their authority. In *Thoughts on the Education of Daughters* she instructed parents to teach girls to think for themselves, a theme she developed further in *Mary, a Fiction* by creating a heroine whose "thinking powers" differentiated her from Richardson's Clarissa and Rousseau's Sophie. "In an artless tale, without episodes, the mind of a woman, who has thinking powers is displayed. The female organs have been thought too weak for this arduous employment; and experience seems to justify the assertion. Without arguing physically about *possibilities*—in a fiction, such a being may be allowed to exist; whose grandeur is derived from the operations of its own faculties, not subjugated to opinion; but drawn by the individual from the original source."[5]

The French Revolution brought about a revolution in her own writing. The lady novelist anonymously penned the first published response to Edmund Burke's *Reflections on the Revolution in France*. Wollstonecraft questioned the foundations of Burke's conservatism, drawing on the ideas of Plato, Machiavelli, Locke, and Hume to give authority to her reply to the Right Honorable Gentleman. When reviewers responded that the rights of women were the proper theme of the female pen, Wollstonecraft wrote *A Vindication of the Rights of Woman,* putting radical and conservative men alike on notice that the time had come for a serious discussion of women's citizenship: "The rights of men asserted by a fair lady! The age of chivalry cannot be over, or the sexes have changed their ground. . . . We should be sorry to raise a horse-laugh against a fair lady; but we were always taught to suppose that the rights of women were the proper theme of the female sex; and that, while the Romans governed the world, the women governed the Romans."[6]

Building on the argument of her first vindication in her second rights tract, she explicitly linked the objectification of women to the subjection of her sex. Just as she had critiqued Burke for his sentimental portrait of Marie Antoinette, Wollstonecraft criticized Rousseau for making Sophie a creature of sensibility rather than sense, born to feel rather than think. She rejected his model of sexually differentiated instruction, which disguised female ignorance as innocence, and offered her own system of female education for independence. The feminist author recognized that Rousseau's representation of womanhood enchained females in a system of domestic servitude. In her final fragment, *The Wrongs of Woman, or Maria,* Wollstonecraft returned to the novel for her arguments about women's rights to reach a wider audience of female readers. Here she threw off what she termed the "chains of theory," so that she could address the multiple ways in which her sex had been wronged by the revolutionary men who refused to grant the rights of mankind to women.[7]

As we enter the twenty-first century a provocative question for political scientists, feminist or not, is how to read Mary Wollstonecraft. Recent readings have attempted to situate her either strictly within the canon (as a political theorist) or strictly outside it (as a literary figure). Both of these approaches, though useful, are inherently misguided and seem to miss the theoretical and literary subtleties in the corpus of Wollstonecraft's work. For example, Virginia Sapiro's path-breaking examination, *A Vindication of Political Virtue,* demonstrates how, in her argument for women's rights, Wollstonecraft contested the gendered construction of reason and virtue in political theory. Sapiro situates the pioneering feminist as a canonical thinker alongside Locke and Rousseau.[8] Yet, although she admits that Wollstonecraft's works have largely been overlooked by mainstream political theorists, Sapiro's analysis offers little explanation as to why Wollstonecraft has been marginalized within the conversation of political thought. To explain why Wollstonecraft's writing has not been included in the canon I pose the question of how this revolutionary woman was authorized to write about political rights.

The question of feminist authority requires an interdisciplinary approach to gender and theory. I differentiate Wollstonecraft's polemical tracts from her sentimental novels in order to explore the gender politics of genre and to place her work within the emerging tradition of women's political writing. The reason that I distinguish her novels from tracts is that, in the eighteenth century, women were closely identified with the novel both as readers and as authors. By turning to the novel we gain a richer analysis of women's contribution to political culture at the end of the eighteenth century. This analysis lets us explore the influence of other women writers upon Wollstonecraft's ideas of political authority and feminist identity. A central aim of my study is to situate her challenge to political theory not just within the context of the canon but among the women who were her intellectual ancestors as well as her feminist successors. Professor Sapiro downplays the genre question in her analysis of Wollstonecraft's treatment of gender by not distinguishing between the novels and the pamphlets. Sapiro thus elides an important aspect of the sexual politics of writing and rights.

On the other hand literary theorist Gary Kelly in *Revolutionary Feminism* does a better job of theorizing genre, placing Wollstonecraft's works within the discursive context of the period, but he is nonetheless blindsided by the politics of gender. Clearly Wollstonecraft wrote about the relationship of property rights to political rights, but her theory of gender modifies her class analysis. In Kelly's treatment, Wollstonecraft becomes a symbol of a political or social agenda that upon closer study we can see is not her own. Case in point, he focuses on the issue of class representation, making Wollstonecraft a model of "bourgeois professionalism," which stands at odds with her life and writings. In this view the revolutionary feminist embraced the emerging public and private split because it offered women greater power in their domestic duties.[9] This reading seems curious in light of Wollstonecraft's *personal* struggles for acceptance as a woman author in a male-dominated public realm, and her concern throughout her writing with the serious difficulties that confront women who pursue economic independence outside the home. More serious is that Kelly's thesis obscures a central theme of Wollstonecraft's writing: that women must represent themselves within the household and—in her most radical formulation—even in the Houses of Parliament, since women who could govern themselves and manage households were certainly capable of wider participation in society. "I may excite laughter, by dropping an hint, which I mean to pursue, some future time, for I really think that women ought to have representatives, instead of being arbitrarily governed without having any direct share allowed them in the deliberation of government."[10]

Thus, each of these thoughtful texts does not come to full

terms with the radical implications of gender difference in Wollstonecraft's theory. So, just as she has been reclaimed for the canon of the twenty-first century, her powerful contestation of the sexual politics of the eighteenth century has been lost. For over two hundred years the interpretation of her writings has in many ways been determined by the reader's judgment of Wollstonecraft the woman author, her life often becoming the subject of analysis rather than her ideas.[11] This cycle of interpretation finds her the champion of women's rights and a misogynist, a model of republican virtue, and a woman masquerading as a man, a masochist, a lesbian, and a prude.[12] By exploring the books of this woman, we become profoundly involved in the historical process of the construction of both sexual difference and philosophical discourse. To understand Wollstonecraft we must critically examine how notions of gender and sexuality were inscribed within the Enlightenment ideals of humanism and rationality. Her treatises and novels confront a discourse of difference that excluded women from the theory and practice of political rights.

In this study I trace the transformation of Mary Wollstonecraft from a female reader into a feminist author and examine her "war with the words" of the "canonized forefathers."[13] I argue that her writing represents a profound interrogation of the central philosophical figures of her century, which directly challenged the male authors who in their philosophical tracts and sentimental novels depicted women as irrational and infantile beings. For Wollstonecraft these characterizations, rather than indicating the intellectual limits of a woman's mind, were evidence of the gender limitations of Enlightenment humanism. These images were doubly dangerous because females, denied the wide experience of the public sphere, relied upon books to bring the wisdom of the world home to them. Mary Wollstonecraft's thesis novels and rights tracts revealed much about how many English women saw themselves and their situation in the late eighteenth century. It was this attempt to give voice to her own vision of self and society that most distinguished her contribution to political thought from those of the fathers of the philosophical canon. She entered the conversation of political theory because she could not "silently pass over" the servile representation of womanhood in the books that were placed in the hands of her sex. "As these volumes are so frequently put into the hands of young people, I have taken more notice of them than, strictly speaking, they deserve; but as they have contributed to vitiate the taste, and enervate the understanding of many of my fellow-creatures, I could not pass them silently over."[14] I investigate how Wollstonecraft read and revised the texts traditionally chosen to educate women so we can more fully comprehend the revolutionary lessons of her books for female readers at the explosive end of a century of Enlightenment. My examination locates her feminist theory within a broader tradition of women's writing on the education of their sex and introduces forgotten female voices into the conversation of political thought.

The goal of my analysis is to demonstrate how Wollstonecraft's writing subverted the patriarchal plot of political theory in which she argued women were "born only to procreate and rot."[15] The feminist author battled the sexual segregation of human life, claiming that every man and woman possessed an unsexed soul derived from God, which destined them for perfectibility. In this philosophical battle of the sexes, she took aim at the fathers of the canon because she believed they had made no attempt to tutor the girl in her intellectual odyssey toward womanhood. As a female reader Wollstonecraft realized that the canon provided no models of female authority, since femininity was associated with a passive domesticity. Thus as a feminist author she warred with the canonical tradition, claiming that the works of the theoretical fathers were unable to give meaning and value to women's lives. More than anything else this articulation of the claims of women for a subjectivity at once both rational and passionate signified the feminist aims of Wollstonecraft's project. Her very presence at the theoretical table highlighted the historical absence of other women from the political debates that shaped their age. Today feminist political theory requires that we amplify her words and explore the silence of women in the canonical conversation of political thought.

The denial of women's contributions to intellectual history erases their intellectual heritage. When Mary Wollstonecraft decided to become an author she proclaimed herself the "first of a new genus."[16] Indeed, her writing represents a new species of political thought that bears some family resemblance to the writings of the canonized forefathers but her feminist politics problematizes this patriarchal inheritance. The feminist author is the descendant of a female intellectual tradition that stretches from Aphra Behn and Bathsua Makin to Mary Astell and Catharine Macaulay. Wollstonecraft's vindication of her sex echoes the arguments of seventeenth-century women writers that females as rational beings must be educated to fulfill their duties to God and Man. This said, she was not interested solely in reviving the "ancient education of the gentlewoman" but sought to extend rational education to women of all ranks. She did not justify educating women only in terms of increasing their value as helpmates to their husbands. Instead she argued that increased educational opportunity would allow women to participate more fully in their society. Coming of age in an era of democratic revolution, Mary Wollstonecraft was the *first* to make an explicit and systematic argument for women's political rights as *autonomous citizens with duties to themselves and their country.*

Today Mary Wollstonecraft is often regarded as the first feminist. She was not the first woman to claim the authority to write about sexual politics (as we shall see). Her writing should be placed along a continuum of female playwrights, scholars, novelists, and diarists whose words helped to shape and reshape the long eighteenth century. In her own lifetime she modeled her work after the books of Catharine Macaulay, Hester Chapone, and Anna Laetitia Barbauld. Wollstonecraft was definitely not alone in examining the idea of female reformation or the ideals of the French Revolution. Her intellectual circle, while it included Thomas Paine, William Godwin, and Thomas Holcroft, also encompassed Helen Maria Williams, Mary Hays, and Amelia Opie. These other radical writers both molded her understanding of the rights debates and modeled their own responses after her influential arguments. However, by reading Wollstonecraft as a *feminist political theorist,* we can see that she was right when she labeled herself first and new, for her writing brought to life a series of questions that do not exist within the work of the fathers of the canon. She occupied a position of outsidership that was highly critical of the categories of mainstream political thought. She rejected the idea that sexual difference was natural as well as the traditional binary opposition of reason to passion. Her writing focused on the incompatibility of the Enlightenment model of the autonomous adult male with the identity and experience of girls and women. Either the canonized forefathers have ignored women entirely, populating their republics of the mind with a fraternal order of parthenogenetic men, or they have represented women as irrational, dependent, and infantile beings who must be ruled by the male members of the body politic.

My reading of Wollstonecraft's writing questions the role of gender in political theory and the development of feminist political theory as an oppositional discourse. My analysis situates her work within a more inclusive intellectual context among the men and women who motivated her to become a rebel writer. Wollstonecraft's theory offers a remarkable challenge to the historical conversation of political thought, one that is missed if we read her works as representative of canonical writing that silences its feminist critics. The canon itself—its categories and mode of reasoning, its truth claims and conditions—determines what we accept as political theory as well as what we expect of political writing and political writers. I read Wollstonecraft's texts as an immanent critique of the canon, a war of words that serves to caution us, as we work to place worthy women among the great men on the syllabus and add their writing to the curriculum, that we should carefully consider the politics of membership and exclusion within the canon.

The following chapters offer a close textual analysis of Mary Wollstonecraft's didactic works, sentimental novels, and political tracts. Chapter 1 examines her encounter as a female reader with the images of woman within the canonical tradition. I analyze how her reading of Rousseau's *Emile* and *Nouvelle Heloise* led her to reject the role of the marriage plot in political thought and to begin a personal quest for feminist authority. Chapter 2 demonstrates how Wollstonecraft's emphasis on the vulnerability of girls and the dependence of women gave her a unique vision of class conflict and family politics. I explore how the themes of gender and generation found in Wollstonecraft's girlhood correspondence and earliest publications—*Thoughts on the Education of Daughters* (1787), *Mary, a Fiction* (1788), *Original Stories* (1788)—become the basis of her mature political theory. Chapter 3 examines Wollstonecraft's theoretical battle with Burke. Her *Vindication of the Rights of Men* (1790) was the first reply to Burke's *Reflections on the Revolution in France* and represented a rhetorical attack on monarchical politics and aristocratic property. Here she used a gender analysis to humanize and unify the actions of Marie Antoinette and the Parisian market women who marched to Versailles to demand bread from their queen.

The critical response to this pamphlet set the stage for Wollstonecraft's second rights tract, *A Vindication of the Rights of Woman* (1792). In Chapter 4 I situate this celebrated treatise on women's rights within the larger tradition of female writing on education and within eighteenth-century debates about women's nature and the nature of politics. I examine how Wollstonecraft's argument for the political rights of her sex is different from earlier tracts that advocated educating girls to make better wives and helpmates.

Chapter 5 focuses on Wollstonecraft's attempt to embody politics in her final fiction *The Wrongs of Woman, or Maria* (1798). Here the feminist author attempted to politicize the female reader by creating a series of cautionary tales of class conflict and sexual politics. I argue that, taken together, these inset narratives form an alternative story of political society, which demonstrates how marriage "bastilled" women for life even in an age of revolution. The study concludes with an analysis of efforts to fictionalize the philosopher, in William Godwin's *Memoirs of the Author of "The Rights of Woman"* (1798) and Frances Sherwood's novel *Vindication* (1993). I suggest that continuing controversies concerning Wollstonecraft's life and the various interpretations of her work in modern feminist theory offer a new way of speaking about the challenge of feminist politics to canonical political thought.

For over two centuries Mary Wollstonecraft has been read and revised by her female readers. Her arguments have been appropriated by women as a means of speaking about their own confrontations with social prejudice and political authority. Perhaps Wollstonecraft's great contribution to feminist theory and practice has been the political language of vindication itself. Feminist political theorists have used her words to enter and engender larger debates about the meaning of individual liberty and civic equality. Mary Wollstonecraft's analysis of gender and genre informed her arguments about the political connection between writing and rights, opening the door for feminist activists and scholars to use multiple discursive formats and forums to articulate their own response to women's subjugation. If her work is merely situated somewhere after Jean-Jacques Rousseau but before John Stuart Mill, her battle with the canonized forefathers is over, and the power of her challenge to political theory is lost to the generations of women who by reading Wollstonecraft have been motivated to write and to rebel.

CHAPTER ONE

Political Theory and the Female Reader

> Woman, who is weak and who sees nothing outside the house, estimates and judges the forces she can put to work to make up for her weakness, and those forces are men's passions. . . . She must, therefore, make a profound study of the mind of man—not an abstraction of the mind of man in general, but the minds of the men around her, the minds of the men to whom she is subjected by either law or opinion. She must learn to penetrate their sentiments by their words, their actions, their looks, their gestures. Men will philosophize about the human heart better than she does; but she will read in men's hearts better than they do.
> The world is the book of women.
>
> —Jean-Jacques Rousseau, *Emile*

Jean-Jacques Rousseau proclaims that the world is the book of women. Yet in Rousseau's books women are portrayed as neither philosophers of human nature nor authors of social contracts but, rather, as readers of male hearts and manipulators of masculine desire. Women are twice removed from politics, unfit for public participation by their inability to reason and to control their passions. In the *Social Contract,* Rousseau makes explicit the argument of *Emile* and *La Nouvelle Heloise,* that the stability of the state depends upon the use of patriarchal authority within the small fatherland that is every man's family.[1] The sexual division of labor in both the household and the republic divides the rights of men and women, the duties of fathers and mothers, and the educations of brothers and sisters. Given the sexual politics of Rousseau's theory, it is not surprising that when he tells the story of a woman's life he is really singing a song of self.[2] In his creation myth, woman is formed entirely for man. Her experience is cut in half; like Persephone she is separated from her mother in the dawn of her life and drawn into a wifely world of shadows. She loses her individual identity through marriage, becoming one with her husband in the legal fiction of coverture. Motherhood divides woman within herself and multiplies her responsibilities to family and community. These are the lines of Rousseau's book of women, the words that describe Sophie.

The heroine of Mary Wollstonecraft's books is "not a Sophie" but a "woman of thinking powers," whom the feminist author describes as "a world in herself." In many ways Wollstonecraft's relationship to the philosophical tradition of the Enlightenment can be assessed by carefully examining her radical reading of Rousseau and her rejection of his book of women. Throughout her writings Rousseau is the target of an ongoing philosophical battle of the sexes, which she defines as a war of words. For Wollstonecraft the paper-doll figures Sophie (of *Emile*) and Julie (the title character of *La Nouvelle Heloise*) can never fully represent the historical experiences of her mother, sisters, or self. She recognized that there was another way to read these fictions of femininity, a critical method that required her to use her own life as the referent for truth. However, her arguments about the construction of gender and subjectivity are not marked by a facile biological essentialism. Throughout Wollstonecraft's writing there is an insistence on the artifice of masculinity and femininity. To her mind, notions of sexual difference are as much conditioned by culture as they are determined by nature. Therefore, fundamental questions of sex roles and power do not return her to a hypothetical primordial state but propel her forward into an examination of texts, and into an investigation of how gender and subjectivity are constituted in both treatise and novel.

Historically the female figure appears within political theory at a distance, caught in the gaze of the male author and objectified as a biblical helpmate or a sexual plaything. When a woman reads the works of the great men of political philosophy she undergoes an identity crisis as a reader. Reading Plato's *Republic*, she must identify with the citizen men of Athens and laugh with Glaucon and Adeimantus at the mere suggestion that women can be educated to rule the just society. The female reader must come to terms with the functionalism of Aristotle's *Politics*, a biological destiny that denies women humanity. She must become the young Augustine, tempted by the pears on the tree in the *Confessions*, and through conversion renounce the female flesh. Does she see herself as Fortuna in Machiavelli's *Prince*, the capricious ruler of half of men's lives? Or is she the wife and mother, a body the prince may not touch? The female reader may fight for life in the Hobbesian state of nature of the *Leviathan*, brutalized but free, the first sovereign if she chooses to care for her child. Perhaps she is the mother in Locke's *Two Treatises on Government*, exercising parental authority with her husband over their children, all the while knowing that he alone represents the household within the state. Indeed, the history of the "woman question" in political thought is a story of gender trouble. Feminist theorists have recognized that the citizen is a man and a man is everything a woman is not.[3] Reading the canonical texts of political theory, a woman must either make the imaginative leap to manhood or reject the images of woman in the works of the fathers of the canon. To claim the authority to represent herself, a woman must confront the sexual politics of theory.

For over two thousand years the traditional answer to the woman question in politics has been that women were not political. Moira Gatens turns this assumption on its head. "Theory can be taken to problematize *women* or women's interrogation of the theory can be taken to problematize the terms of the *theory*."[4] I read Mary Wollstonecraft's work as a case study of one woman's interrogation of the problematic terms of theory. Wollstonecraft, arguably the eighteenth century's most rebellious female reader, became its most revolutionary feminist author by contesting the portrayal of women as "insignificant objects of desire and propagators of fools" in political thought.[5] I approach the books of this historical woman as examples of the confrontation of the female reader with the images of womanhood within the texts of the "canonized forefathers."

Nowhere was this encounter more dramatic than between Wollstonecraft and Rousseau's heroines, Sophie and Julie. Rousseau captured her imagination because he told stories of sexuality and society that illuminated the power of individual women. But he sparked her indignation by institutionalizing a sexual double standard that severely limited the sphere of women's actions. His explicit discussion of heterosexuality politicized the family, as he argued that women's sexual mastery over men in the home could spill over into civil society and disrupt the state. The citizen of Geneva worried about the feminization of politics as men vied with each other for the attention of women. Rousseau's books made it clear that to restore virtue to the republic, the legislator must necessarily segregate men and women into separate spheres.

Ultimately, in her transformation from a female reader into a feminist author, Mary Wollstonecraft became a woman whose own authority could not be contained within the *Social Contract*. She dismisses Sophie and Julie as "fanciful creatures," the products of lust rather than logic. Instead, Wollstonecraft argues that females must be educated to think for themselves and, contrary to Rousseau, that thinking women are capable of self-government and civic virtue. Her novels and tracts dispute the philosophical opposition of authority to femininity, forming the basis of a feminist political theory that examines the complex relationship between sexual difference and political equality. Wollstonecraft radicalized the connection between political writing and political rights by creating alternative tales of gender and citizenship. These alternative tales, developed in rights tracts and didactic novels, subverted the philosophical framework of Rousseau's "book of women."

Mary Wollstonecraft challenged Rousseau's objectification of women in order to theorize a new subject position for woman. Her feminist theory suggests that, in order to understand the absence of women as active participants in public life as well as authors of political tracts, it is necessary to focus on the images of woman present within these texts. The relationship of women to politics is bound by textual representations of the weaker sex, perpetuated in philosophical tracts and popularized in fiction. By reading woman into the text, Wollstonecraft became conscious of the inability of conservative and radical men alike to see women as autonomous subjects and democratic citizens. Thus, her feminism is characterized by the powerful confrontations between woman and the word, between literature and philosophy, that make Wollstonecraft's works such a significant contribution to the study of gender and politics. Her books are the products of a self-consciously inventive woman attempting to give new meanings to many of the concepts that form the basis of both historical political thought and modern political discourse. To embody feminist authority (literally, in the case of Mary Wollstonecraft), we must consider the relationship of the female reader to political theory; and to understand why Wollstonecraft's story has not been included in the history of philosophy, we must examine the divergent roles of the quest and marriage plots in canonical political thought.

THE FEMALE READER

> Girls brought up in this idle way have an ill regulated imagination. Their curiosity, not being directed to substantial things, is turned towards vain and dangerous objects. They read books which nourish their vanity, and become passionately fond of romances, comedies and fanciful adventures. Their minds become visionary; they accustom themselves to the extravagant language of the heroines of romance, and are spoiled for common life.
>
> —François de Fénelon, *De l'Education des Filles*

Jean-Jacques Rousseau's treatises and novels were filled with warnings about the effect of reading on females. To ensure the chaste heart of a young lady, many of the conduct books of the eighteenth century echoed the advice of the seventeenth-century French prelate François de Fénelon, that in the education of girls it was important to control their access to books. Indeed, as Fénelon's philosophical disciple, Rousseau went even further, arguing in *Emile* that if he had his preference he would keep a girl illiterate rather than teach her to read. This is rather ironic, since it was his attempt to "bring the heroine of the sentimental novel into reality" in his portraits of Sophie and Julie that made girls and women so "passionately fond" of his books.[6] Joan Landes and Robert Darnton have noted the widespread influence of Rousseau's works upon female readers, while Nicola Watson has traced the revolutionary impact of *La Nouvelle Heloise* among Jacobin women writers.[7] However, Rousseau worried that females often misinterpreted the meaning of his books and confused their place in the world created by his theory. "When they do a bad job of reading it, it is their fault, or else some passion blinds them." He cautioned reading women that the "true mother of a family is hardly less of a recluse in her home than a nun is in her cloister."[8]

It must be admitted that books of any sort have little importance in Rousseau's experiential model of education, the first principle of which is "[n]o book other than the world, no instruction other than the facts. . . . The child who reads does not think, he only reads; he is not informing himself, he learns words."9 The tutor Jean-Jacques states, "I hate books. They only teach one to talk about what one does not know." He recommends only one book to Emile, *Robinson Crusoe*, a tale of shipwreck and self-sufficiency.10 For Emile to become a man he must become the master of his desires. As Penny Weiss has argued, his sexually differentiated pedagogy was aimed at educating boys and girls for their respective places within society and the family.11 Since social place was closely associated with biological function for women, female literacy was neither necessary nor desirable for Rousseau. The prohibition on reading has dramatic implications for the development of the female intellect because girls cannot experience the world on their own. Unlike boys they are forbidden adventure and independence because in the patriarchal social contract a woman's place is in the home. To emphasize the dangers of misplaced feminine desire, Rousseau offers the cautionary tale of a female reader—identified by Joel Schwartz as the "girl like Sophie"—in book 5 of *Emile*.12

Few scholars have remarked on the fact that Rousseau actually tells the story of Sophie twice; but there is only one happy ending, and that happiness is fleeting. The first Sophie disregards her mother's warning and reads Fénelon's *Adventures of Telemachus*. The young girl's imagination breaks out of the walled-off world of her parents' country home to follow the hero, Telemachus, as he retraces his father's legendary footsteps in the *Odyssey*. This literary transgression into the forbidden realms of fiction introduces the chaste Sophie to the pleasures of romance. Certainly for Rousseau, a young woman should not have worldly knowledge of this type of book. Like Fénelon, he advised guardians to monitor what girls read to ensure that young female readers did not abandon their morals in a lush fictional landscape. However, *Adventures of Telemachus* is not a sentimental novel. It is a classic quest, the story of a boy's journey to manhood. Throughout this developmental grand tour, Telemachus is accompanied by Mentor, an elderly sage who is really the Goddess of Wisdom, Minerva, in disguise. Telemachus's successful resolution of this voyage of personal discovery is secured by the wise guidance and practical protection of Mentor.

This intellectual odyssey holds special dangers for the untutored girl. As a female, Sophie is denied the widespread experience and the specialized education of Telemachus or Emile that gives reason to judgment. Girls destined for marriage do not require texts, tutors, or travel for moral development. Literary critic Carolyn Heilbrun has argued that the stories of men's and women's lives can be differentiated by their adherence to either the quest plot or the marriage plot.[13] To write about a woman's life usually has meant to write about marriage and family. In canonical political theory, man's quest for political identity has been accomplished through the creation of sexual difference. It has been reified in the traditional gender distinctions of the public man and the private woman. Women have been excluded from this historical quest because philosophers have argued that knowledge of men and politics unfits a female for marriage by taking her out of her proper sphere. In the history of political philosophy the stories of women associated with marriage have been subsumed within the masculine quest for the good society. Feminist theorists such as Carole Pateman have detailed how this classical story of subjection is retold within modern social contract theory and the political consequences of this storytelling for women as citizens.[14]

Rousseau speaks for the canonized forefathers when he states, "The quest for abstract and speculative truths, principles, and axioms in the sciences, for everything that tends to generalize ideas, is not within the competence of women."[15] Women, who are physically weak and who have an intellect defined by practical reason, are incapable of the rigorous theoretical thinking required in the quest for wisdom and virtue. Thus, nothing good can come to Sophie or society from her misguided reading of the *Adventures of Telemachus*. The tutor Jean-Jacques tells the story of "the girl like Sophie" in order to articulate the proposition that women, like men, can love virtue. Instead, Rousseau's story demonstrates that virtue has different meanings for the sexes: men quest for virtue by themselves, but women can experience virtue only vicariously through marriage to virtuous men. Sophie becomes infatuated with the image of Telemachus and refuses to marry because no man can live up to the virtues of the fictional hero. Her once proud parents come to consider their daughter a madwoman, suffering from a "mania for virtue" unsuited to her sex. Since her story cannot be resolved through the socially accepted marriage plot, Rousseau has this Sophie die of a broken heart.[16]

The death of the first Sophie is the tragic contrivance of what Rousseau terms the "abuse of the fatal science" of reading. "After all, where is the necessity for a girl to know how to read and write so early? Will she so soon have a household to govern? There are very few girls who do not abuse this fatal science more than they make good use of it."[17] Jean-Jacques rewrites his steps, having left the grieving parents at the grave instead of the altar, where he then leads his reader along another path to meet a second Sophie, a girl whose mind is formed by "conversations and observations not reading."[18] This Sophie lives longer, because she is saved from the despair of her sentimental sister by being united with a "real-life" man of virtue, Emile. A dutiful daughter, she has spent her life as her mother's companion helping to manage her parents' household. Rousseau goes to great lengths to assure us that Sophie has the appropriate feminine virtues: cleanliness, modesty, and most important, a mind that is the equivalent of a tabula rasa. Jean-Jacques heightens Emile's desire for this country girl by telling him that he will have the pleasure of teaching her everything she needs to know about love and life. After a brief courtship, the action leaves Sophie behind as Jean-Jacques, like Mentor, accompanies Emile on his quest through the capitals of Europe to gain knowledge of government and men. Two years later Emile returns to Sophie and her family. In the last pages of the book they are wed, and the tutor steps aside, having created the citizen and his helpmate.

Emile and Sophie do not live happily ever after, however. At the end of his life, Rousseau returned to his fictional family and wrote a sequel to *Emile, Les Solitaires*. The unfinished novel, left among his papers at his death, reworks the story: Emile and Sophie, now the parents of a young boy, grow tired of their pastoral idyll in the countryside and move to Paris. Both husband and wife are drawn into the sexual and political intrigues of the city; while Emile is at the gaming table, Sophie frequents a literary salon. Falling in with a literary crowd, Sophie conceives a bastard child. Unwilling to live a double life, she guiltily confesses her transgression to her husband, and Emile abandons her and their son. Thus, the story of Sophie comes full circle, as Emile relates the fatal dissolution of their marriage in one last letter to his tutor, Jean-Jacques. *The moral of the story is that the quest for knowledge is deadly for Sophie, the girl named for wisdom.* But what Rousseau does not acknowledge is that a woman ignorant of the ways of the world will often become the victim of the worldly. As long as Sophie remains within the confines of the marriage plot, she is the model of female virtue. Once she strays from the role assigned her as a wife within the history of political thought, however, she becomes the image of virtue in distress. Read this way, the stories of both the girls called Sophie in *Emile* become cautionary tales, depicting the conflicts between a woman's search for knowledge and the limitations on female lives imposed by patriarchal authority.

Mary Wollstonecraft's books from first to last reveal her deeply conflicted attitude toward Rousseau's writing about women and their place in his philosophical world. The feminist author responded to the tutor Jean-Jacques's argument that females should not read by countering that the problem was not so much with the female reader but, rather, with the books she read. Wollstonecraft thought that, in the absence of the experiential education of the public sphere, the type of books a girl read would largely determine the kind of woman she would eventually become. In her first published work, *Thoughts on the Education of Daughters*, Wollstonecraft remarked that it is "an old, but a very true observation, that the human mind must ever be employed." She maintained that reading is the mind's "most rational employment," because it subjugates the senses while it nourishes the understanding. For this reason alone, girls should be encouraged to read. However, the type of books that were typically offered to girls counteracted the benefits of reading. The problem with the sentimental novel was that it played upon the senses of the reader instead of strengthening her mind. Wollstonecraft argued that girls and women should read geography, history, even philosophy, because such texts steered clear of the emotional hazards of the senses by objectifying human actions. They could broaden women's knowledge of men and society. Yet, in her own efforts to turn the philosophical page, she would come to realize that women, objectified by the marriage plot, were not considered subjects with a political history of their own. There were no classical dialogues that introduced the girl to the ideas of the well-lived life and the good society. Sophie, created to please, did not require the careful tutoring of Emile. It seemed there was a major drawback to her course of rational reading—the very sensibility that made women the heroines of the sentimental novel excluded them from the action in the history of philosophy.

Emile and (as we shall see) *La Nouvelle Heloise* exemplified this dilemma because they popularized the gender ideology that men were born to think and to act in the world while women were born to feel and to wait at home. Cora Kaplan has written, "It was Wollstonecraft . . . who identified the novel as the popular literary genre directed at women readers that would feed and reinforce denigrating 'sentimental' definitions of femininity."[19] And it was Rousseau whom Wollstonecraft identified as the "Prometheus of Sentiment."[20] She repeatedly argued that his stolen fire was not intended to enlighten women but to make them the keepers of the flame, tied by ignorance and custom to the family hearth. Rousseau had claimed "everything that is to reach the heart must come from it."[21] Both *Emile* and *La Nouvelle Heloise* became eighteenth-century best-sellers because they set the hearts of female readers aflame.

Wollstonecraft confronted the paradox of his popularity with her sex. "He denies woman reason, shuts her out from knowledge, and turns her aside from truth; yet his pardon is granted, because 'he admits the passion of love.'" She reasoned that his sentimental reading of womanhood posed real dangers to the women who read his volumes, because by defining femininity as sensibility he made women slaves to love, incapable of mastering their desires or governing themselves.

> This cruel association of ideas, which every thing conspires to twist into all their habits of thinking, or, to speak with more precision, of feeling, receives new force when they begin to act a little for themselves; for they then perceive that it is only through their address to excite emotions in men, that pleasure and power are to be obtained. Besides, the books professedly written for their instruction, which make the first impressions on their minds, all inculcate the same opinions. Educated then in worse than Egyptian bondage, it is unreasonable, as well as cruel, to upbraid them with faults that can scarcely be avoided, unless a degree of native vigor be supposed, that falls to the lot of very few amongst mankind.[22]

Kaplan explains, "Wollstonecraft's implicit theory of reading assumes the reader will identify herself with the female heroine. The reading of popular fiction and the fantasy induced by it depend at one level on the identification of reader and heroine, and the subsequent acting-out of a related narrative trajectory." Female readers who imitated Sophie or (even more worrisome) identified themselves with Julie were headed for trouble, as seduction gives way to domination. Wollstonecraft asserted that female readers must not be seduced by Rousseau's book of women or be drawn in by his promise that marriage will produce an illusory empire of pleasure. "It is not empire,—but equality, that they should contend for."[23]

Wollstonecraft's criticisms of novels in general, and those of

Rousseau's in particular, were especially powerful, because for literate females in England in the late eighteenth century, private reading often took the place of public instruction. G. J. Barker-Benfield explains: "That women first became literate in significant numbers is a profoundly important feature of seventeenth- and eighteenth-century history." He claims that by 1750 in Britain, "60 percent of the men and 40 percent of the women could read. Between 1754 and 1800, the rate of increase of literacy among women continued to be greater than among men."[24] It was a fact of life that girls were neither educated for independent thought nor taught a trade for economic security. For the poor, childhood was an unobtainable ideal, as even the youngest females were placed in service. If sent to a charity school, the daughter of the lower orders was taught to obey the wishes of the wealthy. A girl of the middling classes, if she was given any formal instruction at all, may have been sent to a dame school to learn how to read, sew, and draw. Even the daughters of the privileged classes were educated only in accomplishments that would increase their value on the marriage market. Patriarchy and primogeniture denied females of noble birth the classical education afforded the oldest son. Destined for domesticity, either through marriage or service, a girl's lessons in all ranks of society tended to reinforce the intellectual boundaries placed upon a woman's knowledge of the world beyond the household. Rousseau's *Emile* and *Nouvelle Heloise* provided a philosophical and fashionable justification for limiting female education at a time when female literacy was on the rise. Addressing her arguments to females cloistered within the home, Wollstonecraft charged that books were a poor substitute for experiential learning; that women, too, needed to quest after knowledge; and that this intellectual journey required them to challenge the gender ideology that supported the separation of the private and public spheres.

It is her attention to the quest of the female reader for wisdom and the power to govern herself that differentiates Mary Wollstonecraft's feminist theory from the works of the canonized forefathers. She argued in *A Vindication of the Rights of Woman* that the false sexual distinctions noted by Rousseau and other male authors who had written on female education were motivated by their desire to maintain patriarchal privilege. "Educate women like men, says Rousseau, 'and the more they resemble our sex the less power they will have over us.' This is the very point I aim at. I do not wish them to have power over men; but over themselves."[25]

Men perpetuated the subjection of women by educating girls only for marriage and justified the exclusion of women from politics by the separation of the family from the state. Their books reinforced women's role as helpmate by stressing that femininity was associated with sentimentality rather than with rationality. Wollstonecraft challenged the "system of education, which I earnestly wish to see exploded, seems to presuppose what ought never to be taken for granted, that virtue shields us from the casualties of life; and that fortune, slipping her bandage, will smile on a well-educated female, and bring in her hand an Emilius or a Telemachus."[26] Her own experience of life suggested a different story for women: "there have been many women in the world who, instead of being supported by the reason and virtue of their fathers and brothers, have strengthened their own minds by struggling with their vices and follies; yet have never met with a hero, in the shape of a husband." Therefore, Wollstonecraft reasoned, women should focus on developing the power of their own minds rather than rely upon the romantic resolution of the marriage plot. If female readers doubted her conclusions, they need only turn the pages of Rousseau's *Nouvelle Heloise,* a history recounted in the "letters of two lovers who live in a small town at the foot of the Alps," to see that this story of heroes and husbands ends in the tragic death of the heroine.[27]

PHILOSOPHICAL PLOTS

> Who knows even if, knowing my sensibility, you are not using a deeper plot to seduce me?
> —Julie to Saint Preux, *La Nouvelle Heloise*

Who could guide a woman on her quest for wisdom? A self-educated Mary Wollstonecraft was wary of the tutor Jean-Jacques and his fictional alter ego, Saint Preux. She believed that the story of Abelard and Heloise retold by Rousseau in *Julie, ou La Nouvelle Heloise* illustrated the perils of entrusting the body and mind of a young woman to a male tutor with more experience of the world. Rousseau provides an explicit comparison of the similarities and differences between the historical relationship between Peter Abelard and Heloise and the fictional romance between Saint Preux and Julie following the return of her father, the Baron d'Etange, to his family:

> When the letters of Eloise and Abelard fell into your hands, you remember what I said to you about reading them and about the conduct of that priest. I have always pitied Eloise. She had a heart made for love, but Abelard has ever seemed to me only a miserable creature who deserved his fate and who was a stranger as much to love as to virtue. After having passed this judgment on him, ought I to imitate him?

Saint Preux terms Abelard a "vile seducer," just as Julie would label Saint Preux in her first letter. Then he distinguishes their love from the ill-fated medieval pair. "It is different, my Julie, with two lovers of the same age, both seized with the same passion, united by mutual attachment, under no particular engagements, both enjoying their original liberty, and forbidden by no law to pledge themselves to each other."[28]

This epistolary novel is the tale of the education and seduction of the noble Julie d'Etange by her common-born tutor, Saint Preux, and the attempt to reform both pupil and preceptor through her arranged marriage to the godlike Monsieur Wolmar. The restriction of women within the private spaces of the family often has been justified by the claim that it protects women from the perils of the public sphere. But Julie's danger is within the walls of her home under the watchful eye of an indulgent mother. When the Baron d'Etange returns to his family after an extended absence he realizes too late the threat posed by Saint Preux to his daughter's virtue. His words are a warning to parents. "I shall be little surprised if the same philosophy which taught her to throw herself at the first man she saw may teach her even to disobey her father" (242).

Saint Preux, the tutor chosen to educate a beloved daughter, breaks his trust with her parents by confessing his love to the young woman. In her response to her teacher, Julie writes of her predicament, "Led imperceptibly into the snares of the vile seducer, I see, without being able to stop myself, the horrible precipice toward which I am running" (32). Saint Preux rejects her characterization of him as a vile seducer, claiming instead that he should be understood as a man of feeling. Unwilling to turn to her mother for help, Julie looks to her cousin, Claire, for guidance. The pupil argues that the tutor is a "man of merit" and that his virtue makes him dangerous. "I regret the lessons I am taking without you, and I am afraid of becoming too learned. Our tutor is not only a man of merit; he is virtuous and therefore more dangerous" (36). Throughout the story it is virtue that forms the fatal attraction between the student and her teacher, just as the virtue of Telemachus corrupted the heart of the first Sophie in *Emile*. After a year of studying together, Saint Preux acknowledges that he and Julie have done little more than "random reading" and that Claire, who has not been disturbed by their passion, has become the most learned of the three.

Thus, the tutor devises a new plan—a curriculum meant to curb the desires of the lovers by excluding poetry and books about love, the texts usually associated with female education. Julie reads Petrarch, Tasso, Metastasio, French drama, and Plutarch's *Lives*. As their lessons progress, she suspects Saint Preux of engaging in a plot to win her heart—he has taught her to love virtue so that she would fall in love with him. Julie inquires, "Who knows even if, knowing my sensibility, you are not using a deeper plot to seduce me?" (47). Given her suspicions, and Saint Preux's impassioned state, Julie proposes a role reversal. "I confess that I am younger, but have you never noticed that if reason ordinarily is weaker and more quickly extinguished in women, it is also formed earlier, just as a frail sunflower grows and dies sooner than an oak?" Female judgment must mature early because girls must protect and preserve their virginity. Julie claims that girls are "charged with such a dangerous treasure that the care of preserving it soon awakens the judgment" (48). Julie carefully forms a judgment of the devices and desires of her young tutor. "Surely, to make use of the means of education to corrupt a woman is of all seductions the most damnable, and to wish to soften a mistress with the aid of novels is indeed to have few resources of one's own." Instead of novels, the tutor has called to his aid Plato's *Republic*, a book that Rousseau asserts was designed for true lovers. But his lessons seem lost on Julie, who notes that her tutor is most effective when he pleads his heart rather than his principles. "If you had used philosophy to forward your designs, if you had tried to establish maxims favorable to your interest, those very methods of deceit would soon have undeceived me, but the most dangerous of your seductions is not to use these methods at all" (50). Saint Preux agrees, stating that there is nothing that he and Julie can learn about love from the pages of a book.

What could Saint Preux possibly teach Julie? For his part, the tutor doubts the efficacy of his pedagogy. "And what did you intend to learn, incomparable daughter, from my vain and sorry knowledge? Ah, it is from you that one must learn all the goodness, all the probity possible in a human soul, and, most of all, that divine union of virtue, love, and nature, which never existed except in you!" (61). Since a woman's virtue consists in maintaining her virginity, neither teacher nor student worries that their unconventional study of philosophy could lead to her eventual corruption. As the months pass, Julie's display of domesticated womanly virtue serves only to further enflame her lover's passion. When the Baron d'Etange returns home from a year engaged in a legal dispute over the family's property, he is surprised by Julie's learning. His pleasure over her progress in music and drawing is clouded, however, by his concern that Saint Preux had neglected to teach her heraldry. To neglect heraldry is to ignore the different class positions of the tutor and his pupil. Baron d'Etange is quick to ask about Saint Preux's fortune and birth. When he is informed that the tutor is not of noble birth he insists that Saint Preux be paid for his services, because he cannot "bear the idea of being indebted to a man who was meanly born" (63). The baron believes it is essential for his daughter to have a knowledge of her place in society, because this will make it clear whom she should marry. Saint Preux's courtship of the noble Julie represents the potential for a radical realignment of society through love relationships. To ignore heraldry is to ignore heredity, and with it to deny the authority of parents to arrange appropriate marriages for their children and thus maintain the social status quo. Women's part in the marriage plot is to reproduce society through the generations, not to introduce revolution by acting on their feelings and subverting the designs of tyrannical parents.

The consequence of the sexual double standard inscribed in the quest and marriage plots in philosophy is that the love which creates heroes such as Saint Preux inevitably destroys heroines such as Julie. After their physical intimacy, Julie acknowledges the horror of her fate, that in the consummation of their love she herself has been consumed. "Love, this fatal love which destroys me, gives you new value; you are elevated while I am degraded, and your soul seems to have profited from the debasement of mine." Calling Saint Preux her only hope, Julie makes her new status painfully clear. "It is for you to justify my crime, if you can, cover it with the honesty of your sentiments, let your merit efface my shame, and *excuse with the strength of your virtues the loss of mine that you occasioned. Be my whole being, now that I am nothing.* The only honor I have left is wholly in you, and as long as you are worthy of respect, I shall not be completely reprehensible" (84; my emphasis).

Julie is well aware of the consequences of her actions, but her masochistic response to her predicament suggests she embraces a sexual double standard that denigrates womanhood. "I know my fate, I sense the horror of it, and yet one consolation is left me in my despair. It is the only one, but it is sweet. It is from you that I expect it, my dear friend. Since I no longer dare to think of myself, I think with more pleasure of the one I love. I give you all the esteem that you have taken from me, and you become only more dear to me by compelling me to despise myself" (84). Once a woman has lost her virginity she is lost to virtue, lost to herself. Now that Julie is nothing, she must live through Saint Preux, for the only way she can experience virtue is vicariously through the actions of her lover. Therefore, she instructs him to act upon the virtues he tried to teach her, or else she has sacrificed her virginity to delusions of his merit and her loss is complete.

It is in *La Nouvelle Heloise* that we see Rousseau's gender ideology most clearly. Sexual differences reflect innate moral differences, and therefore the virtues of men and women cannot be the same. Men quest for the wisdom to govern themselves while women marry to preserve their chastity. Masculine virtue is a civic ideal, and as such it requires a knowledge of men and society, of nations and politics. Feminine virtue is a physical state secured through an innocence that is corrupted by knowledge of men and society, of nations and politics. For Rousseau there is no virtue for women outside of the marriage plot. Thus, sexuality must be confined to marriage because only through matrimony can women maintain the veil of virtue, through private and chaste lives as wives and mothers. The divine Julie's affair with the mortal Saint Preux represents the fall from the passionate precipice that she once feared. Her cousin, Claire, underscores her fallen stature in a letter rebuking their former tutor. "Those sublime sentiments have grown weak, that divine flame has cooled, and that angel is now no more than an ordinary woman. Ah, what a soul you have seduced from virtue!" (230). It is here that the history of two lovers ends and the separate stories of man and woman begins.

Julie's story demonstrates that it is the destiny of women to marry. The Baron d'Etange and his friend Wolmar try to rehabilitate Julie through an arranged marriage and a cloistered life. Their project ultimately fails because, having once given herself to love outside of wedlock, she is victimized rather than vindicated by marriage. Julie must marry to obey the will of her father, but she proclaims that she will marry only with Saint Preux's consent. She must decide her destiny either by dishonoring her family or by being faithless to her lover. Yet how is she to make this life-or-death decision? Her knowledge of the passions leads her to value sentiment over reason, and her thought processes are described as deluded, bordering on madness. Julie's education has not provided her with the necessary mental resources to make her own decision; she must rely on the wisdom of others. Unable to govern herself the young woman is governed by her lover, her father, and finally her husband, in turn. On the occasion of her marriage, Julie writes to Saint Preux that all is changed between them, and she prophetically announces that her new life will end only with her death. She begins, "Bound by an indissoluble tie to the fate of a husband, or rather to the will of a father." Julie's marriage reinforces the bonds between Monsieur Wolmar and the Baron d'Etange while her words reflect her overidentification of her husband with her father (254). The bride reasons that love is not necessary in marriage, in fact it may prove a distraction, since the purpose of marriage is to enable the partners to perform their civic duties. Julie describes her bond with Wolmar by claiming that each completes the other. "Each of us is precisely what the other needs; he instructs me and I enliven him. We are of greater value together, and it seems that we are destined to have only a single mind between us, of which he is the understanding and I the will" (262). Perhaps most indicative of her transformation is her acknowledgment that, given what she has learned in her short time as a wife, if she were allowed the freedom to choose her own husband Julie would pick the older and wiser Wolmar, not the young and learned Saint Preux.

Mary Wollstonecraft recognized that Rousseau's books were dangerous because they promulgated the philosophy of moral differences between the sexes and promoted the separation of family and state. She understood that he used the novel to romance female readers into embracing the marriage plot and accepting their inferior status within the social contract. What makes *La Nouvelle Heloise* so instructive and insidious is that the words of sexual difference come from Julie, the heroine becoming the mouthpiece for

Rousseau's gender ideology. In *Emile* the tutor mouthed similar maxims about the appropriate moral relationship of the sexes and the political consequences of these gender differences for citizens of the republic. Before the *Social Contract,* and even before the sage observations of the tutor Jean-Jacques, the justification for the segregation of men and women into separate spheres is found in Julie's letters. It is Julie who, after reading the *Republic,* discounts Plato's sexual egalitarianism by arguing that the souls of men and women must not resemble each other and neither should the duties of the sexes. This argument will change little whether on the lips of the angelic Julie or in the edicts of the Legislator.

When most readers encounter a discussion of women within historical political thought, it is within the context of the marriage plot in philosophy, which assumes that daughters are destined to lives as wives and mothers within the privacy of the family home. Given the scripted lines of sexual difference reified in the distinctions between marriage and quest, women can only experience vicarious virtue through the actions and adventures of their husbands and sons. In *La Nouvelle Heloise,* philosophy colludes with the marriage plot to reconcile all the characters (both male and female) to society. Marriage is the cure for the corruption of sexuality in both the individual and the society. In the *Social Contract,* Rousseau argues that "man is born free and everywhere is in chains."[29] The citizen of Geneva reconciles men to the bonds of government by creating democratic government. Men are free to the extent that they only obey rules they make themselves. Self-government is the garland over men's chains. Similarly, the author of *Emile* and *La Nouvelle Heloise* attempts to reconcile women to their role in society as wives and mothers by creating complementary marriages. Since husband and wife are one, women are free to the extent that they obey the man they love. Rousseau's philosophical plot requires women to buy into an ideological illusion that marriage will make them whole. Because woman is not born free, she must be reconciled by romance to her chains—the bonds of matrimony.

Mary Wollstonecraft's transformation from female reader to feminist author is signified by her rejection of the marriage plot as woman's story in the history of political philosophy. Her objective is to end the subjection of women to men by exposing the seductive methods of Rousseau's philosophical plot. She understood that women were not born free in Rousseau's world because, in his book of women, biology was destiny. Therefore, Wollstonecraft repeatedly argued against the idea of an essential sexual character in either men or women, and she called on her country to establish coeducational day schools to instruct boys and girls to practice virtue at home and abroad in society. In *A Vindication of the Rights of Woman,* she wrote that "the grand end of their [women's] exertions should be to unfold their own faculties and acquire the dignity of conscious virtue." It was plain to her that in the quest for virtue there was "only one eternal standard," which applied equally to both sexes.[30]

In political theory the stories of men and women differed as the quest and marriage plots diverged. The different journeys of ordinary men and women were largely determined by the separation of the public and private spheres of everyday life. As if to symbolize this division of the world, in Rousseau's book, the hero Saint Preux circumnavigates the globe while the heroine, Julie de Wolmar, leaves her home at Clarens only to die. For Wollstonecraft Julie's fate signified that the ultimate problem of vicarious virtue for women was that it undermined the just republic by limiting women's lives. She argued that the social contract must be founded upon sexual equality. Women must be educated to participate fully in the experiences of the public sphere in order to justly exercise their rights as citizens. "To render the social compact truly equitable, and in order to spread those enlightening principles, which alone can meliorate the fate of man, women must be allowed to found their virtue on knowledge, which is scarcely possible unless they be educated in the same pursuits as men."[31]

THE QUEST FOR FEMINIST AUTHORITY

> In many works of this species, the hero is allowed to be mortal, and to become wise and virtuous as well as happy, by a train of events and circumstances. The heroines on the contrary, are to be born immaculate; and to act like goddesses of wisdom, just come forth highly finished Minervas from the head of Jove.
> —Mary Wollstonecraft, *The Wrongs of Woman, or Maria*

Janet Todd has noted there have been more biographies of the life of Mary Wollstonecraft than scholarly treatments of her writing.[32] Yet it has largely been this interest in the revolutionary life of the feminist author that has kept her work alive and introduced it to following generations of female readers. Here I add a few more pages to the growing biography of Mary Wollstonecraft in order to demonstrate how her personal quest for feminist authority led her to reject the marriage plot, a life choice that involved her in the eighteenth century's most important philosophical debates and political conflicts. She was born on April 27, 1759, in the silk-weaving district of Spitalfields in London into a family that moved throughout England and Wales, the second child and first daughter of Edward Wollstonecraft and Elizabeth Dixon. Today birth order is perceived as having a psychological impact upon children. In British society of the mid-eighteenth century the place of a child's birth in the sequence of children and the sex of that child were determining factors in the life of the child and the status of the adult. The laws of primogeniture and the code of sexual difference ensured that Mary Wollstonecraft would have little in common with her older brother, Ned.

Rousseau's happy images of a community of parents and children in which future citizens are educated stand in stark contrast to the miserable reality of the Wollstonecraft home. As a child Mary witnessed the violent alcoholic outbursts of her father. Edward Wollstonecraft, raised to the status of gentleman by an industrious and pious father, often raised a fist to his wife, Elizabeth, and beat their children. The father's cruelty to his spouse, children, and pets made a lasting impression upon his oldest daughter. We get a glimpse of Mary's childhood from her semiautobiographical first novel, *Mary, a Fiction*. We are introduced to the fictional Mary as she waits outside her parents' room ready to intervene if the argument between her father and mother turns to violence. "Mary . . . would watch at the door, until the storm was over, for unless it was, she could not rest." The young girl suffered at the hands of her mother as well. Throughout her life she would continually refer to her mother's preference for her older brother, the family heir. The attention given Ned as heir to the family money and name generated a deep sense of grievance and rivalry within his sister. Mary details the effects of this patriarchal partiality in developing the portrait of her fictional heroine. "Neglected in every respect, and left to the operations of her own mind, she considered every thing that came under her inspection, and learned to think." In this early novel Wollstonecraft weaves a tale of childhood that produces a woman of intellect. It is significant that it is a childhood marked by abuse and the disregard of parents. She wrote of this fictionalized self, "Could she have loved her father or mother, had they returned her affection, she would not so soon, perhaps, have sought out a new world."[33]

Wollstonecraft's search for a new world was animated as much by the desire for love as for learning. She developed her literary talent and her analytical skills in the process of trying to communicate her need for attention, affection, and friendship. Her relationships with other girls such as Jane Arden and Fanny Blood were formative. Wollstonecraft's primary education was largely the result of her correspondence with these girls (see the next chapter), and the fictionalized accounts of these friendships form the basis of much of her early writing. Her friendship with Fanny Blood developed from a correspondence in which Fanny instructed the sixteen-year-old Mary in the fine art of composing a letter. These lessons, given as a gift from one girl to another, were of fundamental importance in shaping the thought and later the theory of a woman whose letters to Burke and Rousseau would gain the attention of the British nation.

At twenty Mary Wollstonecraft entered the world of fashionable Bath society as a lady's companion, the servant of Mrs. Dawson, an aged widow. This first attempt at establishing independence from her family might have liberated her temporarily from the hostile atmosphere of the Wollstonecraft home but it made her dependent upon the good nature of an elderly employer. Her time in service ended abruptly when she was called home to care for her dying mother. The conditions within the household were much the same as they had been during her girlhood. After her mother's death Mary left her father's house to live with Fanny under the roof of the destitute Blood family.

At this time an incident occurred that dramatically exposed the problems encountered by a young woman upon entering married life. Mary's younger sister Eliza wed Meredith Bishop, a shipbuilder. The marriage was seen by Wollstonecraft's father and brother Ned as a good match. After the birth of their first child, Eliza was deeply depressed and begged Mary to ask their older brother, now a solicitor, to arrange a period of separation from her husband. When Ned made it clear he would not intervene on his sibling's behalf, Mary constructed an elaborate escape from the Bishop home, taking Eliza and abandoning her infant daughter. Mary and her sister went into hiding to escape British laws that required runaway wives to be returned to their husbands. While Meredith Bishop searched for his wife and for a nurse for his child, Mary contemplated the future. Now she needed to create a household for Fanny, Eliza, and her youngest sister, Everina, who left home after their father remarried (taking the family maid as his second wife). Mary considered the few options open to a woman of her class to make a living wage and decided to open a day school. The four women could teach girls a little bit of writing, drawing, sewing, French, and music. After an unsuccessful attempt in Islington, Wollstonecraft and her sisters opened a second school in Newington Green, a neighborhood recognized for its dissenter population. Here Mary was introduced to the radical Unitarian minister Dr. Richard Price and his circle of friends. In these discussions she first encountered the flame of political rebellion that would add brilliance to her life.

Mary Wollstonecraft's intellectual journey had only begun in Newington Green. For years her fondest wish had been to form a household with Fanny Blood. But within a year Fanny, who had long been engaged to marry, sailed to Lisbon to become a bride. Soon the news of a pregnancy would bring Mary to Portugal. Fanny suffered from consumption, and the strain of an advanced disease only increased the pain of childbirth. Fanny Blood Skeys died hours after her child was born, a son, who was dead the next day. Wollstonecraft sailed back to England where she found that her school had suffered the ills of mismanagement, losing pupils and the few boarders who had helped to pay her many creditors. The Blood family grieved the death of their daughter and turned to Mary for financial help in their time of mourning. She learned that there was money to be made in writing about education. Wollstonecraft used the ten pounds sterling she received for her first book, *Thoughts on the Education of Daughters,* to buy passage for the Blood family to their ancestral home in Ireland.

Faced with death and debt herself, Mary Wollstonecraft left the country of her birth to enter Ireland as a servant, the governess to the Lord and Lady Kingsborough of Mitchelstown Castle in County Cork. By all accounts the young author did not make a suitable governess. Mary's ideas about the behavior of the King children were at odds with those of the children's mother, Lady Caroline. She was put in charge of the lessons of the three King daughters. The oldest, Margaret, became particularly fond of her governess and later in life was to write an autobiographical fragment in which she detailed Wollstonecraft's unconventional ideas about girlhood independence. In letters from this period Wollstonecraft often lamented the wild nature of the girls and ridiculed the opulent lifestyle of their mother, who would lavish affection on her dogs and yet cruelly beat her children. The battle for control of the children added a chill to the Palladian mansion of one of Ireland's wealthiest families. The rivalry between the two women exploded one evening when Lady Caroline witnessed her servant blush after receiving a bow from Lord King. The children's attention was not the only source of conflict within the castle. Miss Wollstonecraft was dismissed on the pretext of "corrupting her charges."[34] She found herself homeless and unemployed only months after joining the King household. But she did not leave Ireland empty-handed. Mary Wollstonecraft took with her the manuscript of her first novel, *Mary, a Fiction*. Once in London, she visited her publisher, Joseph Johnson, and in the course of an afternoon her future became that of a woman of words.

The year was 1788, and in London as in Paris there were new voices of dissent. Joseph Johnson had made his trade the publication and circulation of radical thought. In this year before the French Revolution, Johnson and the Scottish freethinker Thomas Christie began a new journal, the *Analytical Review*. Johnson welcomed Wollstonecraft into his literary household, publishing her novel and hiring her to write reviews of other fictions within the pages of the *Analytical*. Mary Wollstonecraft had finally entered a "new world." For a time she lived in rooms above Johnson's bookshop in St. Paul's Churchyard. His dinner table was the scene of famous debates. In this politicized atmosphere Wollstonecraft thought and wrote and was introduced to other influential thinkers whose works would shape a new century. The passions released by the French Revolution crossed the Channel and roused the Johnson circle. Mary poured her energy into her writing, translating the ideas of the Continent for an English audience.

During the next two years, a relatively unknown lady novelist, she wrote the twin political tracts that would make her famous. In November 1790, *A Vindication of the Rights of Men* appeared, the first of many replies to Edmund Burke's *Reflections on the Revolution in France*. In this text she attacked the venerated ideas of the Right Honorable Burke who had condemned the French

Revolution and its English supporters, singling out Wollstonecraft's friend Dr. Price from Newington Green. In 1792 Johnson published *A Vindication of the Rights of Woman*. Here the feminist author developed a model of female education aimed at creating a citizen woman capable of governing herself and her nation. Wollstonecraft argued: "The *divine right* of husbands, like the divine right of kings, may, it is hoped, in this enlightened age, be contested without danger."[35] The spirit of a republican age was incompatible with the notion of vicarious virtue and the subjugation of women to men, both inherent in the marriage plot. She proclaimed that women must articulate the story of their own lives and act for themselves. To become democratic citizens and to participate in the public world, women must challenge social custom and change personal habits. Wollstonecraft called for a revolution in female manners, inciting other women to claim the feminist authority of representing themselves and their own interests in word and deed. The female reader could become a revolutionary agent of change by putting down her book and taking part in the historical dramas of her nation.

With the publication of *A Vindication of the Rights of Woman* the world did indeed become the book of Mary Wollstonecraft. In this text she analyzed the lives of woman upon the historical page and in turn began to question the meaning of her own life. Wollstonecraft put her theory into practice by embarking on a quest of her own to experience the revolution in France for herself. It was the beginning of the Committee of Public Safety's reign of terror in Paris. An Englishwoman of letters was quick to make friends with others who had gathered to mark a moment in the history of human rights. Soon after her arrival in Paris Mary wrote to Johnson that she had seen the carriage of Louis XVI drawn through the streets to his trial. "I am going to bed—and, for the first time in my life, I cannot put out the candle."[36]

The darkness that encircled her would soon be brushed away by the entrance of an American expatriot, Gilbert Imlay. Wollstonecraft found a militarized Paris an inhospitable setting for their blossoming romance and the author took up residence in the country village of Neuilly. Mary and Imlay were continually together and from this union she conceived her first child. In the fall of 1793 the French government ordered the arrest of all English citizens. Imlay and Wollstonecraft went to the American Embassy in Paris and received a certificate stating that she was his wife, allowing her to stay in France. During her pregnancy she wrote *A Historical and Moral View of the French Revolution,* a book she was warned to hide from the authorities and that she finished only days before her daughter, Fanny, was born in Le Havre.

In her letters to Imlay, Wollstonecraft described the physical experience of male and female as speaking a "new language" to her, one that altered her conceptualization of the rights of men and women. The birth of her daughter forced her to redefine the connection between woman and mother, adult and child. Yet, shortly after Fanny was born, Imlay returned to London and took up residence with a young actress in the West End, leaving Mary to nurse their child in loneliness. Once again she was confronted with the neglect she had felt as a girl. A series of letters between Wollstonecraft and Imlay collected in the nineteenth century by the publisher Charles Keegan Paul chronicle her confusion, anger, and desperation as she slowly realized he would not be returning to his family. Wollstonecraft considered her options as an unwed mother, aware that Fanny would be stigmatized as an illegitimate child by English law and society. She decided to return to England in the hope that, once confronted with his daughter, Imlay would accept the responsibilities of a father. In London, Wollstonecraft used the name Mrs. Imlay believing that this matrimonial prefix would protect Fanny from the slurs of bastardy. But her appearance only aggravated Imlay's irresponsibility. Tormented by the lack of money as well as by the loss of love, she found she could not write. Unable to communicate and thus alleviate her sorrow, Mary Wollstonecraft took an overdose of laudanum.

She was revived to the sound of Imlay's promises. He devised a plan for her to act as his surrogate in litigating a business dispute in Sweden. Once the transactions were completed he vowed that he would meet Mary and Fanny in Hamburg. Thus, Wollstonecraft, who had always held the deepest contempt for commerce, traveled with her small child and a nurse to the wilds of Scandinavia in an effort to regain both love and self-respect. The hazardous journey returned Mary to her pen. *A Short Residence in Sweden, Norway, and Denmark* is a text that details a woman's coming to consciousness of her strengths and weaknesses in a picturesque landscape. Fashioned from her letters to Imlay, this small book did not bring the beloved back to the lover. However, the narrative would draw a different man to the lonely writer, another solitary walker who would eventually become her husband.

Gilbert Imlay did not come to Hamburg. Mary and Fanny once again sailed for England. By 1795 the republican aspirations of the revolution had failed, and the reactionary forces in England used the uncommon means of the Seditious Acts to quiet the noise of the common man. Mary sought to drown her own voice forever by plunging into the Thames from the Putney Bridge. Once again she was pulled from the dark waters of death. Soon Joseph Johnson published her travel writings and reintroduced Wollstonecraft to his intellectual circle. Mrs. Imlay began to renew her old acquaintances. One such visit brought her to the doorstep of another of Johnson's authors, the anarchist philosopher William Godwin. The renowned authors of *A Vindication of the Rights of Woman* and *An Enquiry Concerning Political Justice* began a passionate affair. Godwin wrote of their relationship, "It was friendship melting into love."[37] Their intimacy sparked a new life, and Wollstonecraft (pregnant again) and Godwin, the two outspoken critics of marriage, exchanged vows in St. Pancras Church in the spring of 1797. In this short summer Mary Wollstonecraft's happiness was complete. William Godwin became a father to Fanny and eagerly awaited the birth of their child. Mary worked on a novel, *The Wrongs of Woman, or Maria,* a tale that would personalize the political theory of her rights tract.

Mary Wollstonecraft repeatedly tried to establish a new story for women that could transcend the limitations of the marriage plot and allow women to quest for knowledge and meaning in their lives. At the end of her own life, she was working on a book that she hoped would accomplish this personal and political goal. In *The Wrongs of Woman, or Maria* Wollstonecraft presented the female reader with another heroine different from Sophie and Julie, Rousseau's beloved characters. Maria is a woman whose wrongs contest the tradition of political rights. Proponents of the philosophy of the Rights of Man had created revolution in France and rebellion in England, but few of the radicals went so far as to attack the sexual double standards of society or to champion the rights of women within the marriage contract. Women remained chained by an ideology of sexual difference that justified their exclusion from the freedoms of the public sphere.[38]

To vindicate the rights of woman was to challenge the world as most women knew it. On two continents revolutionaries had proclaimed the independence of freeborn men and had written constitutions that guaranteed their natural rights. Yet in the wake of these democratic revolutions Wollstonecraft's *Maria* could still ask, "Was not the world a vast prison, and women born slaves?"[39] The feminist author of *A Vindication of the Rights of Woman* had argued that women, like men, were born free. In *The Wrongs of Woman* she analyzed the processes whereby women were compelled to forfeit their birthright and become enslaved by romantic notions of sensibility to the men who should be their equals.[40] At the center of her critique was the relationship between Rousseau's books and the female reader. It is through reading *La Nouvelle Heloise* that Maria falls in love with her fellow prisoner, Darnford, just as Sophie's reading of the *Adventures of Telemachus* set the stage for her initial idolization and eventual disappointment with Emile. In *The Wrongs of Woman, or Maria* the feminist author exposed the danger posed to the female reader by an overidentification with the heroines of romantic novels. Mary Wollstonecraft argued that, when a woman sees herself in Jean-Jacques Rousseau's sentimental heroines, she becomes complicit in her own seduction and subjugation.

An examination of Mary Wollstonecraft's life and work reveals the profound influence of Jean-Jacques Rousseau. However, it was her death that made Wollstonecraft's own story most like those of his heroines. The feminist author who had created a new life for women in her writing died following the complications of childbirth on September 8, 1797. Her novel *The Wrongs of Woman* was left unfinished. A bereaved Godwin edited her final fiction and published it in a posthumous collection that included his *Memoirs of the Author of "The Rights of Woman."* Paradoxically, the *Memoirs,* a grief-stricken tell-all, quickly made Wollstonecraft's story another cautionary tale for female readers. Godwin's attempt to vindicate his wife by examining how she combined theory and practice in the actions of a revolutionary life was quickly rejected by a reading audience tired of revolution. To anti-Jacobin critics her death in childbirth was seen as a symbol of the unchangeable nature of sexual difference. The tale of Mary Wollstonecraft as morality play was told to future generations in order to underscore the costs of female impropriety and to display the danger of love outside of marriage. The manner of her life and death became a warning to female readers not to follow in her rebellious footsteps.

CHAPTER TWO

A Voice from the Void

> Before I go on will you pause—and if after deliberating you will promise not to mention to anyone what you know of my designs (though you may think my requesting you to conceal them unreasonable) I will trust to your honor—and proceed. Mr. Johnson whose uncommon kindness, I believe, has saved me from despair, and vexations I shrink back from—and feared to encounter; assures me that if I exert my talents by writing I may support myself in a comfortable way. I am then going to become the first of a new genus.
>
> —Mary Wollstonecraft to her sister Everina, November 7, 1787

Mary Wollstonecraft mused that she would be the first of a new genus when she chose to live as an author. Yet in the autumn of 1787, it must have seemed highly unlikely that she would leave any mark at all upon posterity. The vast majority of the women of her generation were married and were the mothers of children. The facts of Wollstonecraft's life were very different. At twenty-eight and unmarried she had already exhausted most forms of respectable employment for a middle-class woman of the late eighteenth century. She had earned her bread for over a decade as lady's companion, seamstress, teacher, and governess. When Mary Wollstonecraft claimed the authority to write, and (more significant) to write about political rights, she broke with her personal past and created a wave in the history of political thought that had not been seen since Socrates discussed women's capacity to be Guardians in the *Republic*. The political intent of her writing was nothing less than the complete subversion of the traditional philosophical plot in which she claimed women were born only to "propagate and rot."[1]

Wollstonecraft's political theory, born of a feminist consciousness, has been largely ignored by mainstream political theorists, the descendants of the canonical tradition. Her work has been considered illegitimate because she refused to acknowledge the patriarchy of the canonized forefathers. As Carole Pateman has noted, the genesis of political theory is singularly masculine:

> Only men—who can create political life—can take part in the original pact, yet the political fictions speak to women, too, through the language of the "individual." A curious message is sent to women, who represent everything that the individual is not, but the message must continually be conveyed because the meaning of the individual and the social contract depend on women and the sexual contract. Women must acknowledge the political fiction and speak the language even as the terms of the original pact exclude them from the fraternal conversation.[2]

Historically, only men have had the generative capacity to bring political theory to life in dialogues, tracts, and treatises. Wollstonecraft's criticism of the canonical tradition directly confronted the sexual politics of gender and generation and created a new form of feminist political analysis that made it possible to theorize women's lives.

Yet a mere ten years after she proposed her brave plan to live as an author, in what was surely one of the tragic ironies of history, Mary Wollstonecraft died from complications of childbirth. Today she has been reborn in the works of many scholars who have used her writings to construct a political history for women. The name of the woman author whose own authority was constantly under attack has become a basis for legitimating the work of a new generation of feminist writers. She has been read as a humanist, who in arguing for women's rights embraced the Enlightenment ideals of reason and self-government. She has also been read as a feminist, who recognized in her analysis of the situation of women the false universalism of Enlightenment humanism. However, while illuminating important aspects of Wollstonecraft's feminist theory, these readings fail to examine the complex ways in which her writing focuses our attention on the sexual politics of authority.

To read Mary Wollstonecraft is to ask how a woman is authorized to write political theory. The history of political thought has often been represented as a conversation that invites everyone to take their place at the theoretical table. Feminist theorists, beginning with Wollstonecraft, argue that women have been excluded from the canonical conversation.[3] Wollstonecraft's writing, unauthorized by the canonical tradition, interrupts the fraternal conversation of political thought. Her work, from first page to last paragraph, represents a voice from the void. She invites to the theoretical table subjects that had not been represented within the writings of the fathers of the canon, foremost among them being the girl. The canon of political thought does not discuss female development or chart a developmental course for women as citizens. Mary Wollstonecraft gave voice to the girl and made her presence felt in the eighteenth-century debates about a woman's place. In speaking of the girl in her early works, and in letting the girl speak throughout her writings, Wollstonecraft articulated what had not been said within the canonical conversation. Indeed, the girl gives voice to the conflicts of gender and generation unacknowledged within the history of political thought. More important, by focusing on the girl we are better able to understand the gender politics of the infantilization of women.

Wollstonecraft's close attention to female development, from girlhood to womanhood, empowered her to attack the subject position of women within canonical political theory. Her critical focus on the girl enabled her to fully visualize women as autonomous subjects and responsible citizens. In her first published works, an educational text and a didactic novel, she began to develop the arguments that form the basis of her twin political tracts, the two vindications. In this manner Wollstonecraft's early writings on the girl anticipated some of the most pressing concerns of contemporary feminist theorists, who from Carol Gilligan to Luce Irigaray have claimed that until we acknowledge the voice of the girl we will not be able to articulate a truly feminist theory.[4]

In this chapter I examine Mary Wollstonecraft's earliest writings. We first encounter the girl in Wollstonecraft's own adolescent letters, where we meet the feminist as a fourteen year old who dreamed of independence. In Wollstonecraft herself we may see an eighteenth-century predecessor of Gilligan's "female resister."[5] This girl was also present in her early publications as she wrote of the duties of daughters and the conflicts of coming of age in a sexist society. Paradoxically, the appearance of the girl in Wollstonecraft's writings has gone relatively unnoticed by many scholars who have dismissed these works as juvenilia. *Thoughts on the Education of Daughters* provides a thoughtful analysis of the effects of social prejudice on female education and economic dependence on women's situation. *Mary, a Fiction* displays a new approach to female friendship and marriage. *Original Stories* offers an original look at the relationship between adults and children. Read alone, these works may seem unremarkable; but if we read them together and place them within their historical context we become aware of how the voice of the girl in Wollstonecraft's writing matured into a distinctive feminist language with which to speak of self. I believe it is here in these early writings that we find an outline of Mary Wollstonecraft's most famous arguments, and it is also here that she found the inspiration and the authority to articulate a theory of women's rights.

THE VOICE OF THE GIRL

> According to my promise I sit down to write to you.
> —Mary Wollstonecraft to Jane Arden, May 1773

Remarkably, we have a great deal of evidence about Mary Wollstonecraft's own girlhood. Even more fortuitous is the fact that the majority of this information comes from Wollstonecraft herself. Her biographer Ralph Wardle collected and edited her personal letters, which begin with correspondence to a childhood friend at the age of fourteen. Wollstonecraft frequently returned to her own youth in her writing and it is here that we first hear the voice of the girl. Her earliest correspondence, with a clergyman's daughter named Jane Arden, reveals a girl's struggle to find the time to read and write. These letters, filled with poetry, country gossip, and demands for a quick and affectionate response, usually ended with her mother's call or the cries of her younger siblings. "I have a hundred things to add, but can't get time for Mama is calling me, so shall reserve them for another letter."[6]

The young Mary was concerned that her letters to the older and better-educated Jane would reveal her grammatical errors as well as her personal faults. "I have glanced over this letter and find it so ill written that I fear you cannot make out one line of this last page, but—you know, my dear, I have not the advantage of a Master as you have, and it is with great difficulty to get my brother to mend my pens." Stuck in what she termed a "dilemma," without "one pen that will make a stroke," she signed her name.[7] Ned, the oldest son, had both books and pens as he was destined for a career at the bar. Mary, the oldest daughter, was destined for marriage and she expended her energy in the tug-of-war of caring for their younger sisters and brothers. These constant battles pitted self-improvement against familial obligations and taught lessons that took a toll on her spirit as well as on her handwriting.

Even at this young age Mary Wollstonecraft dreamed of independence. But her daydreams reveal a very practical account of the necessary exchange of money for liberty, an exchange in which eighteenth-century English women, considered by law as property themselves, were at a decided disadvantage. In a subsequent letter the fourteen-year-old girl details the settlement of a "great fortune" of three hundred pounds on the Miss N——s, noting that "a woman of any oeconomy may live very genteelly on 150 pounds a year." These wild speculations aside, the letter concludes, "I am afraid you cannot read this as all the children are plaguing me."[8] Just a few years later, beset by financial problems as she struggled to support herself and her sisters without a legacy, Wollstonecraft wrote another letter in which she figured that three young women working at embroidery and watercolor landscapes could manage to scrape by on their collective earnings of a pound a week.[9]

However, at fourteen Mary's desire for a singular friendship, rather than the endless needs of child care, put an end to this first and formative correspondence. Jane Arden, the daughter of a preacher and self-styled philosopher, had a wider circle of acquaintances than Mary, daughter of a father whose dissipated ways would soon cost him the title of both gentleman and farmer. Even in a country town like Beverly in the northern county of Yorkshire, everyone had their place in the social hierarchy. On a visit to the Ardens, Mary believed herself to be displaced by a new arrival. She quickly picked up her pen. "Before I begin I beg pardon for the freedom of my style.—If I did not love you I would not write so; —I have a heart that scorns disguise, and a countenance which will not dissemble: I have formed romantic notions of friendship."[10]

Indeed, in this letter the young Wollstonecraft drew a vivid portrait of herself in ink that flowed with jealousy and was blotted by an awareness of hurt pride. "I am a little singular in my thoughts of love and friendship; I must have the first place or none.—I own your behavior is more according to the opinions of the world, but I would break from such narrow bounds." In the great chain of being, even a child at play must know her place. But in girlhood Wollstonecraft refused to play by the rules of the social game. She argued that she had been intentionally snubbed by Mrs. Arden. "When I have been at your house with Miss J——— the greatest respect has been paid to her; every thing handed to her first;—in short, as if she were a superior being.—Your Mama too behaved with more politeness to her."[11] Wollstonecraft's words speak to a self-consciousness of position as well as her knowledge of the social conventions that afforded the newcomer primacy of place. This awareness of women's situation and class position was a theme that would distinguish her writing throughout her career. Wollstonecraft's desire "to have first place or none" would lead her repeatedly to break the "narrow bounds" of the world of opinion.

Six years later, at the age of twenty, Mary Wollstonecraft resumed her correspondence with her girlhood friend Jane Arden. Neither woman had married and each of them had left their families to make their own way in the world. She wrote, "I often recollect with pleasure the many agreeable days we spent together when we eagerly told every girlish secret of our hearts—Those were peaceful days; your's since that period may have been as tranquil, but mine have been far from otherwise."[12] In these letters Wollstonecraft, now employed as a companion to an elderly woman in Bath, tried to bring their friendship up to date, giving an account of herself to Arden who was living in Norfolk as a governess. Her letters from Bath are a sad corrective for anyone who has read Jane Austen's fiction. Under different circumstances a young lady in this spa town would have enjoyed many entertaining diversions, but Wollstonecraft as a working woman had little experience of these pleasures, even though for two years she had lived within walking distance of the Pump Room, the Promenade, and the Assembly Rooms. She wrote to Arden, "Bath is remarkably full at present, and nothing is going forward but Balls and plays without end or number.—I seldom go into public;—I have been but twice to the rooms." The social season in full swing, Wollstonecraft sat on the sidelines while the choreography of marriage twirled ceaselessly around her.

> I am quite a piece of still life, not but that I am a friend to mirth and cheerfulness; but I would move in a small circle;—I am fond of domestic pleasures and have not spirit sufficient to bustle

> about. . . . There is no prospect of my quitting this place in a hurry, necessity not choice ties me to it (not but that I receive the greatest civility from this family)—yet, I am detained here only by prudential motives, if I was to follow the bent of my inclination, I shod [sic] haste away. You will not wonder at this,—when you consider that I am among Strangers, far from all my former connections: —The more I see of the world, the more anxious I am to preserve my old friends, for I am now slower than ever in forming friendships;—I would wish to cherish a universal love to all mankind, but the principal part of my heart must be occupied by those who have for years had a place there.

Her half-hearted assertions to the contrary, she concluded, "I wish I could write any thing that would entertain you, but I mix so little with the world, that I am at a loss for news."[13]

To the sympathetic reader Mary Wollstonecraft seems to have lost her sense of self. Certainly there is something new about these letters. It is her concern about boundaries; her adult world suddenly appears to be so much smaller than the Yorkshire countryside of her childhood. Perhaps in the quiet, monotonous hours of her enforced seclusion she began to develop her theory that men's superior ability to reason as well as their physical strength were not the products of nature but of the social conventions that allowed men the freedom to interact with the world. Wollstonecraft was drawn inward to explore a mental landscape that may have been familiar to many women in her situation. "My wishes and expectations are very moderate.—I don't know which is the worst—to think too little or too much.—'tis a difficulty to draw the line, and keep clear of melancholy and thoughtlessness."[14] What had happened to the young girl whose knowledge of her own heart enabled her to so powerfully speak her mind?

Wollstonecraft's letters demonstrate that her resignation to her predicament gradually turned to resentment, and ultimately to resistance. It seems she was painfully aware of how her marginalized position as a woman in service placed her at the edge of social life and restricted her participation in the wider world:

> To say the truth, I am very indifferent to the opinion of the world in general;—I wish to retire as much from it as possible,—I am particularly sick of genteel life, as it is called;—the unmeaning civilities that I see every day practiced don't agree with my temper;—I long

for a little sincerity, and look forward with pleasure to the time when I shall lay aside all restraint. . . . This is the gayest of all gay places; nothing but dress and amusements are going forward;—I am only a spectator—I have lost all my relish for them:—early in life, before misfortune had broken my spirits, I had not the power of partaking of them, and now I am both from habit and inclination averse to them.

At this point in her life the weight of dependence and the isolation of a life in service had broken the spirit of the girl who had "formed romantic notions of friendship" and who wanted "first place or none."

I beseech you; struggle with any obstacles rather than go into a state of dependence:—I speak feelingly.—I have felt the weight, and would have you by all means avoid it. . . . Your employment tho a troublesome one, is very necessary, and you have the opportunity of doing much good, by instilling good principles into the young and ignorant, and at the close of life you'll have the pleasure to think that you have not lived in vain, and, believe me, this reflection is worth a life of care.[15]

If we look closely at this correspondence, we find Mary Wollstonecraft writing about the extravagance of the court of George III at Windsor, composing her letter on top of a chest of drawers that she used as her desk. The author of *A Vindication of the Rights of Woman* sometimes appears within these letters only to vanish into the page, the strength of her argument diluted like the watered-down ink she used to save a few pence. "I have put so much water in my ink, I am afraid you will not be able to read my faint characters, and besides my candle gives such a dreadful light."[16] Short on time, candles, and money she yearned to be her own mistress. It was in a letter from this period that Wollstonecraft learned of the Arden sisters' plan to live together, earning their keep by running that peculiar eighteenth-century institution, the dame school.

Soon after, Wollstonecraft determined to follow a similar course and set up a household with Fanny Blood, a young woman who had been her constant friend since their introduction by the Reverend Clare five years earlier when the Wollstonecraft family lived in Hoxton outside of London.

> I know this resolution may appear a little extraordinary, but in forming it I follow the dictates of reason as well as the bent of my inclination; for tho' I am willing to do what good I can in my generation, yet on many accounts I am averse to any matrimonial tie... To my great satisfaction, I found Miss Blood in better health than I expected from accounts I had of her.—She received me as she ever has done in the most friendly manner, and we passed a comfortable week together, which knew no other alloy than what arose from the thoughts of parting so soon.—The next time we meet, it will be for a longer continuance, and to that period I look, as to the most important one of my life: this connection must give the color to my future days, for I have now given up every expectation and dependence that wod [sic] interfere with my determination of spending my time with her.[17]

Thus, we find evidence of one of the keynotes of Wollstonecraft's feminism as she repeatedly claimed in these early letters that she would never marry. The force of her aversion to an institution she would later liken to prostitution, slavery, and imprisonment was displayed in an angry letter to Jane in acknowledgment of the marriage of Arden's sister. Just four weeks after the wedding, Wollstonecraft was not sure that her well wishes would still be appropriate:

> I was just going to desire you to wish her joy (to use the common phrase) but I am afraid my good wishes might be unseasonable, as I find by the date of your letter that the honey moon, and the next moon too must be almost over—The joy, and all that, [here she has crossed out "sort of thing" but it is still legible to the reader] is certainly over by this time, and all the raptures have subsided, and the dear hurry of visiting and figuring away as a bride, and all the rest of the delights of matrimony are past and gone and have left no traces behind them except disgust:—I hope I am mistaken, but this is the fate of most married pairs.[18]

She followed this outburst by misquoting Ecclesiastes as the wisdom of Solomon and ended the letter by reiterating her own commitment to live free or die: "'there is nothing new under the sun' for which reason I will not marry, for I dont want to be tied to this nasty world, and old maids are of so little consequence—that 'let them live or die, nobody will laugh or cry.'"

Here, Wollstonecraft, a self-styled old maid who had survived the social disaster of having a younger sister marry before she herself made the trip to the altar, made a resolution of much consequence: *"It is a happy thing to be a mere blank, and to be able to pursue one's own whims, where they lead, without having a husband and half a hundred children at hand to teaze and controul a poor woman who wishes to be free."*[19] Better indeed to be a blank than to follow the scripted lines of womanhood filling the role of biblical helpmate and domestic drudge. Better still for a woman to avoid the perils of the marriage plot entirely by supporting herself. Mary Wollstonecraft knew well that few couples lived happily ever after. As her parents' daughter she had witnessed firsthand the death and destruction that often sealed the marriage contract. Her younger sister Eliza Wollstonecraft Bishop had suffered postpartum depression after giving birth to her first child. Mary, called to care for her sister, watched as she sobbed uncontrollably and ranted about the abuse she received at the hands of her husband. In time Mary became convinced that Eliza was sinking into madness and that she would never recover as long as she remained within her husband's house. So she helped her sister run for her life, leaving behind her infant daughter, to seek refuge in a boardinghouse while Meredith Bishop scoured London for his fugitive wife. In this desperate situation it was up to Mary to devise a new story for herself and her sister.

The harsh realities of poverty and legal limbo that Mary confronted as she and Eliza began to plot a different chapter in their lives would become the basis of the realism that marks her books. Mary and Eliza enlisted the aid of their younger sister, Everina, and the help of Fanny Blood to open a dame school. First in Islington and later at Newington Green, the four women worked to teach their students and earn a living. Just as their independence seemed secure, however, Fanny Blood announced that she would marry and follow her husband, Hugh Skeys, to Portugal. Once again the marriage plot seemed to twist the life out of a young woman, as Fanny, already weakened by consumption, sickened under the weight of her first pregnancy. Mary borrowed money from her Newington Green neighbor, the widow of the preacher James Burgh, to travel to Lisbon and attend her friend during her confinement. She arrived at Fanny's bedside only to see her die and to help Hugh Skeys bury his wife and infant son.

Burdened and embittered by her experiences of marriage and

childbearing, Mary Wollstonecraft would rework these events over and over again in her didactic novels and polemical tracts. Maybe then it is not surprising that her words to Jane Arden resonated with a hard-won wisdom. It is here that she began to write her own "book of woman" as she asserted her birthright to a better life. "Some may follow St. Paul's advice 'in doing well,' but I, like a true born Englishwoman, will endeavour to do better."[20] In the following years, what had begun as a dream of negative liberty, freedom from the familial obligations of gender and the womanly duty of generation, was transformed with age and experience into a dream of positive liberty, freedom to become a new type of being. But what would that new being be? Wollstonecraft was determined not to marry or bear children. Her determination was the product of her own experience of the darker side of the marriage plot. Regardless of the risks, she asserted her independence as a freeborn Englishwoman. Freed from the constraints of gender and generation that were the lot of many of her sisters in England, she resolved to become the "first of a new genus." She continues, "I tremble at the attempt yet if I fail—I *only* suffer—and should I succeed my dear Girls will ever in sickness have a home—and a refuge where for a few months in the year, they may forget the cares that disturb the rest."[21] Mary Wollstonecraft had decided to create herself anew as a woman author.

VERBALIZING THE VOID

> In the following pages I have endeavoured to point out some important things with respect to female education. It is true, many treatises have been already written; yet it occurred to me, that much still remained to be said.
> —Mary Wollstonecraft, *Thoughts on the Education of Daughters*

What could a young woman with little formal instruction of her own add to the eighteenth-century discourse on education? Mary Wollstonecraft brought her observations of the relationship between the inferior education of the girl and the limited opportunities available to the woman. In her first published work she analyzed her own situation and reflected on the position of women within late-eighteenth-century English society. Her resolve to live free of the marriage bond and the ties of motherhood had required her to earn her own subsistence. She had made a meager living by trying her hand at the various forms of respectable employment available to a woman of the middling classes. Wollstonecraft believed that her experience as a working woman, combined with the lessons she had learned as a schoolmistress in the dissenting community of Newington Green, gave her the authority to enter the debate about female education.

Wollstonecraft knew *Thoughts on the Education of Daughters* would be compared to other popular tracts such as Dr. Gregory's *Father's Legacy to Daughters* and Dr. Fordyce's *Sermons for Young Ladies*. She would deal with the inadequacies of these texts later in *A Vindication of the Rights of Woman*. But for now she prefaced her book with the statement that, from her perspective as a woman and a daughter, there appeared "much that still needed to be said." Her audience consisted of parents like her own who had not given much thought to the education of their female children. Wollstonecraft's formal education had consisted of nothing more than a few years in the village school when her family lived in Beverly in Yorkshire. From an early age she believed that this education had not prepared her for the struggles of life. To supplement her knowledge of the world and support herself in the trials she faced, Wollstonecraft had engaged in a program of reading and self-improvement. She hoped her book would reach an audience of female readers similarly employed in a program of self-help, so that they might find comfort and counsel in her words. Emboldened by her project Wollstonecraft refused in her preface to apologize for her efforts, as was the literary custom of many of her contemporaries who, as Mary Poovey has noted, made a rhetorical ritual of begging the public's pardon for daring to put their ideas on paper. "I will not swell these sheets by writing apologies for my attempt." Instead she claimed that her writing would not be in vain if it might "prove useful to one fellow-creature, and beguile any hours, which sorrow has made heavy."[22]

Wollstonecraft's first published work, *Thoughts on the Education of Daughters,* displays her search for an authoritative voice with which to address her audience. There is a tension within this text; conventional advice for modifying girls' behavior similar to that found within other eighteenth-century conduct books often mingles on the same page with radical calls for girlhood freedom. For example, she wrote, "I must own, I am quite charmed when I see a sweet young creature, shrinking as it were from observation, and listening rather than talking." But in the following paragraph she indicated a contradictory desire for the girl to actively engage in the pleasurable pursuit of ideas. "Above all, try to teach them to combine their ideas. It is of more use than can be conceived, for a child to learn to compare things that are similar in some respects, and different in others. *I wish them to be taught to think*—thinking, indeed, is a severe exercise, and exercise of either mind or body will not at first be entered on, but with a view to pleasure" (11; my emphasis).

A few pages later the shrinking girl has lost her charm. The author who claimed that there was still much to be said on the subject of female education disregarded the customary edict that children are better seen and not heard. She argued, "Children should be permitted to enter into conversation; but it requires great discernment to find out such subjects as will gradually improve them." She suggests that stories about animals are a proper object of children's attention, providing lessons that "form the temper and cultivate the good dispositions of the heart." She recommends a series of books for children including Dorothy Kilner's *The Life and Perambulations of a Mouse* and Anna Laetitia Barbauld's *Hymns in Prose for Children.* Her own contribution to this literature, *Original Stories From Real Life,* contains a number of tales that teach children to treat animals humanely (10). Later, in the preface to *Original Stories,* she protested she would have had no reason to write her book if parents would just talk with their children.

Her wish that the girl be taught to think materialized in her argument that girls be given the cognitive tools to develop independent thought. "It may be observed, that I recommend the mind's being put into a proper train, and then left to itself" (21). Throughout her letters of this period, she made frequent mention of the idea that a mind of genius would educate itself. Perhaps this maxim brought resolution to her conflicted thoughts about the inadequacy of her own education. She argued that freedom of expression and action were necessary for independent thinking.

> Fixed rules cannot be given, it must depend on the nature and strength of the understanding; and those who observe it can best tell what kind of cultivation will improve it. The mind is not, cannot be created by the teacher, though it may be cultivated, and its real

powers found out. . . . I would have everyone try to form an opinion of an author themselves, though modesty may restrain them from mentioning it. Many are so anxious to have the reputation of taste, that they praise authors whose merit is indisputable. I am sick of hearing of the sublimity of Milton, the elegance and harmony of Pope, and the original untaught genius of Shakespeare. (21)

The role of the teacher was to cultivate the girl's understanding, not to impose an artificial order on a young mind that would restrict the free flow of ideas. Wollstonecraft claimed that a girl's potential for wisdom was determined by her own "nature and strength," not by the social markers of birth and rank. Thus, in her scheme for female education, the "real power" is vested in the girl. Indeed, she was concerned about the potential dangers of the teacher/student relationship, a concern that prefigures her argument in *A Vindication of the Rights of Woman*. Wollstonecraft read Rousseau's *La Nouvelle Heloise* as a dangerous depiction of the evils of trusting the moral education of an innocent girl to a man with a world of experience.

Wollstonecraft's *Thoughts on the Education of Daughters* is an important text because it displays her attempts to differentiate the girl from the woman. It is here that she first created the continuum of female development from childhood to adulthood that forms the foundation of her later theoretical writings. *The aim of her pedagogy, teaching a girl to think for herself, is also the first principle of her political theory, namely, that rational women have the right to govern themselves.* For Wollstonecraft, it was education, not marriage, that determined female maturity. Her analysis of the situation of her sex began in the intimacy of the nursery and concluded with a chapter concerning women in public places. In tracing this path she carefully distinguished the girl from the woman, using the capacity for rational thought rather than social customs of courtship and marriage to differentiate the seasons of a female life.

One of the most interesting components of her analysis of girlhood education and womanly maturation is her treatment of beauty, a discussion that would have serious implications for her response to Edmund Burke's *Reflections on the Revolution in France*. Wollstonecraft quickly dismissed the social conventions of female beauty, which pitted the exercise of the mind against the development of the body, conventions that for centuries had been used to justify keeping women in the bondage of ignorance. Throughout her argument she contrasted the glow of youthful beauty to the "mind illumined face" of the mature woman. "The lively thoughtlessness of youth makes every young creature agreeable for the time; but when those years are flown, and sense is not substituted in the stead of vivacity, the follies of youth are acted over, and they never consider, that things which please in their proper season, disgust out of it. It is very absurd to see a woman, whose brow time has marked with wrinkles, aping the manners of a girl in her teens" (12–13). The woman who "apes the girl" and mimics the happy "thoughtlessness" of youth robs herself of the humanity of her wrinkles. Wollstonecraft was concerned that women act their age and proudly display the markings of their maturity. She suggested that society should focus its attention on the benefits bestowed by the careful actions of the thinking woman rather than applaud the frivolous attributes of the pretty girl.

Following the form of other books within the genre, Wollstonecraft devoted sections of her text to such items of female protocol as dress, artificial manners, card playing, and temper. Yet she deviated from the path taken by male authors by including a chapter entitled "Unfortunate Situation of Females, Fashionably Educated, and Left Without a Fortune." It is here that Wollstonecraft first speaks directly in print about the void in women's lives created by the sexual politics of gender and generation. This chapter is unique within the context of eighteenth-century conduct books in that it considers how patriarchal privilege encoded in the customs of primogeniture and coverture limited the life choices of educated women in England. In this short chapter Wollstonecraft pointed out much of what remained to be said concerning the education of daughters. She began with a disclaimer, "I have hitherto only spoken to females, who will have a provision made for them by their parents. But many who have been well, or at least fashionably educated, are left without a fortune, and if they are not entirely devoid of delicacy, they must frequently remain single" (25).

Educated daughters of once wealthy families were not likely to attract eligible bachelors of the appropriate class. Mary Poovey argues that the marriage of daughters became an increasingly expensive burden upon families during the eighteenth century in England. The sons of the landed aristocracy were attracted to the daughters of the mercantile elite by the offer of large endowments. Finances were not the only obstacle to matrimony. Poovey writes, "The disproportionate number of socially and economically suitable bachelors also meant that a woman had less choice as to her future husband; the complaisance of male suitors, who took their success for granted, is a commonplace of eighteenth-century novels, as is the sad circumstance of uncourted daughters."[23] As Wollstonecraft herself had learned, a young woman's entrance into the world was mediated by money. Without a large settlement to entice the interest of a beau, the accomplished woman might be excluded from the mating rituals of courtship and later exiled from polite society by her poverty.

Wollstonecraft's letters attest that she was well acquainted with the hardships confronted by daughters of families in financial decline. Speaking for herself, she wrote, "It is hard for a person who has a relish for polished society, to herd with the vulgar, or to condescend to mix with her former equals when she is considered in a different light. What unwelcome heart-breaking knowledge is then poured in on her." This knowledge darkens the colors in the landscape of a woman's life. "The painted cloud disappears suddenly, the scene is changed, and what an aching void is left in the heart!" (26). The intimate nature of Wollstonecraft's comments in this text led Claire Tomalin to remark:

> A striking omission from her book, as from her letters, was any mention of her pupils. There were plenty of personal references, but they were almost all to herself. She never could write without inserting more or less veiled remarks about her own emotional state, and though they read a little curiously in the middle of an educational manual, they make it abundantly clear that she was far more interested in the state of her own life and the prospects that lay ahead of young women than in their years at school.[24]

At this stage in her own intellectual development Wollstonecraft suggested that her sisters in woe, the "unfortunate, fashionably educated women," turn to religion to fill the void in life that was traditionally filled by marriage and child rearing (25). Subsequently, in *Mary, a Fiction,* she would modify her view that women should look to the afterlife, imagining a heaven without marriage or marrying. Even in this first book we see her emphasis on futurity to make right present wrongs. Her own experience of hardship would quickly lead her to replace an attitude of religious resignation with the spirit of political revolution.

In the remaining chapters of *Thoughts on the Education of Daughters*, Wollstonecraft examined the conventional roles of women. Her analysis of marriage provides her definitive statement that education differentiates girls from women. Early marriages are particularly harmful in that they interrupt or restrict the rational development of females. Wollstonecraft foreshadowed the arguments of modern feminist political theorists concerning female "vulnerability in marriage" by asserting that girls and women "forced to act before they have had time to think" were at a decided disadvantage upon entering the marriage contract.[25]

> Early marriages are, in my opinion, a stop to improvement. If we were born only "to draw nutrition, propagate and rot," the sooner the end of creation was answered the better; but as women are here allowed to have souls, the soul ought to be attended to. In youth a woman endeavors to please the other sex, in order, generally speaking, to get married, and this endeavor calls forth all her powers. If she has a tolerable education, the foundation only is laid, for the mind does not soon arrive at maturity, and should not be engrossed by domestic cares before any habits are fixed. The passions also have too much influence over the judgment to suffer it to direct her in this most important affair; and many women, I am persuaded, marry a man before they are twenty, whom they would have rejected some years after. Very frequently, when education has been neglected, the mind improves itself, if it has the leisure for reflection, and experience to reflect on; but how can this happen when they are forced to act before they have had time to think, or find that they are unhappily married? (31)

By defining female maturity by education, not marriage, Wollstonecraft inverts the order of other models like Locke's *Some Thoughts Concerning Education* and Rousseau's *Emile*. Although both these works moved past the politics of generation to focus on childhood neither Locke nor Rousseau, both famous tutors, could get beyond the politics of gender to educate the girl. Wollstonecraft argued that the education of the girl was first and foremost for her own benefit. "Reason must often be called in to fill up the vacuums of life; but too many of our sex suffer theirs to lie dormant" (32). For women, reason could supplement religion as they tried to fill the empty spaces of traditional femininity. Wollstonecraft bitterly attacked early marriages because she believed that they carried a girl away from her lessons to become a prisoner of the hearth and possibly the companion of the wrong man.

> When a woman's mind has gained some strength, she will in all probability pay more attention to her actions than a girl can be expected to; and if she thinks seriously, she will chuse for a companion a man of principle; and this perhaps young people do not sufficiently attend to, or see the necessity of doing. . . . Many are but just returned from a boarding school, when they are placed at the head of a family, and how fit they are to manage it, I leave the judicious to judge. Can they improve a child's understanding, when they are scarcely out of the state of childhood themselves? (31)

Marriage limited the sphere of a woman's actions and further restricted the exercise of her reason. "Women are said to be the weaker vessel, and many are the miseries which this weakness brings on them. Men have in some respects very much the advantage. If they have a tolerable understanding, it has a chance to be cultivated. . . . Nothing, I am sure, calls forth the faculties so much as being obliged to struggle with the world; and this is not woman's province in a married state" (32). Wollstonecraft argued that, if indeed woman was the "weaker vessel," much of this weakness was the result of institutions and conventions that inhibit or stunt the cognitive growth of the girl into the thinking woman.

Her final chapter details the position of women in "Public Places." Wollstonecraft concludes her thoughts on female education by again redirecting our vision. We are asked to observe the funeral of the "fine lady," an uneducated woman who like a child is of "so little use" to society. "In the fine Lady how few traits do we observe of those affections which dignify human nature! If she has maternal tenderness, it is of a childish kind. We cannot be too careful not to verge on this character; though she lives many years she is still a child in understanding, and of so little use to society, that her death would scarcely be observed" (48). Her warning to girls is clear: get an education or else. Females, if raised to please males, would remain children all their lives without the rational education needed to mature as human beings. Only thinking women have the ability to govern themselves and the hope of escaping the female void of dependence by the reasonable management of their households and their substantive contributions to society.

In *Thoughts on the Education of Daughters* Wollstonecraft presents many portraits of women who have been buried alive, suffocated by their situation as women in a society in which they are economically powerless and civilly dead. In writing this educational text she articulated the connection between the obstacles that restrict the education of girls and the social and political impediments to female autonomy. She identified marriage as the primary institution that denied women the opportunity to explore the meaning of their own lives by restricting their access to and their vision of the world into which each one was born. Her own place in the world was uncertain following the failure of her school in Newington Green. This first book focused her thoughts on her experience as a teacher. She wrote that "a teacher at a school is only a kind of upper servant, who has more work than menial ones." In the next sentence she commented that the role of a governess was "equally disagreeable" (25).

Thoughts on the Education of Daughters may have made Wollstonecraft an author, but it gave her little authority with her numerous creditors. Instead of settling her debts, she used the money she received for her book from Joseph Johnson to settle Fanny Blood's family in Ireland. She would soon follow them across the Irish Sea. Given her own "unfortunate situation," a penniless Wollstonecraft accepted the position of governess on the Kingsborough estate for the sum of forty pounds a year.

THE MIND OF A THINKING WOMAN IS DISPLAYED

> In delineating the Heroine of this Fiction, the Author attempts to develop a character different from those generally portrayed. This woman is neither a Clarissa, a Lady G———, or a Sophie.
> —Mary Wollstonecraft, *Mary, a Fiction*

In the advertisement to *Mary, a Fiction,* Wollstonecraft promised her reader that in this "artless tale, without episodes, the mind of a woman, who has thinking powers is displayed." She observed that both popular opinion and historical experience seemed to confirm the belief that "female organs have been thought too weak for this arduous employment." But she countered that, "Without arguing physically about *possibilities*—in a fiction, such a being may be allowed to exist, whose grandeur is derived from the operations of its own faculties, not subjugated to opinion; but drawn by the individual from the original source."[26] The "original source" from which Mary Wollstonecraft drew the generative power to create her heroine were her reflections on her own life. The semi-autobiographical *Mary, a Fiction* traced the development of a woman of mind from her infancy and childhood to her marriage and rebellion against her husband and the opinions of a world that deny women their own thoughts and restrict their actions. Wollstonecraft, who had argued in *Thoughts on the Education of Daughters* that most parents neglect the education of their female children, resolved this pedagogical dilemma in a new way in *Mary*. She wrote to her sister Everina as well as her friend the Reverend Henry Gabell that the novel served to demonstrate an idea she had drawn from her reading of *Emile*, that "a genius will educate itself."

Most literary critics have found little evidence of genius in *Mary*. Wollstonecraft wrote a few months before her death that she thought the novel a "crude production," and that she would rather not share it with "people whose good opinion, as a writer, I wish for."[27] Yet it was in writing this novel that Wollstonecraft began to see herself as the "first of a new genus." Here she further developed the central idea of her earlier educational tract, that a woman needed her own mental resources in order to survive the "warfare of life." In this manner *Mary* fulfilled Wollstonecraft's pledge to show the intricate workings of the mind of a woman with thinking powers. But the novel accomplished far more, by demonstrating the continuity of Wollstonecraft's own thoughts about women's situation and expanding her critique of women as property in marriage relations. Ultimately, the novel represents her first attempt to pose the larger philosophical question of the existence of a thinking woman at the end of the Enlightenment.

Mary, a Fiction is an alternative tale of a woman's situation that differs in dramatic detail from the stories of Clarissa, Lady Grandison, or Sophie. The plot revolves around the coming of age of a young woman, fashionably educated and left *with* a fortune. Here Wollstonecraft continues her discussion of female development begun in *Thoughts on the Education of Daughters,* yet unlike the dispossessed daughters of her educational tract, the Mary of fiction inherits the family fortune when her older brother dies of a "violent fever" at boarding school. The death of the brother gives new life to the sister. Her position within the family has changed. "She was now an heiress, and her mother began to think of her of consequence, and did not call her the child" (18). From society's perspective this transfer of wealth transformed the inconsequential girl into a woman of substance.

Marriage is the consequence of her inheritance, and her father gives the fictional Mary away as a bride to settle a patrimony dispute. But the marriage portrayed here is macabre in every aspect. Instead of the literary conventions of a church ceremony, the heroine is wed at her mother's deathbed to fulfill her parent's last wish. "The clergyman came in to read the service for the sick, and afterwards the marriage ceremony was performed. Mary stood like a statue of Despair, and pronounced the awful vow without thinking of it; and then ran to support her mother, who expired the same night in her arms" (20). This morbid scene juxtaposes the marriage and quest plots in gothic style as the daughter is symbolically wed over the dying body of the mother. "Her husband set off for the continent the same day, with a tutor, to finish his studies at one of the foreign universities" (20). Mary is schooled in the double standards of patriarchy while the young husband completes his education with his tutor and the grand tour of Europe. "As her mind expanded, her marriage appeared a dreadful misfortune; she was sometimes reminded of the heavy yoke, and bitter was the recollection" (22). The woman of thinking powers, in a moment of grief, unthinkingly becomes a wife. The remaining chapters of the novel detail the fictional Mary's struggle with this contradiction.

A revolutionary female emerges from this conflict of womanhood as the unthinking wife is transformed into the thinking woman who scorns her wedding vows. Mary establishes a household with a female friend, travels to Lisbon when her friend becomes ill, and after the friend's death turns her intellectual attention and sentimental affections toward an older man who is not her husband. Unwilling to dismiss her unconventional ideas or repress her feelings she exclaims, "With these notions can I conform to the maxims of worldly wisdom?" (47). Certainly *Mary, a Fiction* did not conform to the model of the feminine novel of the late eighteenth century. Mary "gave her hand" to her husband only in the last two pages of the novel with the wish "that earth would open and swallow her" (72). Wollstonecraft concludes the book with one last journey into the mind of the thinking woman:

"in moments of solitary sadness, a gleam of joy would dart across her mind—She thought she was hastening to that world where there is neither marrying, nor giving in marriage" (73). The fictional Mary, like the author herself, had not yet discovered a world in which women were free to pursue their intellectual interests as well as their erotic desires.

At the end of the eighteenth century the novel as a literary genre allowed the woman writer in general to explore the boundaries of convention and to challenge the ideological borders that separated men from women and adults from children. It offered Wollstonecraft a literary public space, an entry into the debates about power and membership in a radical community that was attempting to redefine and revolutionize discourse. It also served as a popular literary form for politic polemic. Before Jean-Jacques Rousseau wrote *The Social Contract,* he was the author of *La Nouvelle Heloise;* William Godwin followed *Political Justice* with *Caleb Williams.* J. M. S. Tompkins's remarks on this novel still hold true today:

> Conspicuous as the male philosophers are, it was the women in the revolutionary circle who focused the horrified attention of the public. The ethics of the woman's novel, that established harmony of submission, delicacy and self-control, were rudely shaken. Mary Wollstonecraft in her *Vindication of the Rights of Woman* (1792) had said that independence was the soil of every virtue, and had based delicacy on candor instead of concealment. She had written *Mary, A Fiction* (1788) in which "the mind of a woman, who has thinking powers, is displayed," and had exhibited the development of these powers as consequent of the most unconventional behavior. She had spoken freely of passion and saw it as an educative force.[28]

Mary Wollstonecraft was first able to speak freely within the context of the novel. *Mary, a Fiction* represents her early theoretical attempts to analyze and respond to the powerlessness of women within the home and civil society. It was here that she began to equate women's condition as wives with slavery (55). Modern readers will recognize that this is not the type of story that has yet been told within the history of political thought. Rather, *Mary* is an experimental novel, displaying the conflict between a thinking women who would make her own way in the world and the obstacles she encounters from the world of opinion. It is also a cautionary tale that has not received sufficient attention from Wollstonecraft scholars; it depicts an existential crisis of a girl becoming a woman. Her argument raises the question of how traditional political theory, which blurs the boundaries between the child and the adult, serves the purposes of fathers and husbands when the property in dispute is female. Wollstonecraft develops the power of the mind of her fictional heroine. But could this woman with thinking powers overcome the body of literature that conditioned men to treat girls as women and women as perpetual children?

ORIGINAL STORIES FROM REAL LIFE

> I will tell you a story, that will take stronger hold of your memory than mere remarks.
> —Mary Wollstonecraft, *Original Stories*

The market for children's literature was rapidly growing at the end of the eighteenth century. The social and economic forces that had produced an increasingly literate population and with it a booming demand for novels, namely, the rise of an urban middle class and the growth of commercial trade, were the same forces that produced a market for chapbooks and primers. Sarah Trimmer's *History of the Robins,* first published in 1786, was a bestseller. For Mary Wollstonecraft, already the author of a conduct book and a sentimental novel, writing a didactic book for children may have seemed a logical step in popular publication. Yet her *Original Stories from Real Life; with Conversations, Calculated to Regulate the Affections, and Form the Mind to Truth and Goodness* (1788) is an odd book indeed. Geoffrey Summerfield argues in his study of eighteenth-century children's literature that "*Original Stories* has a strong claim to be the most sinister, ugly, overbearing book for children ever published."[29] Summerfield's claim aside, this book was one of Wollstonecraft's most successful publications. The book went through three editions in her lifetime with the second and third editions illustrated by the radical poet William Blake. The subtle changes she introduced to each edition (which trace the progress of the French Revolution and her reaction to the Terror of Robespierre) indicate her desire to bring her argument in line with her larger theoretical project.

We find in this children's reader an outline of Wollstonecraft's most important ideas concerning virtue, society, commerce, and charity. She presented in this text her most systematic analysis to date of the relationship of adults to children as well as her most sympathetic examination of the role of servants within a household and the conditions of the poor within society. *Original Stories* is a book of mind-numbing brutality and heartfelt humanity. Wollstonecraft first sought to train the heart in the habits of compassion, and then, once these habits were ingrained, to instruct the mind in the lessons of rationality. In this text she introduces the female tutor Mrs. Mason, a character drawn from her own experience as a governess in the Kingsborough household and who shares the name of a servant from her school at Newington Green. Mrs. Mason is charged, after the death of their mother, with the care of the daughters of a relative, fourteen-year-old Mary and twelve-year-old Caroline. The girls are described as "ignorant but not prejudiced"; Mary "has a turn for ridicule" and Caroline is "vain of her person."[30] Mrs. Mason makes it plain that she is not training the girls solely for the marriage market but to play a larger, more influential role in the world as women.

In her preface Wollstonecraft situates herself as an author and educator. She justifies her project as a corrective to the corruption of society. "These conversations and tales are accommodated to the present state of society; which obliges the author to attempt to cure those faults by reason, which ought never to have taken root in the infant mind" (359). Unlike the earlier work *Thoughts on the Education of Daughters*, which owed its pedagogical principles to Locke, from its first pages *Original Stories* demonstrates her debt to Rousseau. Wollstonecraft argues that habit and reason are formed in childhood and that the best method for teaching children to act as reasonable beings is for parents and teachers to model rational behavior. Using a simple style well suited to advance truth, she argues that "knowledge should be gradually imparted, and flow more from example than teaching; example directly addresses the senses, the first inlets of the heart; and the improvement of those instruments of the understanding is the object education should have constantly in view, and over which we have most power." Yet Wollstonecraft believes that it is wishful thinking to expect that parents dissipated by their own pursuit of pleasure can act as rational role models and thoughtful teachers to their children. Her critique of society is focused on the vices of the "present generation," chief among them is the fact that most parents have neglected their natural duty to educate their offspring. Anticipating her argument in both vindications she looks to the future and focuses her attention on the next generation: "we must therefore pour premature knowledge into the succeeding one; and, teaching virtue, explain the nature of vice. Cruel necessity" (359). Thus, the conversations and tales found within this text powerfully assault the senses, rendering an immediate response to alleviate suffering in animals and humans, a response that defines goodness and points the way to virtue in men, women, and society.

The influence of the tutor Jean-Jacques is evident upon first opening this book. Here we find Wollstonecraft enlightened by the insight that children develop in stages, a first principle of *Emile*. However, while the lessons Mrs. Mason teaches her pupils have more in common with those offered Emile than those offered Sophie, there are other fundamental differences in Wollstonecraft's educational project. Since her aim is to address the ills of contemporary society, she introduces a discussion of divinity earlier than does the tutor Jean-Jacques. There is no Savoyard vicar in *Original Stories*, but instead (just as some modern Christian teenagers distinguish themselves by wearing "What would Jesus do?" jewelry), Wollstonecraft's pupils aim in all things to resemble God.

Mrs. Mason teaches her pupils by example. Emulating Emile's tutor she never lets the girls out of her sight and follows his technique of imparting wisdom "imperceptibly by rendering [lessons] amusing" (367). What does she teach her charges? Her first lesson is the meaning of goodness. Mrs. Mason takes the girls on a walk through the countryside. She leaves the path to avoid stepping on a snail. When the girls find this amusing she instructs them to observe nature to see that God made every being to be happy by placing them close to the source of their food. In an argument that progresses up the food chain, Mrs. Mason moves from the relationship of snails, to children, and finally to adult men and women. She says to Mary, "You are often very troublesome—I am stronger than you—yet I don't kill you" (368). Her lessons on the treatment of animals begins with an acknowledgment that "might does not make right" and ends with an admonishment to goodness. "Do you know the meaning of the word Goodness? I see you are unwilling to answer. I will tell you. It is, first, to avoid hurting anything; and then, to contrive to give as much pleasure as you can" (368).

In *Emile* Jean-Jacques takes charge of his pupil as an infant and introduces him to the world, first by exploring the relationship of objects in nature and later, when Emile has reached adolescence, by examining the relationships of men in society. Mrs. Mason begins educating her charges at this later stage and uses arguments from nature to illustrate the often brutal relationships among men and women within civilized society. Mary and Caroline after pondering the fate of garden insects are soon forced to act on their precepts when they encounter an "idle boy" with a gun who shoots a pair of larks in flight on the morning air. When Mrs. Mason comes upon the boy, he drops the pair of birds and runs away. The first lark who had just moments before been a vision of flight and song now suffers in pain, and Mrs. Mason uses her heel to put it out of its misery. She carefully attends to the broken wing of the second lark and instructs the girls to carry the nest home with them so that they can care for the injured creature and its brood. In their rambles the girls soon meet with another boy toying with the nest of another bird. Responding to the anguished cries of the mother bird, Mary and Caroline bargain away their pocket money to buy the nest from the boy and return it to its proper place in tree. Mrs. Mason rewards the girls for their good actions and reinforces the morning's lesson. "Now we will return to breakfast; give me you [*sic*] hand, my little girls, you have done good this morning, you have acted like rational creatures." Blake's first illustration brings to life the next line of the text. "Look what a fine morning it is. Insects, Birds and Animals, are all enjoying existence" (370). The copper plate engraving shows Mrs. Mason, eyes cast down to the path at her feet and her arms outstretched. She is flanked by Mary and Caroline whose eyes look to the distant future.

The subsequent chapters move from the treatment of animals to the distinction between animals and man, differentiating human beings from brute creation by the ability to cultivate the mind and enlarge the heart. Mankind has been ennobled by the Divine, who has instilled humanity with the capacity to exercise virtue. Thus, it is not enough to understand the meaning of goodness; to be good one must act on these principles. These distinctions will be the focus of careful analysis in Wollstonecraft's tracts on political rights. And it is in light of her arguments in her two vindications that *Original Stories* takes on a greater significance, because within this didactic reader for children we find the origins of her analyses of man and society that are the theoretical basis of these better-known books.

It is here that Wollstonecraft first approaches the conditions of the political prisoners in France, making reference to the Bastille in a treatment of the debtors imprisoned in England. The story of "crazy Robin" is the tale of a tenant farmer who borrows money from his landlord to support the needs of his large family. Misfortune strikes and when he defaults on the loan he is sent to debtors' prison where his remaining children die of jail fever. Robin goes mad at the loss of his children. After his release from prison Robin and a faithful dog return to the countryside where he once lived with his family. Mrs. Mason tells the girls that she sought to comfort the poor wretch and often brought food to the cave where he lived with his dog. Just as Robin is returning to humanity through the good graces of Mrs. Mason, he and his dog encounter a "young gentleman" on horseback. When the dog causes the rider's horse to start, the gentleman levels his gun at the dog, shoots, and rides off. Mrs. Mason finds Robin in the cave mourning the death of his dog and dying himself. His last words are the sobbing "Will anyone be kind to me?"

There is a much fuller awareness of class politics in this text than in the earlier *Thoughts on the Education of Daughters* and *Mary, a Fiction*. Mary and Caroline are fortunate daughters in that they have been placed in the care of a governess who wants to educate them to provide for themselves if ever they are confronted with the misfortunes of life. Thus, the girls are introduced to a variety of characters who share their life stories of hardship and salvation. These tales offer moral lessons that reinforce the interdependence of society and demonstrate the need to act for the welfare of individuals and the community. Mrs. Mason's pedagogy combines theory and practice in living lessons that transform Mary and Caroline from children into young adults.

Throughout the text there is an emphasis on dialogue between Mrs. Mason and the girls. She teaches by example, telling stories about real people within their community, asking questions and probing the girls' answers. In this way the governess tutors the girls in questions of justice, equity, and virtue. She encourages them to think about their own actions and to question the motivations of others. When Mary and Caroline are introduced to the world through a stay in London, she uses this opportunity to discuss values and virtues. Even a shopping trip to purchase pocketbooks becomes an opportunity to discuss a most unladylike topic, the merits of trade and commerce. Mrs. Mason steers the girls to a family-owned shop with well-made goods but little inventory. When the girls want to make a purchase elsewhere to save some money, she tells them she never looks for a bargain but seeks value. The shopkeeper breaks down in tears and tells her customers that her son is in prison for debt, run to ruin by the importation of cheaper foreign-made goods. Without credit they have been unable to renew their stock and have lost their customers. Mrs. Mason listens carefully to her tale and uses the encounter to teach the girls that their purchases buy this family hope. She promises to help the shopkeeper, and the girls leave the storefront poorer but wiser.

In the pages of *Original Stories* there are no "useless" fine ladies such as those mockingly eulogized in *Thoughts on the Education of Daughters*. The women whose stories fill the pages of this children's reader are working women like Mrs. Trueman who is given a liberal education but then dispossessed of her inheritance by the laws of primogeniture. Eventually she becomes a clergyman's wife, the mother of a fine family, whose useful arts make her the center of village life. Mrs. Mason also relates the history of Anna who, born to wealth, is deprived of her station in life by the failure of a family friend to aid her father in a time of financial hardship. After her father's death in poverty, she must make a living as the village schoolmistress. Each woman fulfills an important social role beyond the household. They are the masters of useful arts, not mistresses of frivolous accomplishments. None of these women is a victim. Their rationality helps them triumph over the adversity of their ordinary lives and this makes them examples of Wollstonecraft's new type of heroine, women who display the power of thought; as such they are fitting role models for Mary and Caroline.

PERSONIFYING THE POLITICS OF SEXUAL IDENTITY

> Every day she made theories by which life should be lived; and every day she came smack up against the rock of other people's prejudices. Every day too—for she was no pedant, no cold-blooded theorist—something new was born in her that thrust aside her theories and forced her to model them afresh.
> —Virginia Woolf, *Women and Writing*

If there is one principle that has historically united feminist theory in all its multivocal diversity it is the idea that the personal is political. Wollstonecraft's theory emerged without apology from the complex experiences of her daily life. As a self-educated woman she developed an educational program geared toward human perfectibility rather than propping up the social status quo. Political theory has often been an aristocratic activity requiring an elite education and money to buy the time to read, think, and write. An eighteenth-century daughter of the English middle class, Mary Wollstonecraft did not have a classical education. She could not read the ancient dialogues in Greek or the history of Rome in Latin. Yet she taught herself to read critically and to write eloquently on the most controversial issues of her time, issues that were often avoided by men with Oxbridge credentials. Wollstonecraft was keenly aware of the sexual politics that denied women a classical education. Many modern readers may view this lack of a formal education as a handicap for a woman who chose to vindicate the political rights of her sex by proclaiming war on the canonized forefathers. But Wollstonecraft associated a classical education with corrupt aristocratic men. Writing in an era of democratic dissent she looked to her own experiences to make sense of the past and the present.

Indeed, Mary Wollstonecraft did not profess an academic distance from the struggles of her own life, whether it was the violent domestic battles between her father and her mother that scarred her girlhood or the bloody street confrontations of the French Revolution that she witnessed as a woman. Her interpretation of these events was always guided by her notion that reason must be united with sensibility. From Wollstonecraft's epistemological perspective, truth must reconcile the mind with the heart. This radical subjectivity informed her reading and her writing, and most important, it undermined her belief in the objectivity of the men of letters and their ability to imagine women as autonomous political subjects.

The canon has historically provided the classic bildungsroman for young men. For over two thousand years the great book tradition has served to introduce men to the ideas of the well-lived life and the good society. But what if one approached the canon of political thought from the position of female development? Who would introduce young women to the great books?

Mary Wollstonecraft followed the publication of *Thoughts on* the Education of Daughters, Mary, a Fiction, and Original Stories by compiling a literary anthology to aid in the education of her sex. The Female Reader; or Miscellaneous Pieces in Prose and Verse; Selected from the Best Writers, and Disposed under Proper Heads; for the Improvement of Young Women contained psalms from the Bible and passages from Shakespeare, the poetry of Cowper and Charlotte Smith, and the educational ideas of Voltaire and Madame Genlis. Godwin tells us that she intended this text to serve as a companion piece to Dr. Enfield's popular Speaker, a compilation whose purpose was to teach boys the fine art of oratory. However, Wollstonecraft makes it plain in the preface that she knew her readers' digest could not replace a liberal education. "Females are not educated to become public speakers or public players."[31] The distinction between the male speakers and the female readers referenced in the books' titles reveals why many modern feminist scholars have cautioned that the historical record cannot be corrected by simply adding women to the canonical conversation.

The conversation of political thought is singularly androcentric and the language of political theory works implicitly as well as explicitly to silence women. By focusing on Wollstonecraft's unauthorized intervention into the canonical conversation, we can claim a better understanding of the sexual politics of political theory. A critical examination of her writing may help us to understand the obstacles that women face in writing political theory. Recent feminist revisions of the canon focus our attention on women's political writing, asking us to consider why women have not written political theory. The answer must begin with a critical examination of how girls and women have been represented within the canonical texts. Women, when they are present within the text at all, have usually been portrayed as existing within the privacy of the household, excluded from men and the public spaces of politics. As one reads the books that comprise the canon from ancients to moderns it becomes increasingly easy to dismiss women entirely, as they literally disappear from the page, expelled from the political by the theoretical categories of public man and private woman.

Yet feminist theorists, beginning with Mary Wollstonecraft, have claimed that this seeming absence is indicative of a powerful presence. Linda Zerilli has recently argued that woman acts as a signification of chaos in the works of Rousseau, Burke, and Mill.[32]

She contends that woman figures the abyss, the place within the discursive domain where the unified masculine subject begins to unravel. Certainly many eighteenth-century men considered women's presence within the public sphere, whether in the salons of Paris or on the streets of London, unnatural and frightening. How much more terrifying to confront Mary Wollstonecraft, who claimed in the name of the absent woman the authority to speak from this historical void. In the next chapter we shall examine how Wollstonecraft herself responded to the image of woman in Edmund Burke's *Reflections on the Revolution in France* and developed the argument for women's subjectivity that challenged the gender dichotomy of the sublime and the beautiful. Reading Wollstonecraft's books complicates our understanding of the representation of women within the canon as well as of the role of woman as a signifier within the discourse of political theory. Mary Wollstonecraft's feminist political theory enriches our knowledge of women as subjects with a political history of their own.

CHAPTER THREE

The Rebel Writer and the Rights of Men

> The Revolution thus was not merely an event that happened outside her; it was an active agent in her own blood. She had been in revolt all her life—against tyranny, against law, against convention. The reformer's love of humanity, which has so much of hatred in it as well as love, fermented within her. The outbreak of Revolution in France expressed some of her deepest theories and convictions, and she dashed off in the heat of that extraordinary moment those two eloquent and daring books—the Reply to Burke and the Vindication of the Rights of Woman, which are so true that they seem now to contain nothing new in them, their originality has become our commonplace.
>
> —Virginia Woolf, *The Second Common Reader*

Wollstonecraft's *A Vindication of the Rights of Men* represented a revolution in political writing and served to introduce her words into the conversation of political theory. The moment was captured by William Godwin in his *Memoirs of the Author of "The Rights of Woman."* He wrote, "Hitherto the literary career of Mary, had for the most part, been silent; and had been productive of income to herself, without apparently leading to the wreath of fame." While this curious statement consigning Wollstonecraft's early writings to silence seems dismissive, it most certainly reflects her own opinion of her previous work. In the past she had written for money, but when she picked up her pen to respond to Burke's *Reflections on the Revolution in France*, her motivations were personal and political. The publication of her anonymous reply to Edmund Burke in November 1790 would forever change the life of this little-known lady novelist as well as transform the debate about political rights. "From this time she was destined to attract the notice of the public, and perhaps no female writer ever obtained so great a degree of celebrity throughout Europe."[1] Mary Wollstonecraft found her voice in her vindications.

Her *Rights of Men* attracted the notice of the public and the attention of reviewers as it was the first published response to Burke's *Reflections*. It appeared on November 29, 1790, just twenty-eight days after Burke's text. As David Bromwich has noted, Wollstonecraft composed her reply quickly.[2] Godwin tells us that she sent the pages to press as the ink was drying. Reviewers commented upon the author's passionate attack on Burke and critically detailed the analysis of property and privilege that was the foundation of this defense of the rights of men.[3] The first edition of the pamphlet was so successful that her publisher, Joseph Johnson, rushed a second edition into print in December. The December 18 edition was to receive a different type of notice from both the public and the reviewers, as it revealed that the anonymous author of *Rights of Men* was a woman.

For years Wollstonecraft scholars have puzzled over the question of why she wrote her first vindication. Within the political context of her time what could a woman contribute to the debates about the rights of men? According to one critic, her biographer Ralph Wardle, this question even haunted Wollstonecraft: "Perhaps she asked herself why a nobody like herself should presume to challenge the opinions of a man of Burke's stature. She was only a woman, and politics was the affair of men." Wardle finds it inconceivable that Wollstonecraft as a woman writer had anything to add to the discourse on political rights. "She must have realized that she had, after all, nothing new or original to say about the theories on which governments were based."[4] Wardle explained away Wollstonecraft's work by claiming it was the product of "scraps of conversation" or tidbits of theory that she picked up from "the writings of Dr. Price and the habitués of Johnson's book shop, or in Rousseau and Locke."[5] If she had been male rather than female, one might counter that this was not bad company for a young man preparing to enter the discourse on government. For Wardle, however, Wollstonecraft's sex made her reply to Burke an aberration, a theoretical trespass by an "upstart young woman who had hitherto hardly presumed to trespass on the field of legitimate literature, much less the field of politics."[6] The lady novelist did not belong at the theoretical table with the great men of political thought.

Yet as her *Rights of Men* reveals, Mary Wollstonecraft had plenty to say about politics, writing, and political rights. She had already published an educational tract and a novel of her own before she joined Johnson's intellectual circle. As a member of this literary household she authored both *Original Stories* and *The Female Reader*. She translated Jacques Necker's *Importance of Religious Opinions,* Christian Gotthilf Salzmann's *Elements of Morality,* and Madame de Cambon's *Young Grandison.* She augmented her living by writing book reviews for Johnson and Thomas Christie's radical monthly, the *Analytical Review,* contributing over a hundred and fifty book reviews in little more than eighteen months. Her time had been well spent in an intensive course of reading and writing. Days alone perusing the latest fiction, travelogue, or pamphlet were followed by nights at Johnson's table discussing ideas with the coterie he gathered above his shop in St. Paul's Churchyard. What was her position at these gatherings? Did Wollstonecraft's contemporaries view her as an oddity, a woman who had dangerously ventured out of her proper sphere?

In relating his introduction to Wollstonecraft in November 1791, Godwin gives us an intriguing portrait of her participation in those evening discussions. He had finagled an invitation from Johnson in the hope of having a few words with the author of the *Rights of Man,* Thomas Paine. But the evening did not go as he expected. Instead of exchanging ideas with Paine he found himself debating with Mary Wollstonecraft. "The interview was not fortunate. Mary and myself parted, mutually displeased with each other. I had not read her *Rights of Woman.* I had barely looked into her *Answer to Burke,* and been displeased as literary men are apt to be, with a few offenses against grammar and other minute points of composition." It is doubtful that Godwin has correctly dated this meeting, as *A Vindication of the Rights of Woman* was not published until February 1792. Her sins against grammar aside, Wollstonecraft's words on that memorable night made a lasting impression on him. "I had therefore little curiosity to see Mrs. Wollstonecraft, and a great curiosity to see Thomas Paine. Paine, in his general habits, is no great talker, and, though he threw in occasionally some shrewd and striking remarks, the conversation lay principally with me and Mary. I, of consequence, heard her, very frequently when I wished to hear Paine."[7] As would so often be the case, Godwin associated Wollstonecraft with her second vindication rather than her first, which he identified as her "Answer to Burke." In this passage Paine is the author of the *Rights of Man*. This said, Godwin's remarks are strikingly different from Wardle's account of a passive woman silently soaking up ideas and opinions while the men talked. Here we have a picture of Wollstonecraft dominating the conversation. For what was it to privately oppose William Godwin after publicly challenging Edmund Burke?

GENDER AS A RHETORICAL POSITION

> Quitting now the flowers of rhetoric, let us, Sir, reason together.
> —Mary Wollstonecraft, A *Vindication of the Rights of Men*

A year earlier an anonymous Mary Wollstonecraft had issued an invitation to reason with the famed parliamentarian: "let us, Sir, reason together." In doing so she surreptitiously entered into debate with the "Cicero of one side of the House," Edmund Burke.[8] Her *Rights of Men* was written in response to the revolution in France, which marked the explosive end to a century of Enlightenment. The revolution indicated a break with the past, a rupture in normal time and space that formed an environment vibrating with conflict and experimentation. It was also an event that marked Wollstonecraft's break with her personal past as she developed her theories and put them into practice in her everyday life. In an era characterized by both questioning and production of meaning, the boundaries between novel and treatise, between polemical fiction and political theory, were not only permeable but subject to analysis themselves. In this time of crisis and creation, a young woman transformed herself from a novelist to a political polemicist by daring to reply to the *Reflections on the Revolution in France*.

It is often said that opportunity is a matter of being in the right place at the right time, and Wollstonecraft's timing was perfect. Burke had observed that the French Revolution had sparked a number of smaller revolts against the status quo, "revolutions which have given splendor to obscurity, and distinction to undiscerned merit."[9] The publication of Wollstonecraft's *Rights of Men* represented one such revolt. In the *Reflections* Burke took aim at the English supporters of the revolution in France, especially members of the Constitution Society and the Revolution Society. He singled out the Reverend Richard Price who, in his speech *Discourse on the Love of Our Country* commemorating the centennial of the Glorious Revolution, preached the rights of men from the pulpit of the Old Jewry in London. To Burke, Dr. Price was the dissenting leader of a literary cabal that threatened both church and king.

In this revolutionary context an obscure novelist named Mary Wollstonecraft was uniquely situated to respond to Burke's criticisms. As a young schoolmistress in Newington Green she had been befriended by Dr. Price, who had introduced her to the radical notion of self-government. As a member of Joseph Johnson's circle she too had been "schooled in the rights of men." Even so, scholars have asked what right did Mary Wollstonecraft have to defend Dr. Price, or to even enter the debate on rights? What possible experience could a woman have of men and government? What had she observed of human nature that would allow her to form opinions about politics and revolutions, justice and constitutions? For years Wollstonecraft's reply to Burke has been overshadowed by the fame accorded *A Vindication of the Rights of Woman*, perhaps because her earlier tract seemed to raise more questions than it answered. What right, indeed?

To begin with, who was the author of *A Vindication of the Rights of Men*? This question was critical within the framework of the rights debates because Edmund Burke began the *Reflections* by claiming his reputation as a well-known parliamentarian would answer for his argument. "My errors, if there are any, are my own. My reputation alone is to answer for them" (4). The question of authority was central to Burke's critique and with it he linked the issue of anonymity. He questioned the authority of the Revolution Society to act as a public representative of the English nation and to correspond with the National Assembly of France. Burke asked, What authorized this "society" to speak on behalf of the English people? The unknown members of the Revolution Society had sent a congratulatory message to France, a "resolution that stands solely on authority; and in this case it is the mere authority of individuals, few of whom appear. Their signatures ought in my opinion, to have been annexed to their instrument" (7). Burke argued that, in his parliamentary experience, the House of Commons "rejects the sneaking petitions" of anonymous authors "on account of the ambiguity and uncertainty of unauthorized general descriptions, and of the deceit that may be practiced under them" (6). Where were the names of the men who, in the guise of the Revolution Society, had opened a line of communication with the National Assembly? Burke blasted, "The world would then have the means of knowing how many they are; who they are; and of what value their opinions may be, from their personal abilities, from their knowledge, their experience, or their lead and authority in this state" (7).

Yet regardless of their names, numbers, or opinions, women had no official political authority within the British state. Anonymity and its deceptions could prove politically pragmatic for individuals who, despite their personal abilities and knowledge, were barred by their sex from the experience of political leadership.[10] Read in light of Edmund Burke's attack on authority and anonymity, Mary Wollstonecraft's anonymous reply to the *Reflections* becomes a powerful example of sexual subversion. For it was in this pamphlet that she first challenged the authority of the men she identified after Burke as the "canonized forefathers" to define the political by the exclusion of women.

Her *Rights of Men* engenders a series of questions about political life that had not been asked by the fathers of the canon, who denied that women possessed the reason which gave men the right to speak on public issues and to participate in politics. In responding to Burke, Wollstonecraft broke the silence of her sex in the canonical conversation by articulating her understanding of the meaning of the French Revolution, a "most extraordinary event" that she believed signaled the "general diffusion of reason and liberty." Accordingly, she claimed that the democratic reason of the common man was the only legitimate basis for political authority. Instead of the divine right of kings, Wollstonecraft asserted the "sovereignty of reason" in her rebellion against a patriarchal society that equated power with hereditary property and political pedigree. She called for the creation of a government founded on rational discourse to replace coercive monarchical rule (27). But at this time in her career, did Wollstonecraft believe that the enlightened rationality that gave ordinary men the right to govern themselves could authorize an obscure woman writer to reason with the Right Honorable Edmund Burke?

The evidence from her *Rights of Men* is mixed. On one hand she claimed that her defense of natural rights was based upon "the cold arguments of reason, that give no sex to virtue" (46). On the other hand she repeatedly employed gendered language to support her analysis, using the terms "manly" and "masculine" to qualify her own ideas, and "effeminate" and "infantile" to deprecate Burke's arguments. Why? What did this sexual subterfuge mean?

First, Wollstonecraft as a lady novelist was acutely aware that at the end of the eighteenth century authority was largely opposed to femininity. Wollstonecraft wrote that the power of reason "has not only been denied to women, but writers have insisted that it is inconsistent, with a few exceptions, with their sexual character."[11] Second, as a woman who frequently spoke her mind, she was well acquainted with the social conventions of female propriety, which proscribed individual behavior and honored silence. William Godwin claims that Wollstonecraft did not want to be known as an author. "At the commencement of her literary career, she is said to have conceived a vehement aversion to being regarded, by her ordinary acquaintance in the character of an author, and to have employed some precautions to prevent its occurrence."[12] Third, she knew that a majority of the public would censure any woman who had the audacity to enter a traditionally forbidden discursive space and to author an explicitly political tract.

Biographer Ralph Wardle viewed *A Vindication of the Rights of Men* as a trespass. He remarks repeatedly on the shortcomings of the text, arguing that these failures arise from Wollstonecraft's unsuitability as a woman for the task of writing political theory. He criticizes Wollstonecraft for "abusing Burke" and apologetically explains away her rhetorical attacks as the result of her limited knowledge of politics. "Probably Mary resorted to such tactics when she was unsure of herself. She must have realized that she had, after all, nothing new to say about the theories on which governments are based." I strongly disagree with Wardle's assessment that Wollstonecraft "had probably not studied the authorities on the subject" and his characterization of her text as the product of "scraps" of overheard conversations. The anonymous Wollstonecraft draws her analysis from the works of Plato, Machiavelli, Locke, Hume, and Rousseau in a systematic manner that belies Wardle's thesis about the random nature of her thoughts. Her innovative attempt to use these philosophical fathers to dispute patriarchal politics displays her intellectual engagement with political theory. Poovey notes that the *Rights of Men*, as a "political disquisition," represents a radical departure for a woman author. "Wollstonecraft's choice of a project, then, signals her determination to transcend the limitations she felt her sex had already imposed on her. In this first expression of her professional self, Wollstonecraft actually aspires to *be* a man, for she suspects that the shortest way to success and equality is to join the cultural myth-makers, to hide what seemed to her a fatal female flaw behind the mask of male discourse." My reading of the text is not that Wollstonecraft wants to be a man but that she desires a form of authority that has historically been opposed to femininity.[13]

Wollstonecraft's rhetorical strategies speak to the constraints of gender on political discourse, as well as the restraints placed upon women within political communities. Even in this revolutionary age, it appeared that in order to defend liberty and equality it was necessary to be a part of a fraternity from which almost all women were excluded. Certainly Wollstonecraft's participation in Johnson's evening debates indicate that in private she actively fraternized with her fellow writers. But in public how could any woman write with authority on the rights of men?

Wollstonecraft's gender-bending answer to this discursive dilemma was to masquerade as a man, treating gender in her text not as a stable category but rather as a rhetorical position. Schooled in the rights of man, she directly contested Burke's notion of the nature of gender difference and class hierarchy. Throughout the *Reflections,* Burke juxtaposed the ecclesiastical education of the English gentleman with the wild speculative philosophy of the common man. Whereas the clergy taught young nobles and young gentry lessons derived from the ancient experience of the canonized forefathers, self-taught commoners aspired to the lofty metaphysics of the philosophes. The emerging individual of this "enlightened age" had abstractions rather than ancestors. These "new men," with property only in their rhetorical rights, endangered the corporate identity of the men of old who, born to noble rank, were the guardians of hereditary wealth. Burke argued that the French Revolution was the barbarous product of opportunists of lowly birth, whom he accused of speculating in government as so many money jobbers seeking to enrich themselves at the expense of the commonwealth. These "financial philosophers" espoused the theoretical politics of the rights of men in order to undermine the property and principles of the nation for their own personal gain. In the *Reflections,* Burke used the notions of hereditary property and aristocratic politics to discredit the speculative philosophy of these "new men." Wollstonecraft's attempt to give a "manly" definition to her ideas of civic virtue and democratic politics demonstrates that she understood the close connection between reason and authority, manhood and property, in Burke's argument. Critics such as Wardle who have questioned how a "nobody" like Wollstonecraft could respond to Burke have largely missed these determinative factors of gender politics.

Every woman was a nobody in Edmund Burke's England. Born female, no woman could claim the authority of political experience or the right to property in her own body. Wollstonecraft's *Rights of Men* is significant for feminist theorists because it highlights the problem of entering a discourse in which the basic terms of the debate are constructed through the exclusion of women.[14] As Virginia Sapiro has asserted, this text can be interpreted as a radical struggle for power in language.

> The *Vindication of the Rights of Men* certainly shows haste, anger, and a need for editing. But its author appears more than aware of the politics of language. Wollstonecraft's anger revolved around disagreement about representation in all its senses, political, linguistic, and aesthetic. Her words and tone become most personally antagonistic when she debates Burke over fundamental questions of public and private honor and virtue: representation and self-representation, misrepresentation and self-misrepresentation.[15]

Wollstonecraft's literary strategy confused gender identities and thus transcended the literary boundaries that excluded women from political writing. Behind the mask of anonymity, the female author constructed an elaborate ruse to give authority to her response to Burke. Wollstonecraft's manly masquerade allowed her to subvert the privileged position of the masculine in language politics. But her efforts to defend the rights of men by using the "manly" language of reason to rebuke the "effeminate" rhetoric of the famous male orator did more than dispute discursive terrain. She directly called into question the political status of women.[16]

She took on the "gothic pile" of hereditary property, which, when passed down from father to son, reinforced the material dependence and political irrelevance of mother and daughter in a patriarchal society (58). A propertyless woman, she pitted individual liberties against property rights in an analysis of power that attacked the differentiation of sex and status through primogeniture and rank. The revolutionary power of democratic reason was the promise that each man could be his own legislator; but in denying that women possessed reason the rebellion stopped far short of allowing individual women the right to govern themselves. Wollstonecraft's rhetorical strategies reveal a tension between her belief in the theoretical universality of Enlightenment rationality and her practical experience of the prejudices that denied that English women were political subjects in their own right. Thus, her appropriation of the manly authority of Enlightenment reason, added to her analysis of gender and property, provided an immanent critique of the sexual politics of political theory.

Today Mary Wollstonecraft's theoretical hide-and-seek in her first vindication is intriguing because it serves as a powerful reminder that in eighteenth-century England the true identities and interests of individual women were always hidden from public view within the social contract. Her rhetorical ploy brought to the level of meaning the repressed fact that females had no independent political identity of their own and, thus, no subject position from which to speak back to power. As daughters they were the responsibility of their father; upon marriage they were represented by their husbands. Common law proclaimed married women to be civilly dead, as the wife's political being was subsumed within the body of her husband by the codes of coverture. At the time Wollstonecraft wrote her reply to Burke, the male head of the household exercised full legal control short of death over the lives of his wife and their children. Thus her refusal to identify herself as a woman—in a text that refuted the famous orator's representation of women as passive, private, and silent—is a telling commentary on the centrality of gender to political discourse and the marginality of women in political practice. Wollstonecraft's belief in the universal nature of rights was challenged and fragmented by her historical experience of female invisibility, as well as by the misogynistic content and highly stylized form of eighteenth-century political writing. For as a woman she had been denied the practical experience of political life, experiences that traditionally have taught the ruled how to rule. Without the authority of ancestors who could give her ideas political pedigree, Mary Wollstonecraft made pragmatic use of the abstract principles of natural right in order to respond to Burke. Her literary efforts in her first vindication prove that, as a woman author, she needed all the flowers of rhetoric to enter the debate about the rights of men.

ENGENDERING POLITICAL AUTHORITY

> I have not yet learned to twist my periods, nor, in the equivocal idiom of politeness, to disguise my sentiments, and imply what I should be afraid to utter: if, therefore in the course of this epistle, I chance to express contempt, and even indignation, with some emphasis, I beseech you to believe that it is not a flight of fancy; for truth, in morals, has ever appeared to me to be the essence of the sublime; and, in taste, simplicity the only criterion of the beautiful. I war not with an individual when I contend for the rights of men and the liberty of reason.
>
> —Mary Wollstonecraft, *A Vindication of the Rights of Men*

The opening paragraph of her *Rights of Men* sets the stage for Mary Wollstonecraft's rhetorical battle with Edmund Burke. The novice polemicist may not yet have learned all the tricks of the grammatical game but the literary devices employed in her anonymous reply to the senior statesman indicate she had been taught that polite women were silent on matters of politics. Even so, she rebelled against these lessons, refusing at the onset to apologize for her words. "Sir, It is not necessary, with courtly insincerity, to apologize to you for thus, intruding on your precious time, not to profess that I think it an honour to discuss an important subject with a man whose literary abilities have raised him to notice in the state" (7). No apology was needed, for Wollstonecraft's support of the revolution in France appeared to her to be similar to Burke's defense of the American rebellion. In taking up her pen she was engaged in the grand cause of liberty and the pursuit of the literary laurels that brought honor and notice to a skillful author.

Wollstonecraft's answer to Burke was especially significant because Burke's *Reflections* aimed at denying a voice to those individuals who would revolt against the normative standards of gender and generation embodied in the principles and traditions of British politics. She had been at war with these standards all her life because they excluded her sex from those experiences that taught men civic virtue and gave them authority to act in the public sphere. But for Burke the dual spirits of chivalry and religion made sacred those distinctions between men and women that formed the foundation of a patriarchal society with an aristocratic class structure. In the *Reflections* he claimed to revere these distinctions, which he considered to be at the heart of what he termed the "real" rights of men. "Far am I from denying in theory, full as far is my heart from withholding in practice (if I were of power to give or to withhold) the *real* rights of men. In denying their false claims of right, I do not mean to injure those which are real, and are such as their pretended rights would totally destroy" (51; original emphasis). Thus, Burke warned his readers that the radically inclusive logic of rights theory would break down the critical distinctions of sex and class, producing a revolution that was capable of destroying all social bonds and political institutions.

Recently a number of scholars have argued that Burke drew his class and gender framework from his earlier work *A Philosophical Enquiry into the Origin of Our Ideas of the Sublime and the Beautiful* (1757). In this text he created an epistemology grounded in the traditional binary opposition of an active masculinity, which he associated with the sublime, and a passive femininity, which he identified with the beautiful. Vivien Jones has claimed that Burke's categorization of the sexes had a critical impact on the construction of gender difference at the end of the eighteenth century. She has argued that Burke's "apparently complementary oppositions" between the masculine and the feminine reveal "social and moral inequalities" between men and women; thus, the "'softer virtues become the subordinate virtues'; complementarity gives way to hierarchy."[17] These lessons are not lost on Wollstonecraft. She chastises Burke's valorizing of beauty in the place of moral virtue, arguing that his message masks his method of securing female subservience. She suggests that the female readers of Burke's *Sublime and the Beautiful* may have been "convinced . . . that *littleness* and *weakness* are the very essense [sic] of beauty; and that the Supreme Being, in giving women beauty in the most supereminent degree, seemed to command them, by the powerful voice of Nature, not to cultivate the moral virtues that might chance to excite respect, and interefere [sic] with the pleasing sensations they were created to inspire" (45; original emphasis).

In his reading of Burke's *Reflections* Tom Furniss has stated that the "way Burke organizes his thought on a range of issues into gendered binary oppositions . . . is characteristic of the discourse of the period."[18] Furniss contends that Burke revisited his argument from *Sublime and the Beautiful* within the *Reflections* in an attempt to naturalize the opposition of masculine and feminine, and to stabilize gender categories threatened by revolutionary excess. For Burke the art of politics was the sublime activity of men of hereditary rank and courtly privilege. Their noble actions had produced a golden age of European civilization characterized by the spirit of the gentleman and the faith of religion. Burke's rhetorical strategy in the *Reflections* centered on the representation of this civilized world turned upside down, a world in which the boundaries of court culture were in danger of being transgressed by the political ambitions of swinish men and brutish women. The democratic rebellion in France signified a class warfare that he equated with the loss of patriarchal control and the revolting specter of gender uncertainty.[19]

The cultural chaos and political incoherence created by gender uncertainty forms the basis of Linda Zerilli's treatment of the *Reflections*. She argues that woman acts as a signification of the chaos in Burke's political thought. "Burke's recreation of the assault on the royal family at Versailles, which draws on a dark and repressed image of brute passions unconstrained by the civilizing conventions of chivalry and feminine beauty, figures woman as the site of chaos that is at once social and symbolic."[20] Zerilli makes a convincing case that, for Burke, the French Revolution represented an open assault on sexual hierarchy as well as upon monarchical politics.

Yet her provocative linguistic analysis does not examine how historical women like Wollstonecraft contested Burke's representation of woman or the feminine in their own writing. This exploration is critical within the context of the *Reflections*, because Burke blamed the democratic rebellion upon Enlightenment philosophes, who preached the rights of men to a mob composed of both men and women. He described the revolution as revelry, as saturnalia, men and women moving in a bloody masquerade in which gender and class boundaries were subverted.[21] In the National Assembly, the legislators and the people became one, joining forces to attack the very foundations of religion and chivalry by dividing among themselves church lands and feudal estates. Burke characterized the revolutionary congress as a "profane burlesque," in which the government became the site of violence and sexual perversion. He accused the legislators of responding only to the cries of a "mixed mob of ferocious men, and women lost to shame, who, according to their insolent fancies, direct, control, applaud, explode them; and sometimes mix and take their seats with them; domineering over them with a strange mixture of servile petulance and proud presumptuous authority. As they have inverted the order of all things, the gallery, is in the place of the house" (60).

One of the most horrible aspects of the revolution for Burke was that the women who were once mastered by men now proudly presumed the authority to enter the public realm and become sublime actors themselves. Sapiro argues that Burke effectively employs the language of the sublime to evoke his powerful reaction to the class mixing and gender-bending of the French Revolution. "Burke relayed his moral and political message as a nightmare teller would: not merely through a chronological story or a logical argument but by invoking the horror of it all through tone and imagery."[22]

From Zerilli's standpoint it is clear that the female patriots who marched in the streets of Paris presented a vision of womanhood that was irreconcilable with Burke's notion of the passivity of the beautiful feminine. Acting on their own, these revolutionary women did much to explode the religious and chivalric structure and symbols of France. For Burke democratic philosophy threatens to disembody the institutions of French society by overturning the relationships between the sexes. Marie Antoinette is more than a monarch; she is the symbol of patriarchal order and patriotic loyalty. Burke states, "To make us love our country, our country ought to be lovely" (172).[23]

This spectacle of gender parody and class mockery heralded the destruction of Burke's golden age of honor and order. And it was just this gender trouble that made Wollstonecraft's reply so bold in the eyes of her contemporaries.

> When the Right Honorable Author first threw down the *gauntlet*, and entering the ground from whence Sir Robert Filmer was forced so shamefully to retire, stood forth the champion of *hereditary right*, he undoubtedly expected to be opposed by all those men, who in a liberal and enlightened age, had ranged themselves on the side of liberty: but how deeply it must wound the feelings of a *chivalrous knight*, who owes the fealty of "proud submission and dignified obedience" to the fair sex, to perceive that two of the boldest of his adversaries are women![24] (original emphasis)

From her first paragraph Wollstonecraft inverted the rhetorical world of the *Reflections* by proclaiming that "truth was the essence of the sublime and simplicity the only criterion of the beautiful"

(7). She battled with Burke, "attacking the foundation of [his] opinions" (9). She refuted his arguments concerning liberty and property, undermining the patriarchal principles that structure the relationship between men and women. For her the French Revolution signified more than the fall of a crown; it represented a displacement of authority and a reassessment of the meaning of political rights for all citizens. Her thesis was that liberty was the God-given right of all rational beings, a natural right that distinguished human beings from brutes (14). She defined the "birthright of man" as "such a degree of liberty, civil and religious, as is compatible with the liberty of every other individual with whom he is united in a social compact, and the continued existence of that compact" (9). Unlike John Locke, however, she claimed that the protection of individual freedoms—not the protection of property—was the primary function of government. To her mind the two functions were largely incompatible in a democratic community. The "demon of property has ever been at hand to encroach on the sacred rights of men, and to fence round with awful pomp laws that war with justice" (9). Through the redistribution of church lands and aristocratic wealth the French government had heralded a new day of equality and equity for the citizens of the Republic. Merit, not money, would distinguish citizens while ability rather than nobility would characterize the leaders of the French nation.

It was in the spirit of these radical democratic changes that Wollstonecraft offered her own reading of the French Revolution. She, too, noted both monarch and mob; but she framed a different portrait of liberty, property, and gender politics. Indeed, she promised her readers she would show Burke to himself and demonstrate that naked self-interest accounted for his defense of monarchy and aristocracy in the *Reflections* (18). Stripped to the flesh, Burke appeared to her as a mere apologist for a corrupt aristocratic order whose time was past. To make her case, Wollstonecraft repeatedly contrasted the diseased anatomy of the aristocracy to the healthy physique of the middle classes. At the center of her analysis was an attack on the twin evils of female degeneracy and male effeminacy, both of which she associated with the gender politics of court culture.[25] Her portrayal of the servile nature of the aristocracy underscored her belief that kings and courtiers, emasculated by a hereditary effeminacy, were unable to exercise legitimate power in an age of democratic revolution.

Turning to Burke, Wollstonecraft argued that the display of

effeminate sensibility in the *Reflections* proved he was incapable of the manly efforts necessary for philosophical endeavor. "If I were not afraid to derange your nervous system by the bare mention of a metaphysical enquiry, I should observe, Sir, that self-preservation is, literally speaking, the first law of nature; and that the care necessary to support and guard the body is the first step to unfold the mind, and inspire a manly spirit of independence" (16). To Mary Wollstonecraft, her own female body garbed in the cloak of manly reason, Edmund Burke appeared in his nakedness to have been unmanned by sensibility.

Certainly, Wollstonecraft's writing reversed the roles of rank and sex, overturning the moral order encoded in Burke's notions of the sublime and the beautiful. Nowhere was this reversal of order more evident than in the two authors' representations of October 6, 1789. Whereas Burke used the image of the hungry women of the October Days as an example of the brutish nature of democracy, Wollstonecraft represented the same women as suffering subjects of a tyrannical government. She dismissed his image of the "furies of hell, in the abused shape of the vilest women" as just another "empty rhetorical flourish" (30). She directly challenged Burke to redefine the feminine with reference to rank and education in order to see these poor women as human beings. "Probably you mean women who gained a livelihood by selling vegetables or fish, who never had had any advantages of education; or their vices might have lost a part of their abominable deformity, by losing part of their grossness" (30). Wollstonecraft asserted that the condition of womanhood itself provided the human bond that could unite the bread marchers with their queen.[26] "The Queen of France—the great and small vulgar, claim our pity; as they have almost insurmountable obstacles to surmount in their progress toward true dignity of character; still I have such a downright understanding that I do not like to make a distinction without a difference" (30).

It is this distinction without difference that highlights the sexual politics of the rights debate in England and France. Wollstonecraft charged that Burke was blinded by false distinctions in the *Reflections*. How else could one explain his nightmarish depiction of the bread marchers or his celestial description of the young Marie Antoinette, a description she singled out as bearing the tell-tale marks of sensibility, not the *"regal* stamp of reason"? (30). Burke recounts his famous vision thus:

> It is now sixteen or seventeen years since I saw the queen of France, then the dauphiness, at Versailles, and surely never lighted on this orb, which she hardly seemed to touch, a more delightful vision. I saw her just above the horizon, decorating and cheering the elevated sphere she just began to move in—glittering like the morning star full of life and splendor and joy. (66)

In her reply Wollstonecraft contrasted Burke's vision of Marie Antoinette to Dr. Price's view of the promise of democratic revolution:

> Tottering on the verge of the grave, that worthy man in his whole life never dreamt of struggling for power or riches; and, if a glimpse of the glad dawn of liberty rekindled the fire of youth in his veins, you, who could never stand the fascinating glance of a *great* Lady's eyes, when neither virtue or sense beamed in them, might have pardoned his unseemly transport,—if such it must be deemed. (18; original emphasis)

For Wollstonecraft the real horror of Edmund Burke's representation of October 6 was his feigned chivalry in supporting the queen of France, when just a few years earlier he had been among the loudest voices in parliament supporting the Regency Bill, when George III was pronounced mad by court doctors in November 1788 and the Prince of Wales rallied his friends in parliament to declare him regent.[27] Wollstonecraft questioned why Burke had not displayed the same sympathy for the sufferings of his own monarch, Queen Charlotte, during the regency crisis that he now extended to Marie Antoinette. She denounced the parliamentarian: "When you descanted on the horrors of the 6th of October, and gave a glowing, and, in some instances, a most exaggerated description of that infernal night, without having troubled yourself to clean your palette, you might have returned home and indulged us with a sketch of the misery you personally aggravated" (26). Burke's treatment of his own queen left a bad taste in Wollstonecraft's mouth but she was aware that the flavor of his remarks would be savored by many of the powerful. "The rich and weak, a numerous train, will certainly applaud your system, and loudly celebrate your pious reverence for authority and establishments—they find it pleasanter to enjoy than think; to justify oppression than correct abuses.—*The rights of men* are grating sounds that set their teeth on edge; the impertinent enquiry of philosophic meddling innovation" (52; original emphasis). Wollstonecraft surmised that Burke's attack on the National Assembly and his defense of the French monarchy were meant to appeal to a different brand of political epicurean.

But political tastes are subject to change. Whereas in Paris women marched for bread, in London much of the hunger for liberty that Burke had once fed with his support for the colonial cause had now been sated by the revolution in America. Wollstonecraft claimed that Burke had been "the Cicero of one side of the house for years," but with time he had been surpassed by other students in the "school of eloquence" (43). In his slow withdrawal from the public eye he had witnessed the fade of his own "blooming honors." It was this vision, not the revolt in France, that produced "the impassioned *Reflections* which have been a glorious revivification of your fame." Wollstonecraft claimed that in his desire to be a "great man" he had "deserted his post" as the herald of liberty and freedom (43). Burke had switched sides and become a traitor to the rights of men. She asserted that another man was revealed in his text:

> There appears to be such a mixture of real sensibility and fondly cherished romance in your composition, that the present crisis carries you out of yourself; and since you could not be one of the grand movers, the next *best* thing that dazzled your imagination was to be a conspicuous opposer. Full of yourself, you make as much noise to convince the world that you despise the revolution, as Rousseau did to persuade his contemporaries to let him live in obscurity. (44; original emphasis)

Undoubtedly, Wollstonecraft's likening of the pragmatic parliamentarian Edmund Burke to the romantic theorist of the *Social Contract*, Jean-Jacques Rousseau, would have seemed absurd to many of her contemporary readers. Rather than revealing the true nature of Burke's motivations in writing the *Reflections*, this statement may reflect Wollstonecraft's own ambitions. The publication of her first vindication was an exercise in political polemic aimed not so much at cutting a great man down to size but more at increasing the stature of a little-known lady novelist.

Given the discursive context of the early 1790s, Wollstonecraft's rhetorical strategy enabled her not only to enter the debate about the rights of man but also to engender larger theoretical issues about sexual politics.28 However, this elaborate subterfuge ultimately backfired in the last pages of the *Rights of Men*. Contrasting the misery of the masses in London with the hungry women of the bread march, Wollstonecraft queried Burke, "What were the outrages of a day to these continual miseries?" (58). For her it was the wretched conditions in which the majority of men and women lived out their days, not the fate of the French monarchs, that constituted the "present crisis" in politics. Wollstonecraft, too, was "carried away from herself" by the contemplation of this crisis. Indeed, she was overcome by the very sensibility she had tried to pin to Burke. "Man preys on man; and you mourn the idle tapestry that decorated a gothic pile, and the dronish bell that summoned the fat priest to prayer." Full of her own feeling, she chided Burke, "Did the pangs you felt for insulted nobility, the anguish that rent your heart when the gorgeous robes were torn off the idol human weakness had set up, deserve to be compared with the long-drawn sigh of melancholy reflection, when misery and vice are thus, seen to haunt our steps, and swim on the top of every cheering prospect?" In an enlightened age, "Hell stalks abroad;—the lash resounds on the slave's naked sides; and the sick wretch, who can no longer earn the sour bread of unremitting labor, steals to a ditch to bid the world a long good night" (58).

We can only speculate whether Mary Wollstonecraft as a woman writer with her own bread to earn may have tasted the sour flavor of unremitting labor on her tongue before she lashed out at the pensioned Burke.

> Such misery demands more than tears—I pause to recollect myself; and smother the contempt I feel rising from your rhetorical flourishes and infantine sensibility.
>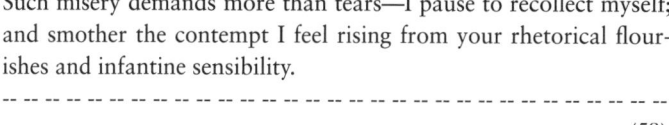
> (58)

What can possibly account for this break in her argument? Was Mary Wollstonecraft overcome by the misery of the masses or silenced by the smothering contempt she felt for Edmund Burke's defense of property and privilege? We find that, when Wollstonecraft the anonymous author paused to "recollect" the self, she was carried away by emotion and that this process of recollection reduced her to responding to Burke with two lines of dashes rather than her own words, leaving an empty space on the printed page. She quickly tried to return to character but instead found herself too shaken to continue. "Taking a retrospective view of my hasty answer, and casting a cursory glance over your *Reflections,* I perceive that I have not alluded to several reprehensible passages, in your elaborate work; which I marked for censure when I first perused it with a steady eye" (58). Knocked off balance by her own recollection of self, she admitted she was at a loss: "And now I find it almost impossible to candidly refute your sophisms, without quoting your own words, and putting the numerous contradictions I observed in opposition with each other" (58). Modern readers are left to ponder whether this gap represents an "embarrassing silence," as Sapiro has asserted, or the first self-conscious moments of *A Vindication of the Rights of Woman.*[29] Her own naked humanity revealed by her tears on the page, Mary Wollstonecraft, at least momentarily, was silenced by sensibility.

Thus, Wollstonecraft's reply to Burke abruptly ends with a textual tear in the fabric of her argument. What should we make of this unusual passage signifying the breakdown of language, a place within the text where she could not express her thoughts or feelings in words? It appears that in the process of writing her answer to Burke, Wollstonecraft's conception of manly authority began to unravel and created a crisis of identity that ended her masquerade. The paradox of this identity crisis is that in her attempt to expose Burke she exposed her own fragmented identity as a female author. Godwin in the *Memoirs* recounted that in the midst of composing her reply, Wollstonecraft told him, she experienced some form of writer's block. "When Mary had arrived at the middle of her work, she was seized with a temporary fit of torpor and indolence, and began to repent of her undertaking." She went to visit Joseph Johnson who volunteered to destroy the pages already in print if that would bring her peace of mind. But this would not do as it went against her political principles and undermined her economic independence. Living by her pen, those pages were her pay. "Mary had wanted stimulus. She had not expected to be encouraged in what she knew well to be an unreasonable access of idleness. Her friend so easily falling in with her ill humor, and seeming to expect that she would lay aside her undertaking, piqued her pride." Had the novice polemicist taken on more than she could handle in challenging Edmund Burke? According to Godwin, "She immediately went home; and proceeded to the end of her work, with no more interruptions than were absolutely necessary."[30]

Therefore, Mary Wollstonecraft, an obscure lady novelist, concluded her reply to the Right Honorable Burke by again attacking the authority invested in name and rank. She argued that even "enlightened philosophers" seemed to give more credit to property than to the rights of men. "They bow down to rank, and are careful to secure property; for virtue, without this adventitious drapery, is seldom very respectable in their eyes—nor are they very quick-sighted to discern real dignity of character when no sounding name exalts the man above the elbows" (60). Perhaps then it was not surprising that when Johnson published her pamphlet at the end of November no name appeared on the title page.

THE PROPER THEME OF THE FEMALE SEX

> We should be sorry to raise a horse-laugh against a fair lady; but we were always taught to suppose that the rights of women were the proper theme of the female sex.
> —*Gentleman's Magazine*, 1791

Wollstonecraft's *Vindication of the Rights of Men* was so successful that less than a month after the publication of the initial anonymous edition a second edition was issued, revealing Mary Wollstonecraft to be the author of the first reply to Edmund Burke. Could a woman, in this revolutionary age, expect her pamphlet on political rights to be judged by the rational standards that her work espoused? Immediately following the republication of this controversial tract, a reviewer for the conservative monthly the *Gentleman's Magazine* wrote, "We should be sorry to raise a horse-laugh against a fair lady; but we were always taught to suppose that the rights of women were the proper theme of the female sex."[31] The reviewer raised the critical question of how a woman could write a defense of the rights of man. Women simply did not write about rights. If a woman should be rash enough to pen a treatise about the rights of mankind, she must restrict herself to the rights of women.

Ironically, the reviewer goes on to suggest that the strongly worded text was the product of a man masquerading as a woman, given that the author attempted to defend the rights of men against the "demon of property." By writing about property and class, Wollstonecraft had certainly crossed the boundaries of both gender and genre. These transgressions by a woman author have often provoked reactions of denial or dismissal. Joanna Russ has commented, "What to do when a woman has written something? The first line of defense is to deny that she wrote it. Since women cannot write, someone else (a man) must have written it."[32] Thus, the reviewer for the *Gentleman's Magazine* asserted in the concluding paragraph of his lengthy analysis:

> Mrs. W., if she be a real and not a fictitious lady, is engaged in a service wherein the great leaders have run themselves aground. Malcontents, who have nothing to lose, may lend their names, and offer their hands, for any mischief. But reflecting minds will see through their stale and shameful tricks and not involve themselves in the ruin of their country. Why will not these devotees of reason give an example of the dispossession of the demon of Property, by dividing their property (if they have any) into aliquot parts between their children and the first beggars who present themselves to ask alms of them? Every experimental philosopher should first try the experiments on himself before he electrifies a whole kingdom.[33]

In *Rights of Men,* Wollstonecraft declared "Security of Property! Behold, in a few words, the definition of English Liberty" (14). She was well aware that, at the end of the eighteenth century, English women were among the least secure and the least free of the king's subjects. The real Mrs. W., an unmarried woman in George III's England, held property only in her name, her hand, and her reflecting mind. She had learned in her reply to Burke that political writing and political rights were the precious patrimony of the sons of liberty. The importance of this hereditary connection cannot be overestimated. For women the political consequence of primogeniture and patriarchy has been a form of powerlessness in which women were treated as property themselves. Indeed, as a woman without property, on what possible ground could Wollstonecraft respond to Burke and defend the political rights of her countrymen?[34]

The answer lies in the literary strategy of Wollstonecraft's first vindication. Over the past two centuries commentators have suggested that what was truly remarkable about her pamphlet was that, in the words of historian George Stead Veitch, "She met Burke on his own rhetorical ground and bettered him." The spirited nature of Wollstonecraft's reply to Burke appealed to many of her eighteenth-century readers and reviewers. Early in the twentieth century Veitch wrote that he found it "strange" that "the only reply to Burke which is adequate on the emotional side should have lapsed into obscurity, for Burke's strength was due as much to the intensity of his feelings as to the power of his mind, and the antagonist who was sufficiently sympathetic to meet him on his own ground had manifest advantages over the other controversialists."[35] Virginia Sapiro echoed Veitch, noting that *Rights of Men* "responded both to *what* Burke wrote and *how* he wrote it."[36] Yet neither of these careful analyses comes to full terms with the gender politics of Wollstonecraft's *Reply to Burke*.

The lady novelist crossed the boundaries of gender and genre in order to confront Burke and in the process reinvented herself as an author. Her rhetorical strategy was based on an elaborate ruse that subverted the traditional conventions of political discourse. An anonymous Mary Wollstonecraft, masquerading as a man, promised her readers she would "show Burke to himself" and in the process displayed the "mind of a woman with thinking powers" to the readers of contemporary political thought. "But it was not my intention, when I began this letter, to descend to the minutiae of your conduct, or to weight your infirmities in a balance; it is only some of your pernicious opinions that I wish to hunt out of their lurking holes; and to shew you to yourself, stripped of the gorgeous drapery in which you have enwrapped your tyrannic principles" (37).

To dismiss gender is to miss the most radical element of this exchange between the novice polemicist and the senior statesman. For it was Mary Wollstonecraft's sex that made it impossible for her to meet Burke on his own theoretical turf. Her writing disputed the ownership of this contested discursive ground. She confounded gender categories by employing literary devices that challenged Burke's notion of authority and left her readers wondering, Who was the author of *A Vindication of the Rights of Men*?

In the weeks following the publication of the first edition of her pamphlet, Wollstonecraft's friends and foes alike speculated on the identity of the author who had publicly championed the rights of men by attacking Burke in print. The author eluded even the Reverend Richard Price who had a personal stake in knowing the name of his recent advocate. It was time for Wollstonecraft to reveal herself and take credit for her words; she sent a copy of her reply to Dr. Price. In a letter posted from Hackney on December 17, 1790, one day before Johnson issued the second edition, which publicly proclaimed Mary Wollstonecraft to be the author, the Reverend Price sent his cordial thanks to his friend from Newington Green:

> Dr. Price presents his kind compliments to Miss Wollstonecraft, and returns her his best thanks for sending him her Vindication of the rights of Men in answer to Mr. Burke, and for the pleasure he has derived from the perusal of it. He has not been surprised to find that a composition which he has heard ascribed to some of our ablest writers, appears to come from Miss Wollstonecraft. He is particularly happy in having such an advocate; and he requests her acceptance of his gratitude for the very kind and handsome manner in which she has mentioned him.[37]

In her reply to Burke Wollstonecraft began her direct attack on the canonized forefathers. The real surprise is that, given the gendered structure of rights discourse, so few scholars have mentioned that the first answer to Burke's polemic was from a woman. Wollstonecraft's literary strategy confused gender identities and thus transcended the literary boundaries that excluded women from political writing. She was not simply a woman writing behind the mask of anonymity. Wollstonecraft appropriated the gendered mantle of political authority, becoming the voice of reason and thereby confounding Burke's construction of female subservience and silence by loudly addressing her reading audience as a man.[38] It is evident from the confusion of the reviewer from the *Gentleman's Magazine* to Dr. Price himself that Wollstonecraft's theory and strategy in her first rights tract did much to confound the distinction of sex in political writing.[39]

The anonymous publication of the *Rights of Men* requires us to recognize the troubled relationship between sex and significance in the history of political discourse and becomes an important departure point for Wollstonecraft's feminist political theory and our own. Ultimately, the fundamental problem of political discourse is a politics that denies women a language to express visions of self. Historically, women have not been represented in the stories of the democratic struggle for power, nor represented in the institutional seats of democratic governments. Misrepresentation and underrepresentation are inherently related, interacting to create a political discourse that materially and spiritually limits women's lives.

Viewed from this perspective, Wollstonecraft's *Rights of Men* was a product of double vision. She mastered the illusion of masculine authority through anonymity and thus entered the patriarchal discourse of political thought. Yet she fractured the philosophical looking glass by consciously turning gendered language upon itself, distorting the terms and markers of sexual difference. Her appeals to manly authority were used to legitimate an argument that called into question the meaning of human rights. Her discursive strategy played on gender uncertainty: who was the author of *A Vindication of the Rights of Men*? Certainly within the discursive context of the late eighteenth century, the identity of this anonymous author would prove to be of enormous importance to the debate about political rights. For the anonymous defender of the rights of men became the notorious champion of the rights of women. In Wollstonecraft's own lifetime her work opened up a debate about the social expectations and political exclusions that restrict women's participation in civil society.

Rights of Men concluded with Wollstonecraft's own visionary scheme for political reform. Instead of the corruption of a court culture, which promoted its own gender crisis, she offered men and women civic friendship as the foundation of political virtue. She argued that this virtue could not be inherited; it could be acquired only by hard work. Real progress in Europe would not occur until there was an end to the patriarchal succession of hereditary honors. "Whether the glory of Europe is set, I shall not now enquire; but probably the spirit of romance and chivalry is in the wane; and reason will gain by its extinction" (29). Only a truly egalitarian nation would be able to achieve the humanistic goals of the Enlightenment. In the *Reflections* Burke had lamented that the philosophy of the rights of man would produce a democratic leveling of France. "On this scheme of things, a king is but a man; a queen is but a woman, a woman is but an animal; and an animal not of the highest order" (67). Mary Wollstonecraft confirmed this new order. "All true, Sir; if she is not more attentive to the duties of humanity than queens and fashionable ladies in general are," but she suggested that this leveling had important civic consequences for women, which could raise them above brute creation (25). She denounces the romantic valorization of women, noting that "such homage vitiates them, prevents them from endeavouring to obtain solid personal merit; and in short, makes those beings vain inconsiderate dolls, who ought to be prudent mothers and useful members of society" (25). Her analysis provides a vivid contrast to Rousseau's commentary on girls and their toys, in which he states that the little girl "awaits the moment when she will be her own doll."[40] Thus, we see the beginnings of the theoretical argument of Wollstonecraft's second vindication. Rational women should be the helpmates not the playthings of men.

In her first vindication she took aim at the outmoded code of chivalry by redefining the masculine and feminine by duty to country and responsibility to self. In her enlightened plan kings and queens, farmers and chambermaids, simply became men and women to be judged by their humanity and reason like everyone else. According to Godwin, the "applause which attended her *Answer to Burke* elevated the tone of her mind" and "increased her confidence in her powers."[41] Emboldened by her success Wollstonecraft proceeded to author a subsequent treatise attacking the patriarchal politics of the canonized forefathers whose writings confined "the rights of humanity to the male line from Adam downwards."[42] In *A Vindication of the Rights of Woman* Mary Wollstonecraft used her newfound authority to claim this birthright for her sex.

CHAPTER FOUR

The Feminist Author and Women's Rights

> A wild wish has just flown from my heart to my head, and I will not stifle it though it may excite a horse-laugh.—I do earnestly wish to see the distinction of sex confounded in society, unless where love animates the behavior.
>
> —Mary Wollstonecraft,
> *A Vindication of the Rights of Woman*

Mary Wollstonecraft's wild wish to confound the distinction of sex in society required challenging the canonical tradition of political writing and transforming the masculinist discourse of political rights to include women. I argue that she would never have written *A Vindication of the Rights of Woman* if she had not first authored *A Vindication of the Rights of Men*. The popular response to her defense of the rights of men and political events in both England and France proved to this rebellious writer that now was the time to call for women's rights. But how to do it? To whom should she direct her call? As a woman author Wollstonecraft was acutely aware of the constraints that sexual distinctions in society imposed on political dialogue between men and women. Thus, in both vindications she employed rhetorical devices that confounded the mark of gender and she developed theoretical arguments that denied sexual difference. This dual strategy gave her the authority to enter the rights debate and to represent her sex in the conversation of political thought.

A Vindication of the Rights of Woman was dedicated to Charles Talleyrand, the minister of education in revolutionary France, and indeed much of her motivation for writing this book came from her reaction to events there. But Wollstonecraft's intended audience were the female readers she addressed in her preface: "My own sex, I hope, will excuse me, if I treat them like rational creatures, instead of flattering their fascinating graces, and viewing them as if they were in a state of perpetual childhood, unable to stand alone."[1] Echoing her challenge to Edmund Burke, Wollstonecraft instigated a revolution in political writing by asserting the authority of her own reason in her argument for the rights of woman. She warned her female readers that the "soft phrases" used by the canonized forefathers in describing the female sex were only "epithets of weakness." She took up her pen to point the way for other women. "I earnestly wish to point out in what true dignity and human happiness consist—I wish to persuade women to endeavour to acquire strength, both of mind and body" (75). Her plan was the product of experience and reflection. "I shall be employed about things, not words!" (76). As the spokesperson for a new genus of thinking women, she would "avoid that flowery diction that has slided [sic] from essays into novels, and from novels into familiar letters and conversation" (76).

Wollstonecraft was the first of many to reply to the *Reflections on the Revolution in France*. Her bold response to Edmund Burke's attack of the humanist ideals of the French Revolution underscored the profound exclusion of women from both the discourse and the practice of Enlightenment philosophy. The reviews of her first vindication proved that for a woman to write about politics was to invite public censure or the outright denial of her authorship.[2] But if the reward for penning a polemic was not the popular recognition of her name, it did offer the author an opportunity to publicize her ideas and extend her agenda. In February 1792 Joseph Johnson published *A Vindication of the Rights of Woman*. Wollstonecraft's second vindication offered female readers a comprehensive plan for personal revolution and political reformation. The publication of this controversial tract produced an international sensation. Within the year it was reissued in London and subsequently reprinted in Dublin, Philadelphia, and New York. After years of translating other writers' work into English, to see her own book translated into French and German must have brought her great satisfaction. She promised a future volume on the relationship of women to the law that would further explore their rights and duties as citizens. Mary Wollstonecraft had at last made a name for herself as a feminist author.

In the *Rights of Woman* she consciously created a feminist theory by confounding the distinctions of sex. She distinguishes biological sex from the system of gender representation and practice of the late eighteenth century. She confounds the social distinctions of sex in two ways. First, she uses gendered language and the guise of anonymity to conceal her sex as an author. Second, she deconstructs the textual representations of women in selected polemics and conduct books to reveal the male authors behind the portraits of femininity, thus she disputes the natural origin of sexual difference.

In her reply to Burke she had condemned the system of rank that produced the "distinctions without difference," which separated Marie Antoinette from the market women of Paris. In her subsequent vindication she argued that the sexual distinctions in society were the "grand cause" of female ignorance and male tyranny. Truth, for Wollstonecraft, was the basis of virtue for both men and women—and the foundation of the private virtues that were necessary for public happiness. The false distinctions that gave a sexual character to the mind, she asserted, detracted from the moral development of women and impeded the general progress of civil society. As long as femininity was defined by weakness, women would gain power through cunning actions that corrupted both the private household and the public sphere. Wollstonecraft took on the stereotypical eighteenth-century characterizations of female nature:

> Dismissing then those pretty feminine phrases, which the men condescendingly use to soften our slavish dependence, and despising the weak elegancy of mind, exquisite sensibility, and sweet docility of manners supposed to be the sexual characteristics of the weaker vessel, I wish to shew that elegance is inferior to virtue, that the first object of laudable ambition is to obtain the character as a human being, regardless of the distinction of sex; and that secondary views should be brought to this simple touchstone. (75)

For over two centuries Wollstonecraft's *Rights of Woman* has been just such a touchstone for generations of women committed to sexual equality. She rejected the "fanciful theories" of male authors that treated females as either irrational creatures or lesser men. Instead, she considered "woman as a whole, let it be what it will, instead of a part of man." For Wollstonecraft, the woman question was a simple one: "the inquiry is whether she have reason or not" (122).

She sought to deny men the authority of defining womanhood as difference by critically analyzing the representations of woman's "nature" in the work of the leading male writers. Her fundamental assertion was that reason separated mankind from brutes and that women as human beings shared with men a rational nature derived from God. She made problematic the traditional opposition of femininity to rationality by revealing the patriarchal motivations behind the portraits of woman that literary men such as Rousseau claimed to have drawn from nature: "Do you wish always to be well guided? Then always follows nature's indications. Everything that characterizes the fair sex ought to be respected as established by nature."[3]

From her vantage point, women at the end of the eighteenth century appeared to be in a most *unnatural* state. Unenlightened views of sexual difference and barbarous social distinctions between the sexes brutalized females by making them creatures of cunning rather than rational beings. Given the present state of society, Wollstonecraft argued that it was impossible to know the exact nature of woman so great were the artificial restraints placed upon the female sex. Repeatedly, she attacked the "boasted prerogative of man" (170), revealed in the writings on female manners that subjected women to the arbitrary rule of masculine prejudice. Her call to rebellion incites women to reform themselves and to resist the dogma of paternalism. "It is time to effect a revolution in female manners—time to restore them their lost dignity—and make them, as a part of the human species, labour by reforming themselves to reform the world. It is time to separate unchangeable morals from local manners.—If men be demi-gods why let us serve them?" (114). She created a political theory that called for both a "revolution in female manners" and the enlightened reformation of society, so that women would have the educational opportunity, economic security, and political recognition they needed to create their own complex identities. To do this she needed to focus on the nature of the woman question in eighteenth-century political thought.

Edmund Burke in *Reflections on the Revolution in France* described women who laid claim to political rights as participating in a political system that reduced queens to women and women to animals. Jean-Jacques Rousseau in *Emile* argued that women involved in political activity transgressed nature and risked becoming men. Wollstonecraft in the *Rights of Woman* linked these discussions of woman's nature to the nature of politics and looked to social explanations for so-called biological differences. First, she claimed in response to Burke that women, like men, were rational subjects who could be ennobled by the pursuit of virtue. An inferior education rather than an inferior intellect had kept women "gentle, domestic brutes" (89). Second, she refuted Rousseau by arguing that women's duties were human duties and, as such, demand rights. No being could be virtuous who was not free. To both men she answered that political tyranny and false refinement, rather than a desire to usurp masculine authority, had drawn women from their sphere. Historically women have always participated in politics. The issue for Wollstonecraft was to legitimate women's participation in the public sphere. To this end she argued that there was no sexual character to virtue. What Burke and Rousseau called virtuous was neither masculine nor feminine; it was a human attribute and a divine gift.

Thus, women must be incorporated into the social contract or remain a constant threat to that contract. As she stated in the first paragraph of the *Rights of Woman,* women must be free within the social contract or retain their natural freedom by remaining "on the barren heath" of the state of nature (65). Any constitution that did not recognize the human rights of woman was unjust and corrupt in its first principles. In this way Wollstonecraft reconciled naturalist philosophy about human nature with political philosophy. For her efforts, the pundit Horace Walpole famously identified her as a "hyaena [sic] in petticoats," an interesting distinction given that naturalists of the eighteenth century like Buffon made much of the fact that hyenas could mimic the human voice, and that female hyenas had a "false penis," which made it difficult to distinguish them from their male counterparts.[4] In the historical conversation of political thought, this notorious distinction would clearly mark Wollstonecraft as different from Burke and Rousseau.

The *Rights of Men* was Wollstonecraft's introduction to the conversation of political theory. This initial confrontation of the anonymous woman with the patriarchy of canonical thought set the stage for her analysis of women's rights in her second vindication. Wollstonecraft's literary strategy in the *Rights of Woman* was built upon the lessons she had learned in her reply to Burke: that writing had a critical impact on rights, and that established authority was opposed to femininity. However, the *Rights of Woman* was written in direct response to the disappointing turn of events in revolutionary France, where, in spite of the implicit universalism in the Declaration of the Rights of Man and Citizens, the new constitution explicitly removed women as active members in the body politic. The French framers were strongly influenced by the writings of Rousseau and drew sharp contrasts between the roles of men and women in the political sphere.[5] The dream of a gender-inclusive body politic was shattered by the institutionalization of sex differences in the educational reforms of Charles Talleyrand based upon his reading of Rousseau. Thus, Wollstonecraft picked up her pen again to vindicate political rights, but this time, she attacked the "male aristocracy" (157) in political thought who had confined political rights to the male line since Adam and Eve left the Garden.

Taken together, her two rights tracts posed a radical challenge to political discourse in the last decade of the eighteenth century. Wollstonecraft transformed what began as a critique of paternalistic government into a full-scale attack on the distinctions of gender and rank that formed the basis of a patriarchal society. Ultimately, the *Rights of Woman*, like the earlier *Rights of Men*, provides a powerful example of the dilemmas of authority and femininity that have had enormous implications for women's political writing as well as for their political rights.

WOMAN'S NATURE AND THE NATURE OF POLITICS

> I plead for my sex—not for myself. . . . It is then an affection for the whole human race that makes my pen dart rapidly along to support what I believe is the cause of virtue.
> —Mary Wollstonecraft, *A Vindication of the Rights of Woman*

In the *Rights of Woman* Wollstonecraft denied that reason was exclusive to men and called into question the very foundations of canonical theory that excluded women from political power. The "horse-laughs" that greeted her second vindication recalled the laughter that met Socrates' claim in book 5 of the *Republic*, that if women share reason with men they might also share the leadership of their communities. "I may excite laughter, by dropping an hint, which I mean to pursue, some future time, for I really think that women ought to have representatives, instead of being arbitrarily governed without having any direct share allowed them in the deliberations of government" (217). For Wollstonecraft, the power to govern oneself was a divine birthright, born of human reason. The radical suggestion that women might rule themselves raised the revolutionary possibility that women might represent their own interests in government alongside men.

Wollstonecraft framed a theoretical space for the thinking woman in the discourse on politics by asserting that she must govern herself. The feminist author argued that the misrepresentation of women's nature within the texts of the leading male writers had important consequences for the political representation of women by men in government. She dismissed the notion that females were naturally irrational and she condemned the servile dependence of women upon men in both family and civil society. She began her *Rights of Woman* by contesting the discourse of difference and creating a theory that moved women from silent objects to speaking subjects. She disputed the natural origin as well as the social significance of sex differences between men and women. Her analysis confronted the textual representations of women's nature within eighteenth-century writing, ranging from polemics to novels. Her task had been dictated in large part by Rousseau, who had ambiguously stated in *Emile* that "woman is man" in all things but sex:

> In everything not connected with sex, woman is man. She has the same organs, the same needs, the same faculties. The machine is constructed in the same way; its parts are the same; the one functions as does the other; the form is similar; and in whatever respect one considers them, the difference between them is only one of more or less. In everything connected with sex, woman and man are in every respect related and in every respect different.[6]

He used the category of "sex" to determine both physical and behavioral traits of each individual. Wollstonecraft argued that Rousseau's complex theorizing about sexual difference in *Emile* and *La Nouvelle Heloise* belied a simple biological reductionism, which conflated the minor physical differences between anatomically similar beings with the major social distinctions that structure our understanding of both our common bodies and our different destinies.

In the *Rights of Woman* Wollstonecraft tried to disentangle the female body from the restrictive clothing of a political system of subjection and a culture of control. Her effort was much the same as Rousseau's attempt to free the infant Emile from the swaddling fabric that deformed the body over time. She removed layer after layer of social cloth and studied the texture of the weave that throughout history had so tightly bound and restricted women's physical and psychic independence. Wollstonecraft argued that women were bound by the textual representations of female nature that inscribed femininity as difference. To her mind woman, born free, was everywhere enchained by a political discourse that posited the equality of all men in reason while prescribing the slavery of all women to the world of opinion.

Wollstonecraft's thesis was that men and women shared a rational nature derived from God. She claimed that, except for physical strength, all distinctions between the sexes were the products of social conventions—a direct challenge to male authors who represented social distinctions as a necessary consequence of natural differences between the sexes: "she is always represented as only created to see through a gross medium, and to take things on trust" (122). Wollstonecraft's strategy complicated masculine authority and openly questioned women's blind obedience to powers outside themselves. She contended that many of the representations of the nature of her sex needed to be subjected to careful analysis by women themselves. In so doing, the feminist author critiqued the construction of sexual difference—in the works of Rousseau, the conduct books of Dr. Fordyce and Dr. Gregory, and in various eighteenth-century novels—in a chapter she titled, "Animadversions On Some Of The Writers Who Have Rendered Women The Object Of Pity, Bordering On Contempt."[7] Wollstonecraft interrupted this desultory conversation among men because she was deeply concerned about the lessons that female readers would take from these texts. If women emulated the passive models of femininity that filled the pages of treatise and novel, she argued, they would be incapable of the public speech and action necessary to confront the real problems and prejudices in their daily lives.

Portraits of women's nature and educational models that praised female weakness and fostered the submission and silence of her sex had restricted women's membership in society, she stated. The female reader schooled only in the lessons of these works learned that, because women were naturally deficient in reason, they were required to rely on the wisdom of men. Wollstonecraft, the female reader turned feminist author, observed that these books provided females with an education "worse than Egyptian bondage" (187).

> I may be accused of arrogance; still I must declare what I firmly believe, that all the writers who have written on the subject of female education and manners from Rousseau to Dr. Gregory, have con-

tributed to render women more artificial, weak characters, than they would otherwise have been; and, consequently, more useless members of society. I might have expressed this conviction in a lower key; but I am afraid it would have been the whine of affectation, and not the faithful expression of my feelings, of the clear result, which experience and reflection have lead me to draw. (91)

Wollstonecraft developed her theory by reflecting on her personal experiences as a self-educated woman. She entered the public debate on the role of women conscious that her words might be interpreted as either arrogant or whining. In writing the *Rights of Woman* she contested the androcentric textual tradition, asserting that her objection "extends to the whole purport of these books, which tend, in my opinion, to degrade one half of the human species, and render women pleasing at the expense of every solid virtue" (91).[8] To vindicate the rights of her sex, Wollstonecraft first needed to deconstruct the textualization of women's nature in the writings of her primary target, Jean-Jacques Rousseau.

No philosopher did more to reinvent the nature of both sexes than Rousseau. Joan Landes comments on the profound impact of "print culture" on the men and women of revolutionary France. The proliferation of pamphlets, letters, political tracts, and fictions contributed to the "active textualization of life" in the late eighteenth century, an era in which both sexes modeled their behavior upon the suggestions of a treatise or the characterizations of a novel. Rousseau's works, in particular, established a new bond between the author and the reader, in which "reading—active, not passive—was an element in the process by which life was remade along domestic and virtuous grounds."[9] In his writings Rousseau sought to return corrupt men and women to nature. However, the consequences of this "return" were very different for women than they were for men. Rousseau created a vision of natural woman whose rustic simplicity he opposed to the real women of intellect, the *salonierres* and bluestockings of Paris and London. Rousseau valorized female ignorance, making female chastity rather than human rationality the focus of womanhood.[10] His concept of nature assured the equality of all men while demanding the subordination of all women. Rousseau claimed in the *Discourse on the Origin and Foundations of Inequality Among Men* that the attempts of previous philosophers to uncover the origins of inequality among men had failed because they imputed to nature characteristics that were the products of the advancement of the arts and sciences in society. No philosopher who had come before him had been able to accurately portray "natural man" within the state of nature. In their search for the foundations of government, "all of them, continually speaking of need, greed, oppression, desires, and pride transferred to the state of Nature ideas they had taken from society; they spoke of the Savage Man and depicted Civil man."[11] As Diana Coole notes, Rousseau's discovery of a "naturalist fallacy" in the writings of Hobbes and Locke can be contrasted with Wollstonecraft's criticisms of the portraits of women's "nature" artfully composed in the works of male authors. "The only natural society, Rousseau continues in *The Social Contract,* is the family, where 'the ruler corresponds to the father.' In other words, he has gratuitously taken as his model of what is natural for women, that configuration which emerged from a particular stage of development, namely the patriarchal family, even though this appeared only with a revolutionary change and was succeeded by another."[12] For Wollstonecraft, "Men, indeed, appear to me to act in a very unphilosophical manner when they try to secure the good conduct of women by attempting to keep them always in a state of childhood" (89). Rousseau's artful efforts to draw a woman from nature culminated in the child coquette Sophie. Indeed, Rousseau states, "To be a woman means to be coquettish."[13]

Conversely, in the *Rights of Woman,* the examination of man in the state of nature was replaced by a study of the infantile status of women in civil society.

> *I have, probably, had an opportunity to see more girls in their infancy than J. J. Rousseau*—I can recollect my own feelings, and I have looked steadily around me; yet, so far am I in coinciding with him in opinion respecting the dawn of the female character, I will venture to affirm, that a girl, whose spirits have not been dampened by inactivity, or innocence tainted by false shame, will always be a romp, and the doll will never excite attention unless confinement allows her no other alternative. (112; my emphasis)

Wollstonecraft ridiculed Rousseau's claim that he had drawn the image of Sophie from nature. "He did not go back to nature, or his ruling appetite disturbed the operations of reason, else he would not have drawn these crude inferences" (151). She pointed to an anomaly in Rousseau's theory; the nature that liberated men from submission to hereditary kings reinforced the subjection of women to fathers and husbands.[14] The fallacy that led philosophers to extend their own patriarchal interests to "natural man," and to transfer contemporary social relationships to the state of nature, was much the same as the philosophical error that placed adult women in a state of childish dependence on men. Wollstonecraft recognized that philosophical arguments that assumed women were irrational and childlike by nature provided the justification for the political segregation of society according to sex.

The feminist author denaturalized the fundamental opposition of femininity to rationality by highlighting the masculine motivations behind theoretical and literary re-creations of woman's nature. She described the crippling effects of these caricatures of femininity upon historical females: "Educated in the enervating style recommended by the writers on whom I have been animadverting; and not having a chance, from their subordinate state in society, to recover their lost ground, is it surprising that women everywhere appear a defect in nature?" (185). The irony of these arguments appeared to her to be that the "civilized" women, who embody the false refinements advocated by male authors, would be more moral if they had been "left in a state nearer to nature" (129–30). Her analysis complicated the multiple readings of nature that have represented women as dependent beings, as she dismissed the "fanciful female character, so prettily drawn by poets and novelists" (120). Her comment on Dr. Gregory's statement that women were by nature fond of dress was typical of her sense of the ambiguity of the term "nature": "I am unable to comprehend what either he or Rousseau mean, when they frequently use this indefinite term." She continues, "If they told us that in a pre-existent state the soul was fond of dress, and brought this inclination with it into a new body, I should listen to them with a half smile, as I often do when I hear a rant about innate elegance.— But if he only meant to say that the exercise of the faculties will produce this fondness—I deny it. It is not natural; but arises, like false ambition in men, from a love of power" (97). We cannot return to a state of nature in order to ascertain the perfectibility or corruption of eighteenth-century men and women. Wollstonecraft suggests that arguments about the "nature" of the sexes are philosophical exercises, and as such they explicitly reveal the work of man in ordering the world. The portraits of "natural woman" are the product of masculine desire rather than disinterested logic

(97). Women in costume, like soldiers in dress uniform, may be adorned in finery, but, ever obedient to the will of their commanding officers, they are not ennobled by the virtues of independent thought and autonomous action.

The study of woman's nature at the center of the *Rights of Woman* was at its core an analysis of the "distinctions without difference" and the "indefinite terms" used to demarcate the boundaries between the lives of men and women. In the determinate relationship between political writing and political rights, women, defined by men as irrational by nature, became the "objects of pity and contempt," and as a historical consequence they were denied political subjectivity (147). Wollstonecraft's focus was thus on the connection between the objectification of woman within the texts of the canonized forefathers on one hand and the subjugation of women within patriarchal society on the other. She recognized that irrational women were forever dependent on rational men for the reason to guide their own lives. "Rousseau declares that a woman should never, for a moment, feel herself independent.... He carries the arguments, which he pretends to draw from the indications of nature, still further, and insinuates that truth and fortitude, the corner stones of all human virtue, should be cultivated with certain restrictions because with respect to the female character, obedience is the grand lesson" (94). Wollstonecraft decried as "nonsense" the assertion that women were irrational and dependent by nature (94–95). She argued, "Reason is, consequentially, the simple power of improvement; or, more properly speaking, of discerning truth. Every individual is in this respect a world in itself" (122). To this feminist author it was time for women to become the heroines of their own life stories; the moment had come for women to take center stage in the historical dramas of a revolutionary world. Wollstonecraft's political theory offered women the emancipatory power of Enlightenment reason, the power to break the bonds of servitude imposed by ignorance.

EDUCATION AND CITIZENSHIP

> Asserting the rights which women in common with men ought to contend for, I have not attempted to extenuate their faults; but to prove them to be the natural consequence of their education and

station in society. . . . Let woman share the rights and she will emulate the virtues of man, for she must grow more perfect when emancipated, or justify the authority that chains such a weak being to her duty.
—Mary Wollstonecraft, *A Vindication of the Rights of Woman*

It was a truth of this enlightened century that girls were poorly educated and that women had no institutional political power. Wollstonecraft's *Rights of Woman* politicized the education of females by engendering the debate about civic duty and civil rights. Making a case for a broader definition of woman's citizenship, she called for the coeducation of boys and girls in national day schools and for expanded vocational instruction for women. Her thesis was that females did not lack reason but, rather, that they historically had been denied a rational education and the wide experience of the world that teaches civic virtue. She theorized that social prescriptions equating female innocence with ignorance were the foundation of the ideological belief that men and women had separate sexual natures and that femininity was inconsistent with rationality.

Analysis of the social distinctions based upon sex was at the center of her rights theory, and these distinctions were nowhere more evident than in access to education. Eighteenth-century Englishwomen were not allowed to fully develop their rational abilities because members of their sex were excluded from the formal education afforded to Englishmen. Wollstonecraft attacked the conventions of female education that focused on the body rather than the mind. She lashed out at parents and teachers who emphasized manners over morals, teaching girls to value pretty accomplishments rather than rational improvements. Since marriage was the fate of the majority of females, these conventional lessons were aimed at making a young lady pleasing to her future husband, a plaything instead of a partner. Wollstonecraft, returning to her argument from *Thoughts on the Education of Daughters*, asserted that given the vagaries of fortune, females needed an education that would provide them with a "well stored mind" and the appropriate skills to cope with the inevitable challenges of life.

The political significance of Wollstonecraft's argument becomes clear when it is placed within the larger historical context of women's writing on the education of their sex. In a chapter on feminist traditions, Virginia Sapiro contends that Wollstonecraft's work stands alone and is not directly connected to the writings of earlier female authors. Then as now an ignorance of women writers creates an intellectual gap in female education.

> From the point of view of traditions of feminist thinking there is one further problem. Even if a woman gained an education, read through scholarly libraries, and perhaps even taught herself Latin, as Catharine Macaulay did, where would she learn about earlier proto-feminist voices? By what means would she become aware of the writing efforts of women before her time? There is no more reason to believe that a typically educated woman of Wollstonecraft's time ("education" such as it was likely to be) would be any more familiar with Mary Astell, Christine de Pizan, or the controversy about women in Renaissance England than a typically educated woman today would be familiar with those writings or the work of Margaret Fuller, Antoinette Brown Blackwell, Charlotte Perkins Gilman, the feminist writing of John Stuart Mill—or Mary Wollstonecraft. Who would lead a woman to these writings as an "educated" person might be led to those in the more commonly accepted canon of great thinkers?[15]

It is exactly these kinds of questions that signify the importance of Wollstonecraft's quest for rational education and independent thought for women. Outside of references to Hester Chapone, Catharine Macaulay, Sarah Trimmer, and Germaine de Stael, in Wollstonecraft's work there is indeed little commentary on the work of other women writers. This said, however, she was a mentor and friend of Mary Hays who authored the six-volume *Female Biography: or, Memoirs of Illustrious and Celebrated Women, of all Ages and Countries*. Hays's volumes contained lengthy references to the writings of Mary Astell and other seventeenth-century women authors.[16]

To truly understand the history of feminist discourse and the unique importance of Wollstonecraft's contribution to the canonical conversation of political thought, the *Rights of Woman* must be situated in the midst of a longer debate about the politics of women's education. At various points within the seventeenth century, women had authored pamphlets and tracts aimed at reviving an "ancient" tradition of educating women of the highest ranks in society. The tutor Bathsua Makin and the scholar Mary Astell both asserted the rationality of their sex in making their cases for the education of elite women.

Makin's *An Essay to Revive the Antient Education of Gentlewomen, in Religion, Manners, Arts, and Tongues. With An Answer to the Objections against this Way of Education*, published in 1673, attacked the "barbarous custom to breed women low." Makin contrasted this modern custom with the pedagogy of an earlier time. "I verily think, Women were formerly Educated in the knowledge of Arts and Tongues, and by their Education, many did rise to a greater height in Learning. Were Women thus Educated now, I am confident that the advantage would be very great: The Women would have Honour and Pleasure, their Relations Profit, and the Whole Nation Advantage." Throughout her essay Makin referenced the examples of women who had demonstrated proficiency in arts and sciences. She devoted special attention to women as linguists, orators, mathematicians, philosophers, and poets. She was the tutor of the Princess Elizabeth, daughter of King Charles I, and she claimed that under her tutelage the princess "could read, write, and in some measure understand, Latin, Greek, Hebrew, French, and Italian" by the age of nine. Unfortunately, Elizabeth died young, leaving Makin to note mournfully, "Had she lived, what a Miracle would she have been of her Sex."[17]

A similar line of reasoning was followed by Mary Astell, in *A Serious Proposal to the Ladies, for the Advancement of their True and Greatest Interest*, first published in London in 1695, almost a hundred years before the publication of Wollstonecraft's *Rights of Woman*. Astell argued for the creation of a women's college that would allow unmarried women to pursue an intellectual life. Her primary aim was to prepare Christian women for the afterlife, and her chief claim was that ignorance cannot prepare a woman for immortality. A "lover of her sex," Astell proposed that wisdom alone makes women truly beautiful. While the body ages and decays, the wise soul grows in beauty. For too long the life of the mind has been monopolized by men. "The Ladies I'm sure, have no reason to dislike this Proposal, but I know not how the Men will resent it to have their enclosure broke down, and Women invited to taste of that Tree of Knowledge they have so long unjustly monopoliz'd. But they must excuse me, if I be as partial to my own sex as they are to theirs, and think Women as capable of learning as Men are, and that it becomes them well."[18] In the proposed college women would practice a religious retirement, and when not involved in private study or communal devotion they would instruct other women. Yet the serious proposal was modest in its demands for female authority. "We pretend not that Women shou'd teach in the Church or usurp Authority where it is not allow'd them; permit us only to understand our *own* duty, and not be forc'd to take it upon trust from others; to be at least as learned, as to be able to form in our mind a true idea of Christianity."[19] Like Makin, Astell promoted competition among her readers with the intellectual exploits of women of years past. Yet neither plan received much private approval or public support, with the result that a century later Wollstonecraft began her *Rights of Woman* by questioning whether women were even capable of a rational education.

Indeed, Mary Wollstonecraft's text responded directly to the changing times reflected within the broad eighteenth-century debate about the meaning and methods of education in a free nation—a debate that went beyond questions of gender to encompass issues of class privilege and racial identity. Wollstonecraft controversially likened women in marriage to slaves, noting that both were recognized legally as property without political rights of their own. Just as it was illegal to educate slaves to read and write because they might throw off their chains in revolt, the idea of teaching women to think for themselves risked overturning the sexual division of labor within the household and challenged the sexual segregation of the political. Traditionally, calls for the education of females had been valued only to the extent that these lessons and petty accomplishments would make women more marketable at marriage—again, as a specially skilled slave might be more valuable on the auction block.

The politically charged nature of her argument for coeducation made it stand out from the other writers of the eighteenth century, both male and female. In *A Father's Legacy to His Daughters*, Dr. Gregory advised his daughters to "hide any learning" they might have obtained, lest they scare away future husbands: "Be even cautious in displaying your good sense. It will be thought you assume a superiority over the rest of the company. But if you happen to have any learning, keep it a profound secret, especially from men, who generally look with a jealous and malignant eye on a woman of great parts, and a cultivated understanding."[20] Wollstonecraft chided Gregory that such sexual subterfuge was unbecoming in a woman. Dr. Fordyce claimed in *Sermons to Young Women* that learning would unsex females.[21] Wollstonecraft responded that such a slur against "masculine" women was merely a "bugbear" (76), a rhetorical slight meant to dissuade women from intellectual pursuits.

Her gender theory is particularly striking when compared to the class politics of the eighteenth century's most famous woman of "masculine mind," Catharine Macaulay. In *Letters on Education*, Macaulay focused on educating the elite in the hopes that a liberal education would liberalize attitudes toward the masses.[22] Wollstonecraft countered that no progress would be made until there was an end to hereditary honors and aristocratic privilege. Whereas Sarah Trimmer suggested that charity schools should teach poor girls to obediently serve fine ladies, Wollstonecraft argued that women from the lower classes should be taught to earn their bread with independence.[23] Unlike Hannah More, Wollstonecraft believed that a woman needed liberty to keep the faith and fulfill her part in God's great plan. Wollstonecraft's plan for national day schools charged the state with the civic education and vocational training of girls and boys in all ranks of society.

The relationship of the citizen to the state is mediated by education, and this frames Mary Wollstonecraft's argument for the extension of political rights to women. She wrote both of her vindications in response to the revolution in France. The foundation of her theory was the Enlightenment principle of the perfectibility of humanity through reason. Her egalitarian politics was grounded in the belief that reason was the birthright of all men and women. The *Rights of Woman*, like her previous *Right of Men*, was a rebuttal to the patriarchal principles of privilege that denied men of the lower classes and women of all ranks the power of reason to rule their own lives. Utter and Bridges have written, "the rights of women in education were almost abreast of the rights of men in politics, and if Tom Paine is the father of the one, Mary Wollstonecraft is the mother of the other."[24] This statement falsely separates the theoretical strands of Wollstonecraft's argument in the *Rights of Woman*. Education is the first step to politically empowering women. The rights of women in education cannot be equated simply with the rights of men in politics. The political rights that the French revolutionaries claimed to be the birthright of all men, regardless of education, were denied to all women. The revolutionary power of Wollstonecraft's feminist analysis was that it theorized the relationship between gender, education, and citizenship.

Wollstonecraft's *Rights of Woman* was published during a decade of constitution writing. She dedicated her tract to Charles

Maurice de Talleyrand-Périgord, the former bishop of Autun and member of the National Assembly in France. She had celebrated the innovations of the French Revolution in her *Rights of Men*, but now she loudly protested the injustice of excluding women from the constitution of the new nation:

> But, if women are to be excluded, without having a voice, from a participation of the natural rights of mankind, prove first, to ward off the charge of injustice and inconsistency, that they want reason—else this flaw in your NEW CONSTITUTION will ever shew that man must, in some shape, act like a tyrant, and tyranny, in whatever part of society it rears its brazen front, will ever undermine morality. (68)

She addressed Talleyrand because in writing the "Rapport sur l'instruction publique, fait au nom du Comité de constitution" in 1791, he had called for the public education of both men and women within the country. Yet following Rousseau, Talleyrand advocated a model of sexually differentiated education, which subordinated the needs of the individual woman to the wishes and wants of her husband and family. Wollstonecraft replied:

> Consider, I address you as a legislator, whether when men contend for their freedom, and to be allowed to judge for themselves respecting their own happiness, it be not inconsistent and unjust to subjugate women, even though you firmly believe that you are acting in the manner best calculated to promote their happiness? Who made man the exclusive judge, if woman partake with him the gift of reason? (67)

The feminist author cautioned the legislator that, in a just republic, women must be the judges of their own happiness. She asserted that Talleyrand was acting the tyrant, "when you force all women, by denying them civil and political rights, to remain immured in their families groping in the dark" (67). Finally, she leveled her most powerful criticism, stating that women who were denied political rights could not be expected to fulfill their political duties within the new state: "Sir, you will not assert, that a duty can be binding which is not founded on reason?" (67). Her theory of women's rights was dependent on extending to women the experiential lessons of the public sphere that were the basis of civic education. "Contending for the rights of woman, my main argument is that if she be not prepared by education to become the companion of man, she will stop the progress of knowledge and virtue; for truth must be common to all" (67).[25] Constitutions that proclaimed the rights of men must take into account the rights of women or both sexes would suffer the torments of divided homes, an unjust polity, and a fragmented society.

Wollstonecraft's analysis of the subjection of women linked the misrepresentation of women's nature in treatise and novel to the absence of women from the constitutions that guaranteed the rights of men. Rather than speak of women as the "fair defects" of nature, she questioned the "defects" of government that combined to deny women the political subjectivity and economic opportunity required for an independent life. Nowhere was the difference between women's rights in education and men's rights in politics more evident than in the plight of the educated "gentlewoman." Once again, she returned to a theme she had first developed in *Thoughts on the Education of Daughters,* remarking that this woman was often "forced by necessity" to enter into an unhappy marriage, her individual happiness sacrificed for the questionable good of the public. In an argument that would be reiterated in the nineteenth century by John Stuart Mill in *On the Subjection of Women,* she called on government to "encourage" educated women to "fill respectable stations" within society:

> In order to render their private virtue a public benefit, they might have a civil existence in the state, married or single; else we shall continually see some worthy woman, whose sensibility has been rendered painfully acute by undeserved contempt, droop like "the lily broken down by the plowshare." . . . It is a melancholy truth; yet such is the blessed effect of civilization! The most respectable women are the most oppressed; and, unless, they have understandings far superior to the common run of understandings, taking in both sexes, they must, from being treated like contemptible beings, become contemptible. How many women thus waste life away the prey of discontent, who might have practiced as physicians, regulated a farm, managed a shop, and stood erect, supported by their own industry, instead of hanging their heads surcharged with the dew of sensibility, that consumes the beauty to which it at first gave lustre. (219)

Wollstonecraft's contention was that the men who hold political power cannot be immune to the interests of spinsters, wives, and widows. Her argument openly questioned the logic of the theoretical separation of men and women in education and politics and contested the relationship of the sexes within the home and the state.

It is troubling that the connection between education and political subjectivity is often overlooked. Wollstonecraft's *Rights of Woman* is commonly read as a treatise on female education. It is often grouped with other writings on the education of women and rarely read alongside other polemics on rights. In this manner, she can indeed be termed the "mother" of women's right to education (recalling Utter and Bridges) while Paine can become the "father" of men's political rights, although the content of their work and the foundations of their theory are very much the same.

The practical and theoretical consequences of this familial division are enormous for women. First, to separate the rights of women to education from the rights of women in politics is to overlook the historical fact that women have been denied political rights because they were denied the right to education.[26] Second, this false separation allows women's contribution to the debates that form the canon of political theory, like the work of Mary Wollstonecraft, to be categorically ignored.[27] At the end of the eighteenth century the politics of public education was the focus of explosive debates. Both radicals and conservatives understood that access to education increased access to political power. Marilyn Butler argues that the question of educating women often became ensnared in the question of educating men of the lower classes: "during the 1780's and the early 1790's they [dissenting intellectuals] and those like them evolve a rhetoric of liberty which is international rather than patriotic, 'levelling' rather than hierarchical, and above all misleadingly unconstrained, since it puts its claims in respect of the individual conscience, which has no class accent. The message that comes across, unspecific yet unmistakable, is *insubordination*."[28] Wollstonecraft, as a proponent of women's political rights, was keenly aware of the sex and class barriers to women's educational rights. Thus, in her argument she did not separate education from politics but wove these theoretical strands into whole cloth.

The political importance of Wollstonecraft's analysis of rights is lost in the didactic reading.[29] The question of women's education has from antiquity been a profoundly political question. Rousseau certainly understood the relationship of education to power. It is significant that he labeled Plato's *Republic*—the one classical work in which women are educated with men for political leadership—an "educational" text. He argued, "In his *Republic*, Plato gives women the same exercises as men. I can well believe it! Having removed private families from his regime and no longer knowing what to do with women, he found himself forced to make them men." Rousseau, not knowing what to do with Plato's politics, was forced to relegate the *Republic* to an educational text. In *Emile* he advocated sexually differentiated education and the subsequent exclusion of women from political participation on the basis that men and women had opposing but complementary natures. There could be no educated "masculine" women in Rousseau's "small fatherland." As Sophie is "constituted" differently from Emile, they "ought not to have the same education."[30]

Rousseau's *Emile, or On Education* made it clear that the access of women to education, and the form of that education, profoundly impacted their ability to exercise political rights. Sophie was educated to comfort men, not to govern herself. Indeed, Rousseau's theoretical construction of womanhood had an enormous influence on the real women of the late eighteenth century. It has been argued that his pedagogy of pleasure alarmed English Puritans. "He would educate women to gratify men rather than ensnare them. Much of the clamor for and against Rousseau in England had to do with his *Emile* and his ideas on the education of women."[31] Yet Rousseau was not alone in modeling women's education to respond to the interests of men. Wollstonecraft stated, "Rousseau, and most of the male writers who have followed his steps, have warmly inculcated the whole tendency of female education ought to be directed to one point: —to render them pleasing" (96). She stressed that the lessons of these patriarchal authors were directed at making women pleasing to men: "Man, taking her body, the mind is left to rust" (145).[32]

Thus, Wollstonecraft denounced Rousseau's theory of sexually differentiated education, asserting his interest was in maintaining the subordination of women to men: "For never was there a sensualist who paid more fervent adoration at the shrine of beauty" (173). She claimed that, in order to make her an obedient plaything, "[h]e denies woman reason, shuts her out from knowledge, and turns her aside from truth; yet his pardon is granted, because 'he admits the passion of love'" (173). Wollstonecraft argued that the female readers who "pardon" Rousseau and model themselves after Sophie mistake their own interests by submitting to the bondage of love instead of fighting for the independence of reason. She attacked the pedagogy of pleasure that sacrificed women's reason to male desire. She argued that the education of women should be dictated by their own needs and not by the whims or whines of men. In this manner the *Rights of Woman,* like *Emile,* echoed the intensely political pedagogy of Plato's *Republic.* The purpose of education was to teach the individual to govern himself or herself; empowered by reason the individual would not be enslaved by his or her own desires or by the desires of others.

Wollstonecraft claimed that Emile and Sophie shared the same rational nature, and she thereby transposed the founding principles of Rousseau's pedagogy to create a model of female education that empowered women. Her theory produced a new being, a woman whose virtue was grounded in reason and whose excellence was tried by experience. "[I]t is a farce to call any being virtuous whose virtues do not result from the exercise of its own reason. This was Rousseau's opinion respecting men: I extend it to women, and confidently assert that they have been drawn out of their sphere by false refinement, and not by an endeavour to acquire masculine qualities" (90). In her opinion it was not women's attempt to exercise reason that disrupted the harmony between the sexes but false notions of femininity and masculinity, which split the world into sexually segregated spheres. These "false refinements" were the real cause of the cunning and manipulative behavior that women resorted to in order to exert influence within the household and the state.

Wollstonecraft believed that Rousseau's opinions added fuel to the battle between the sexes. She argued, "I war not with his ashes, but his opinions. I war only with the sensibility that led him to degrade woman by making her the slave of love" (161).[33] Women who were the slaves of love were in fact enslaved by men. It was the construction of woman's subservient sensibility that became the focus of Wollstonecraft's analysis of relations between the sexes. She asserted that the differences ascribed to sex should instead be traced to the self-interests of male writers in perpetuating a system of sexual subjugation.

> Hapless woman! what can be expected from thee when the beings on whom thou art said to depend for reason and support, have all an interest in deceiving thee? This is the root of the evil that has shed a corroding mildew on all thy virtues; and blighting in the bud thy opening faculties, has rendered thee the weak thing thou art! It is this separate interest—this insidious state of warfare, that undermines morality, and divides mankind! (166)

History demonstrated the danger of man mediating woman's access to truth. Male authors had perpetuated the myth that women's rationality was dependent upon masculine desire. Wollstonecraft returned to the story of Abelard and Heloise to suggest that male desire would always interfere with this transfer of reason. She broke the dependence of women on men by arguing that reason common to both sexes should be the guide for female behavior (62). Women can not depend on their husbands to guide them through the odyssey of life.

> But the system of education, which I earnestly wish to see exploded, seems to pre-suppose what ought never to be taken for granted, that virtue shields us from the casualties of life; and that fortune, slipping of her bandage, will smile on a well-educated female, and bring in her hand an Emilius or a Telemachus. . . . There have been many women in the world who, instead of being supported by the reason and virtue of their fathers and brothers, have strengthened their own minds by struggling with their vice and follies; yet have never met with a hero, in the shape of a husband. (162)

Since to her mind the age of chivalry was dead, Wollstonecraft stood forth the champion of her sex: "[I] throw down my gauntlet, and deny the existence of sexual virtues, not excepting modesty. For man and woman, truth, if I understand the meaning of the word, must be the same" (120). Truth must be the foundation of judgment for both sexes. She argued, "'Educate women like men,' says Rousseau, 'and the more they resemble our sex the less power will they have over us.' This is the very point I aim at. I do not wish them to have power over men; but over themselves" (131).

The thinking woman has the power to govern herself. Educated women would not need to resort to the deceptive practices that subservient females had historically used to sway tyrannical husbands and despotic fathers. When women were educated to become the rational companions of men, the society of the sexes would enter a new harmonious era of equality. Mary Wollstonecraft's political theory rested on the belief that, as a rational being, a woman's first duty was to herself. She defended her sex against the prejudices of the past by claiming that, barred from the institutions of learning, they had been subjected to a "slavery which chains the very soul of woman, keeping her for ever under the bondage of ignorance" (215). In a subsequent paragraph, she links the slavery of women to notions of female propriety:

> For Rousseau, and a numerous list of male writers, insist that she should all her life be subjected to a severe restraint, that of propriety. Why subject her to propriety—blind propriety, if she be capable of acting from a nobler spring, if she be an heir of immortality? Is sugar to be produced by vital blood? Is one half of the human species, like the poor African slaves, to be subject to prejudices that brutalize them, when principles would be a surer guard, only to sweeten the cup of man? Is not this indirectly to deny women reason? for a gift is a mockery, if it is unfit for use. (215)

The primary goal of a woman's education was to enable her to fulfill the duties she has to herself: "the most perfect education, in my opinion, is such an exercise of understanding as is best calculated to strengthen the body and form the heart. Or, in other words, to enable the individual to attain such habits as will render it independent" (90). It was this independence and strength that would transform woman from the silent object of male desire to a speaking subject in the conversation of political thought.

In her call for personal autonomy and independent thought for women, Wollstonecraft fundamentally challenged the discourse of political theory by uniting femininity and rationality. The perfect education for a woman was an education that would allow her to provide for herself intellectually and spiritually. "The being who discharges the duties of its station is independent; and, speaking of women at large, their first duty is to themselves as rational creatures, and the next, in point of importance, as citizens, is that, which includes so many, of a mother" (216). However, Wollstonecraft recognized the need to redefine the "duties" of motherhood in such a manner that would not restrict women solely to a lifetime of mothering.[34] Her brief discussion of motherhood in *Rights of Woman* confronted the functionalism of the philosophical tradition. The ability of women to bear children did not lessen their reason or decrease their humanity. She contended that the sexual distinctions noted in treatise and conduct books could often be attributed to the social conventions of motherhood. Wollstonecraft's novels, *Mary, a Fiction*, and *The Wrongs of Woman, or Maria*, highlight the fact that she believed mothering was not an instinctual effort but a social behavior that reflected the constraints of class, ethnicity, and personal history like any other human activity. In the *Rights of Woman* she remarked that all women, whether or not they had borne children, shared in the rationality that differentiated human beings from animals (74). "Women, I allow, may have different duties to fulfill; but they are human duties, and the principles that should regulate the discharge of them, I sturdily maintain, must be the same" (120).

To her mind the duties of motherhood demanded the extension—not the restriction—of women's political rights. Once again, she distanced herself from Rousseau. He asserted in *Emile* and in *La Nouvelle Heloise* that the first duty of woman was to bear children and that this duty preceded all others, even the woman's duty to herself. He ambiguously claimed that "the female is female her whole life," and that "everything constantly recalls her sex to her." Maternity may biologically differentiate women from men, but in Rousseau's theory paternity determined the power relationships within society that gave meaning to sexual difference. "When woman complains on this score about unjust man-made inequality, she is wrong. This inequality is not a human institution—or, at least, it is the work not of prejudice but of reason."[35] Rousseau's revealing statement demonstrates the actual origin of the "natural" inequality between men and women. According to his logic, woman is "wrong" to argue for her "rights" because inequality is legislated by men who use the language of reason to voice their prejudices. Wollstonecraft extended the claims of Enlightenment humanism to women and began a debate about the relationship of sex, maternity, and citizenship that challenged male authors' representations of women in writing and male representatives of women in political and economic life.

Mary Wollstonecraft is often considered the mother of modern feminism because she was the first to form a model of citizenship in which the political subjectivity of the woman herself was the basis of her rights and duties as a citizen. In Wollstonecraft's writing the citizen woman was an autonomous member of the community. The call for the independence of women was a persistent theme in her texts and, as such, represents the first principle of a theory of the political rights of woman. In the *Rights of Woman* she crossed the boundaries of genre to create an analysis of gender that linked the textual representations of woman as the object of male desire to women's political and economic subjugation to men. She made explicit the connection between the portrayals of women's lives in polemics, conduct books, and novels written by men to the restriction of women's social and political roles.

A WOMAN OF MASCULINE MIND

> I am aware of the obvious inference:—from every quarter have I heard exclamations against masculine women; but where are they to be found?
>
> —Mary Wollstonecraft, *A Vindication of the Rights of Woman*

It is significant that for over two hundred years Wollstonecraft's unique contribution to the debate about the political rights of both men and women has been the subject of controversy. The anonymous publication of *A Vindication of the Rights of Men* allowed this thinking woman to enter the discourse on political rights. The dispute concerning the sexual identity of the author of the first vindication highlighted the powerful social and political restrictions on women in a decade that witnessed the revolutionary extension of the political rights of men. The subsequent publication of *A Vindication of the Rights of Woman* ended the mystery about whether Mrs. W. was a "real or fictitious lady"; however, it signaled the beginning of a more lasting conflict about the relationship of women to political writing. Wollstonecraft, identified as a woman, had to contend with the derisive charges of mimicry and opportunism that attacked her integrity as an author and detracted from the critical consideration of her theory. The *Rights of Woman* received this notice in the *Analytical Review,* just months after its publication: "It might have been supposed that Mrs. W. had taken advantage of the popular topic of the 'Rights of Man' in calling her work 'A Vindication of the Rights of Woman,' had she not already published a work, one of the first answers, that appeared to Mr. Burke, under the title of, 'A Vindication of the Rights of Man.'" Wollstonecraft's call for the independence of women may have appeared prophetic instead of practical. The reviewer concludes:

> The lesser wits will probably affect to make merry at the title and apparent object of this publication; but we have no doubt if ever her contemporaries should fail to do her justice, posterity will compensate for the defect; and have no hesitation in declaring, that if the bulk of the great truths which this publication contains were reduced to practice, the nation would be better, wiser and happier.[36]

Today Wollstonecraft's second vindication continues to be a subject of controversy.

William Godwin reported in *Memoirs of the Author of the "Rights of Woman"* that the attention Wollstonecraft received following her first vindication induced her to write her second. It is telling that many of the reviews of the *Rights of Men* suggested that the woman author should restrict herself to writing about the rights of woman. There is no small irony in the fact that the gentlemen reviewers of the *Gentleman's Magazine* never bothered even to note the publication of the *Rights of Woman* in the journal's "Review of New Publications." This denial of Wollstonecraft's work indicates that many of her contemporaries considered it improper for a woman to attack the sexual distribution of power within society.

Wollstonecraft's "wild wish . . . to see the distinction of sex confounded" strongly indicates her recognition of the discursive boundaries that excluded women from the conversation of political theory (126). Her theory and discursive strategy in both vindications were founded on a humanist appeal to reason that denied sexual difference. She simply refused to concede reason to men. The feminist author answered the "exclamations against masculine women" by arguing that if the virtues that make us human were defined as "manly" she would hope that woman "may every day grow more and more masculine" (74). She defuses the charge that educating women will make women more masculine in a subsequent paragraph:

> Indeed, the word masculine is only a bugbear: there is little reason to fear that women will acquire too much courage or fortitude; for their apparent inferiority with respect to bodily strength, must render them, in some degree, dependent on men in the various relations of life; but why should it be increased by prejudices that give a sex to virtue, and confound simple truths with sensual reveries? (76).

Wollstonecraft's attempt to confound the distinctions of sex represents one woman's strategy to explode the prejudices that equate masculinity with rationality.

Ironically, Horace Walpole's accusations of male identification and mimicry are surprisingly similar to Joan Landes's modern feminist critique of Wollstonecraft's argument in *Rights of Woman*.[37] Landes writes of Wollstonecraft: "She shares the implicitly masculinist values of the bourgeois public sphere, worrying over woman's willful, artificial, and unnatural control over language. Repudiating the female position, she orients herself almost exclusively toward the male logos."[38] Yet Wollstonecraft's attempt, in her rights tracts, to create a theoretical space for the thinking woman complicated the relationship of women to language. Landes's analysis of the "active textualization of life" indicates the significant role that reading played in reshaping the meaning of masculinity and femininity at the end of the eighteenth century.[39] Wollstonecraft's effort to confound the distinctions of sex within writing makes problematic Landes's characterization of Wollstonecraft herself as a female writer seduced and co-opted by the gendered categories of eighteenth-century discourse. A study of Wollstonecraft's writings indicates that the textualization of life evoked by Landes was not totalizing. The author of the *Rights of Woman* did not reflect the graces of Rousseau's Sophie, securing a space to exist by acquiescing to the will of the stronger. Mary Wollstonecraft struggled to distance herself far enough outside of republican discourse to assert that her life was not reflected in these texts.

Mary Wollstonecraft's *Vindication of the Rights of Woman*, like her earlier *Vindication of the Rights of Men*, provides the basis for a radical examination of the relationship between theory and practice, which reveals the contradictions between gender and authority. The feminist author argued that reason was not gendered; yet she continually returned to gendered language to support her argument. These texts demonstrate the constraints of gender and genre she encountered upon entering the conversation of eighteenth-century political thought. Wollstonecraft at once opposed and participated in a debate in which women have been absent as authors as well as citizens. She created a literary space to expound her theory of political rights by confounding the distinctions of sex. Her need to transcend the limitations of gender speaks to the genre boundaries that have historically silenced women writers and our need to take this history into account when reading women's political writing. Wollstonecraft transformed the discourse of political theory as a woman writing about the political rights. Ultimately, the *Rights of Woman*, like the *Rights of Men*, exploded eighteenth-century social constructions of authority and femininity. Even more revolutionary would be her subsequent analysis of the wrongs that women have suffered at the hands of men unwilling to recognize women's rights.

CHAPTER FIVE

Writing the Wrongs of Politics

> But a wife being as much a man's property as his horse, or his ass, she has nothing she can call her own. He may use any means to get at what the law considers his . . . he can rob her with impunity, even to waste publicly on a courtesan; and the laws of her country—if women have a country—afford her no protection or redress from the oppressor, unless she have the plea of bodily fear. . . . When such laws were framed, should impartial law givers have first decreed, in the style of a great assembly, who recognized the existence of an être suprême, to fix the national belief, that the husband should always be wiser and more virtuous than his wife, in order to entitle him, with a show of justice, to keep this idiot, or perpetual minor, for ever in bondage. But I must have done—on this subject, my indignation continually runs away with me.
>
> —Mary Wollstonecraft,
> *The Wrongs of Woman, or Maria*

Mary Wollstonecraft wrote in the advertisement to *A Vindication of the Rights of Woman* that she intended to examine the relationship of women to law in a subsequent volume. "Many subjects . . . call for particular investigation, especially the laws relative to women, and the consideration of their peculiar duties. These will furnish ample material for a second volume, which [will] elucidate some of the sentiments, and complete many of the sketches begun in the first."[1] Wollstonecraft's radical vindication of women's rights was a response to the exclusion of women from the natural rights of men guaranteed by the new French nation. Her argument for the rights of women demanded the critical consideration of the laws that denied political subjectivity to women and perpetuated a system of sexual subjugation in which women were dependent upon men for political representation.

Wollstonecraft's theory of women's rights was grounded in a critique that connected the textual misrepresentations of women's nature by male authors to the political subjection of women to male representatives in government. She revealed a tautology at the very heart of the late-eighteenth-century construction of femininity; that women were, by sex, considered naturally less rational than men, and therefore, females were categorically denied access to formal education as individuals. Thus, when a woman acted irrationally because of her inferior education, her action was used to further justify her exclusion from the civic lessons of public participation. Wollstonecraft challenged this sexual segregation of eighteenth-century society, claiming that women, like men, should be allowed the experiential learning of citizenship. In this manner she made problematic the theoretical separation of private families from the communities in which they were embedded. Wollstonecraft inverted the gender logic of her era that a woman's sensibility would be corrupted if she became involved in the intrigues of politics. To her mind the greatest danger to a woman's virtue was marriage to a man engaged in vice. Therefore, she radically countered that a woman's primary duties to herself, as a rational individual and as a caring mother, demanded public activism to ensure her rights and to meet the needs of her children. Her analysis called into question the value as well as the ability of husbands, fathers, and sons to voice and promote the interests of wives, daughters, and sisters within the privacy of the family home or the public spaces of politics.

Nowhere is her analysis of the political problems and the moral dilemmas created by male representation of females in the laws of England more explicitly examined than within the pages of *The Wrongs of Woman, or Maria*. The feminist author of the *Rights of Woman* found it necessary to create Maria, the vindicating heroine of *The Wrongs of Woman*, in order to embody the injustices created by an oppressive legal code. Wollstonecraft's treatment of the rights of men in her first vindication highlighted the absence of women from the discourse on rights. Her second vindication demonstrated the multiple problems of simply adding women to, or including women in, the already existing rights debate. Mary Wollstonecraft, the defender of the French Revolution in the *Rights of Men*, became a critic of the revolution in the *Rights of Woman* because the democratic constitution that progressively ensured the equality of all men regressively reinforced the inequality of the sexes. In *The Wrongs of Woman* she completed the sketch of women's situation that she had begun in her earlier works. By doing so, she subverted the abstractions of political theory by forming characters who told stories that personalized the physical and mental abuses suffered by women because of patriarchal politics.

The Wrongs of Woman is fundamentally a book about the subject position of women in a male-dominated society. It is the tale of one woman's rebellious actions and the story of how her actions are checked by both men and women who abuse authority. Wollstonecraft further develops her feminist political theory in this novel by returning to her analysis of the dialectical relationship between thought and feeling in the lives of men and women. She qualifies her theoretical exploration of political rights by carefully examining the complicated interplay of sex roles, economic opportunities, and social expectations. The novel offers the female reader multiple stories of individual women and men and their struggles with power and powerlessness. Wollstonecraft portrays the complexity of these relationships by concentrating on the small community of husband and wife. Her critical analysis of marriage challenges the easy union of the sexes that forms the basis of the separation between the private and public spheres in both liberal and republican theory by focusing on the conflicts of interest between spouses.

In *The Wrongs of Woman, or Maria* the wild wish to confound the distinctions of sex, which had fueled Wollstonecraft's examination of women's rights in her second vindication, gave way to the comprehension of the complex realities of sexual difference. Her "main object" in this work is to chronicle the "misery and oppression, peculiar to women, that arose out of the partial laws and customs of society."[2] Wollstonecraft focuses on how the legal status of women gives meaning to the distinctions of sex. Woman, "constituted" as other than man instead of his equal, is "written out" of the new democratic constitutions that structure the legal relationship of citizens to each other and the state in America and France. In the period Wollstonecraft was writing, to treat women as citizens necessarily meant addressing the mediated legal relationship of women to politics. To speak of women as political subjects required not just an examination of how woman's nature was constructed within texts, but also an analysis of how sexual difference was constituted within the law and how it was institutionalized through political practice. Historically, women's relationship to the state has been determined by the marriage contract. As Carole Pateman has argued, women did not contract into the societies created by Hobbes, Locke, or Rousseau. According to Pateman's reading of the fathers of the canon, the social contract was based upon a preceding sexual contract that inscribed the political subjection of women to men. Thus, when the canonized forefathers spoke of women they were speaking of wives; woman's relationship to the state was mediated by man.

For Wollstonecraft to truly vindicate women and to establish their political rights demanded the critical study of the wrongs to which they had been subjected as wives. Her investigation of the legal status of women indicated the power of her theoretical insights into the eighteenth-century discourse on political rights. In *The Wrongs of Woman* she shifted her attention from the portrayal of the distinctions of sex within novels and treatises (sexual difference in theory) to an analysis of the different treatment of men and women before the law (sexual difference in practice). Wollstonecraft, a humanist convinced of the perfectability of all mankind through reason, devoted this text to the corruption of men and women caused by ignorance. She vividly portrayed the difference made by sexual distinctions, institutionalized in law and custom, in the life chances of the young and the old, the rich and the poor.

Wollstonecraft's analysis of the historical oppression of her sex was of central importance in the development of feminist political theory as an oppositional discourse. In her narrative, the story of one woman recalled the stories of many women and the numerous differences among women. The fiction itself is framed as a humanizing conversation between women and about women's lives. Its pages form an ongoing dialogue between two women separated by class but united by circumstance. Maria, the legitimate daughter of landed gentry, shares her story with her guardian Jemima, the illegitimate daughter of a seduced housemaid. Each woman recounts the tales of other women who have suffered wrongs in their homes and in their communities, without legal remedy because, born women, they are denied their birthright as citizens. In the process both women become the unlikely heroines of an alternative history of feminist rebellion, which chronicles their dual struggle for personal freedom and citizenship within their country.

Paradoxically, Wollstonecraft, the feminist author, chose to theorize the dynamics of these issues within the context of a novel instead of a treatise. Why did the author, who in her treatise on women's rights decried the influence of novels on women's education and manners, use the epistolary form of the novel to articulate the relationship of women to the law and their duties to each other? I claim that this change in literary form highlighted a critical challenge to the discourse of political philosophy. Wollstonecraft did not retreat from politics in returning to the novel. Rather, she politicized the relationship of women to both fiction and philosophy by arguing that the sexual distinctions in eighteenth-century discourse structured and reinforced the social distinctions institutionalized by the law. Wollstonecraft radically contested the *very terms* upon which women enter the conversation of political theory. Her work revealed her understanding that the discourse of political theory was not a separate or isolated debate but, rather, a deeply connected and transforming dialogue that drew upon the fictional and factual dramas of human history. Jane Moore comments:

> *The Wrongs of Woman* makes apparent what the *Vindication* suppresses all along: this is the impossibility of treating literature and philosophy as self-enclosed categories. *The Wrongs of Woman* is an eminently "philosophical" fiction: its project, like that of the *Vindication* is to "[exhibit] the misery and oppression, peculiar to women, that arise out of the partial laws of society". And its arguments, although inscribed in the language of fiction are no less "philosophical" for that.[3]

The Wrongs of Woman is an exciting text, because it demonstrates one woman's literary exploration of the very boundaries of political expression. Wollstonecraft finished her sketch of women's rights within a novel, the literary genre that was widely considered the appropriate form for women's writing in the late eighteenth century. Yet her theme of the wrongs of woman transcended the limitations of female propriety, just as her method transformed the conventions of the novel. Wollstonecraft fundamentally confounded the distinctions between the novel and the treatise by using the novel in an expressly political way to reach a wider audience of female readers. Her politicization of the novel represented the culmination of her examination of the possibilities and the limitations of addressing women's rights in eighteenth-century political discourse. The feminist author's analysis of the rights and wrongs of woman in her final book has profound implications for our understanding of gender and citizenship. These implications can best be appreciated by situating Wollstonecraft's *Wrongs of Woman* within the context of her other works. This revolutionary study of the relationship of women to the law called into question the foundations of social contract theory. Wollstonecraft contested the boundaries between home and state by arguing that the separation of spheres in theory could not protect women from the brutality of human nature in practice. The point of this returns me to the questions that began this study. What can we learn about the world of the late eighteenth century by reading the books of Mary Wollstonecraft? How can her writing in treatise and novel challenge our modern understanding of historical political theory? What is her legacy as a feminist author for the female readers of today?

EMBODYING RIGHT AND WRONG

> In writing this novel, I have rather endeavored to portray passions than manners. In many instances I could have made the incidents more dramatic, would I have sacrificed my main object, the desire of exhibiting the misery and oppression, peculiar to women, that arise out of the partial laws and customs of society.
> —Mary Wollstonecraft, *The Wrongs of Woman, or Maria*

Mary Wollstonecraft's second vindication must be read alongside her final fragment, *The Wrongs of Woman, or Maria,* in order for the power of her theory of the relationship of gender to the history of political rights and political writing to be fully appreciated by the modern reader. In the *Rights of Woman* she announced, "The laws respecting woman, which I mean to discuss in a future part, *make an absurd unit of a man and his wife;* and then, by the easy transition of only considering him as responsible, she is reduced to a mere cypher."[4] Wollstonecraft disputed the "easy union" produced by marriage, in which the separate identity and interests of a wife were subsumed within the body of the husband. The laws that gave husbands power over their wives, she argued, were incompatible with any notion of women's civil rights because conjugal right voided the legal existence of women. Sir William Blackstone's seventeenth-century commentary nullified the unique individual existence of wives as persons with standing under the law. "By marriage, the husband and wife are one person in law: that is, the very being, or legal existence of the woman is suspended during the marriage, or at least incorporated and consolidated into that of the husband; under whose wing, protection, and cover, she performs everything."[5] Wollstonecraft recognized that the absence of women's rights within democratic constitutions was closely linked to the suspension of married women's rights within authoritarian households.

Traditionally when readers encounter the image of woman in political philosophy it has been within the context of the marriage plot. At the end of the eighteenth century, marriage for women was still a matter of life and death. Most aspects of a woman's daily life were relatively untouched by advances in the arts and sciences or revolutionary politics. Limited educational opportunities and few chances for economic advancement when coupled with the social customs of marriage and motherhood made women dependent upon men. Common law considered all females either marriageable or married; accordingly fathers were the legal representatives of their daughters, and husbands represented their wives. In her marriage vows a woman swore to obey the wishes of her husband and to submit to his will. Her body became his property and as a *femme couverte* her individual identity was subsumed within that of her husband. Coverture meant that for her married life a woman was civilly dead. Married women might spend the majority of their lifetimes pregnant if they did not die in childbirth. There were no reliable methods of birth control or safe ways to terminate an unwanted pregnancy. The separation of family and state reinforced the isolation of individual women and made it the legal duty of the husband to discipline his wife. A woman had little recourse if she married an abusive man. Divorce was nearly impossible, while the more common separation with bed and board required a mother to leave her children behind and face the future impoverished and alone. In an age defined by the French Revolution, Wollstonecraft's heroine Maria summed up the position of women in England by stating that marriage imposed a life sentence upon her sex.

Yet Wollstonecraft's novel about women's wrongs was not a simple companion piece to her treatise on women's rights.[6] She informed her reader that she intended "to show the wrongs of different classes of women, equally oppressive, though, from differences of education, necessarily various." Wollstonecraft defined these "peculiar" wrongs of women as "matrimonial despotism of heart and conduct." She was concerned that these wrongs "degrade the mind," asserting, "For my part, I cannot suppose any situation more distressing, than for a woman of sensibility, with an improving mind, to be bound to such a man as I have described for life. . . . I should despise, or rather call her an ordinary woman, who could endure such a husband as I have sketched" (84). This is a critical statement. It highlights a significant aspect of this novel, which has gone unrecognized. Wollstonecraft stressed that, as long as marriage remained the only "profession" open to women, their belief system and behavior would be determined by their roles as wives.

Wollstonecraft's concern that a wife's political views will be determined by the husband who supports her has been shared by other advocates of female education and financial independence. In *Three Guineas*, Virginia Woolf responds to a letter from a gentleman who has inquired of her what women can do to help prevent war. In her reply she discusses the political implications of marriage for women, noting that British women were excluded from careers within the professions until 1919. Woolf asserts that since women, as wives, labor within the home and since this labor is unpaid, the wife is dependent upon the salaried husband for her opinions. Thus, Woolf devotes three fictional guineas to three very real causes; a women's college, a society that promotes professional women, and an organization that opposes war. "For to help women to earn their living in the professions is to help them to possess that weapon of independent opinion which is still their most powerful weapon. It is to help them to have a mind of their own and a will of their own with which to help you prevent war."[7] Wollstonecraft prefigures Woolf in her argument that a woman needs to be financially independent of her father and husband in order to express disinterested political opinions. Educating women is critical, because only through education can a woman hope to achieve the money and status necessary for her to take full advantage of the rights and duties of citizenship.

Wollstonecraft remarked repeatedly throughout her works that learning was experiential. A bad marriage had enormous consequences for the uneducated woman, whose only knowledge of the world outside her door might be the conversation across the dinner table. Thus, Wollstonecraft's strong words took aim at passive female behavior. While the fictional husband, George Venables, was a model of brutish behavior, it was with the actions of Maria Venables that the author was most concerned. The woman of improving mind must act to assert her own rights as a rational individual, not shrink away and endure an abusive servitude. Wollstonecraft argued that tyranny within the household enfeebled both the husband and the wife and visited this weakness on the next generation. She did not lay the entire blame for women's wrongs on the shoulders of men but called upon women themselves to take on the responsibilities of reason and the duties that were the companions of rights.

In the chaotic first months of the French Revolution, many political prisoners were granted liberty by a public empowered by the discourse of the rights of men. Wollstonecraft wrote of the taking of the Bastille:

> Thus, was the nation saved by the almost incredible exertion of an indignant people; who felt, for the first time, that they were sovereign, and that their power was commensurate to their will. This was certainly a splendid example, to prove, that nothing can resist a people determined to live free; and then it appeared clear, that the freedom of France did not depend on a few men, whatever might be their virtues or abilities, but alone on the will of the nation.[8]

However, as the revolution progressed it became clear that the new republican rhetoric reinforced the subjection of women to men rather than emancipating them.[9] The French re-created their society by breaking the barriers of class, religion, and region. But even as they redrew the map of France to destroy the old ties of alliance and prejudice, they chose not to disturb the lines demarcating the lives of the sexes. The heroine of *The Wrongs of Woman* declares, "Marriage had bastilled me for life. I discovered within myself a capacity for the enjoyment of the various pleasures existence affords; yet, fettered by the partial laws of society, this fair globe was for me a blank" (146). The words of Maria Venables echo those of the young Mary Wollstonecraft, who had claimed it was better to be a "mere blank" than to lose oneself in the marriage plot. The revolutionary struggle that had freed men from monarchical rule and allowed them to govern themselves in France had not significantly loosened the bonds of patriarchal authority upon women. Rather, the newly restrictive ideology of Republican Motherhood that made it women's responsibility to birth and raise children for the nation emerged as a way to keep women in their place.[10]

In the wake of democratic revolution Wollstonecraft's Maria could still ask, "Was not the world a vast prison, and women born slaves?" (88). The feminist author examined the political inequality of men and women, focusing upon the unequal treatment of husbands and wives before the law. Her depiction of marriage in this novel was truly controversial, even in an era in which the institution of marriage was under attack in the work of other freethinkers. Her own husband, William Godwin, had denounced marriage in his treatise *Political Justice* in 1793. It was the great insight of *The Wrongs of Woman* that no political system was just unless men and women were treated equally according to the rule of law. Separate sphere arguments, which gave men rights over women within the home while denying women rights within the state, jeopardized women's personal safety. In her final fiction Wollstonecraft exposed the costs of the separation of the spheres, graphically depicting the physical violence and sexual abuse suffered in silence by many women within the privacy of the family home.

Thus, the story of Maria emerging from Wollstonecraft's feminist political theory was very different from the fictions of female life created by the men or other women of her era. Maria was the product of a woman who had thought deeply about the relationship of gender to politics and culture. Wollstonecraft formed a character who embodied her own resistance to female stereotypes within literature and philosophy. The feminist author developed a tale that bore witness to the difficulties women encountered in establishing their own identities, their own lives, within societies marked by gender distinctions and the political and economic inequality of the sexes.

Maria's story politicized the personal history of many eighteenth-century daughters. She marries early to escape the mistreatment of a stepmother, hoping for a small portion of individual freedom and lured by the excitement of life in London. Her early marriage proves to have disastrous consequences. Maria's alcoholic husband squanders her dowry and his estate. When Maria refuses to ask a relative for additional money to pay her husband's debts, he attempts to raise the cash by selling her into prostitution. Maria, disgusted by the cruelty of her husband, tries to escape with her child to revolutionary France in order to circumvent the difficulty of petitioning for a divorce within England.[11] Her attempt to flee her marriage ends when she is drugged by her lady's maid on the journey to Dover. Maria's infant daughter is returned to her husband, and she is imprisoned as a fugitive wife in an asylum outside London.

Wollstonecraft opens her narrative by introducing the reader to Maria in the hours following her capture. As Maria comes out of her drug-induced stupor, both she and the reader become conscious of the manacles that impede her free movement. The feminist author's choice of a prison setting symbolized the degree to which women's liberty was limited by patriarchal society. Later in the story we become aware that Maria is being held captive in an asylum whose inmates include both political prisoners and the insane. Wollstonecraft sympathetically portrays those who are "lost to reason," while invoking her reader to question the rationality behind the incarceration of Maria and her fellow prisoner, Darnford, a man of political principles imprisoned by his family in a property dispute. Her treatment of the inmates of the asylum recalls her analysis of madness in *A Vindication of the Rights of Men,* thematically linking the possession of reason rather than property as the only legitimate claim of political rights.

For both men and women, imprisonment is the most graphic example of the loss of one's rights. The beings housed within this prison are separated by lock and key from their families and their countrymen. Maria is under the watch of Jemima, a female guard who has been so brutalized in her womanhood that she has almost lost her humanity. Brought together by circumstance, the two eventually become confidantes. Wollstonecraft used the themes of imprisonment and guardianship to criticize the political relationships outside the asylum walls. These themes were particularly significant to British women of the eighteenth century because throughout their lives they remained under the guardianship of fathers, brothers, and husbands. Wollstonecraft exposed the contradiction that women who share with men the capacity for reason were never granted the liberty to develop their rationality through formal education, the pursuit of a profession, or active public participation.

My reading of Wollstonecraft's use of the asylum in *The Wrongs of Woman* differs from Elaine Showalter's reading. Showalter begins her study of gender and madness with a portrait of Maria as the ultimate victim, a woman stricken with that peculiar "female malady," insanity. "Maria, has been forced into a madhouse by her abusive husband, who wants control of her fortune and liberty to pursue his sexual adventures. To Maria, the 'mansion of despair' in which she is incarcerated becomes a symbol of all the man-made institutions, from marriage to the law, that confine women and drive them mad."[12] This reading misses the critical analysis of gender and society that is central to this text. Wollstonecraft, the feminist author, endeavors to prove to her reader that Maria is not mad, just as Maria's first actions are to convince Jemima she is not insane. Jemima, described as possessing an "understanding above the common standard," remarks after listening to Maria's story that she "must be more carefully watched, for appearing at times so reasonable" (87). Maria exhorts her to "believe me mad, till you are obliged to acknowledge the contrary. The woman was no fool, that is, she was superior to her class; nor had misery quite petrified the life's-blood of humanity, to which reflections on our own misfortunes only give a more orderly course" (87).

Jane Spencer has commented that in the later half of the eighteenth century, female authors often employed madness as a license to strongly condemn the position of women within society. A character's madness could become a literary device for circumventing the propriety that curbed the criticisms of the lady novelist. Spencer adds that, at the time Wollstonecraft wrote the *Wrongs of Woman,* her reputation as a lady was beyond repair, indicating that she did not need to use madness as a foil for free speech. "Wollstonecraft had abandoned the woman writer's respectable role with a vengeance."[13]

The conversations between Maria and Jemima lead us to ask whether a woman's complaints about domestic tyranny are simply the unconnected babble of madness or the concise language of reason. Maria's "madness" consists in leaving the dubious protection of her husband for the even more precarious liberty of the single woman, ostracized by the London society of the 1790s. Wollstonecraft emphasizes that Maria has been imprisoned because her actions as a reasonable woman have been interpreted as irrational by the questionable standards of the "rational" world.

During her imprisonment Maria recounts the reasons for her actions in a series of letters addressed to her infant daughter. Wollstonecraft emphasizes the importance of these maternal words, claiming that for Maria the project of instructing her child gave "life to her diction, her soul flowed into it" (90). Maria describes her memoirs as containing the "observations of her heart," which "only a mother—a mother schooled in misery, could make" (123). After relating her personal history of familial suffering and marital strife, she admonishes her daughter to learn from her mother's mistakes and to become the "mistress of her own actions" (141). Maria's letters contain no soothing words of a mother separated from her child but recall a long list of outrages that she asserts all women suffer within England. She denounces the sexual double standards of eighteenth-century Britain, which deny women the right to own property, the ability to divorce without a decree from parliament, the wages of their own labor, and the right to represent their own interests in their own voices. Ultimately, this written testimony, which began as a release from misery, painfully increases the frustrations of its author. Maria laments, "Why was I not born a man, or why was I born at all?" (134).

Maria is not the only prisoner within the asylum, however. Wollstonecraft introduces the character of Darnford, suggesting that the distinctions of sex free neither man nor woman from the chains of desire. After six weeks of being "buried alive," Maria "began to reflect . . . on the little objects of which attract attention when there is nothing to divert the mind; and how difficult it was for women to avoid growing romantic, who have no active duties or pursuits" (94). To alleviate her boredom and grief Darnford gives her his copy of Rousseau's *La Nouvelle Heloise*. "She had read this work long since; but now it seemed to open a new world to her—the only one worth inhabiting" (95).[14] Maria, the female reader imprisoned by much more than the asylum's walls, carefully considers the margin notes written by the book's owner and begins to conjure up the romantic image of a new Saint Preux.[15] "But if she lent St. Preux, or the demi-god of her fancy, his form, she richly repaid him by the donation of all St. Preux's sentiments and feelings, culled to gratify her own, to which he seemed to have an undoubted right, then she read in the margin . . . 'Rousseau alone, the true Prometheus of sentiment, possessed a fire of genius necessary to portray the passion, the truth of which goes so directly to the heart'" (96). Certainly this "mother schooled in misery" should have been wary of this demigod. As she reads *La Nouvelle Heloise*, Maria falls in love with her fellow prisoner, Darnford, much like Sophie's reading of the *Adventures of Telemachus* led her to idolize Emile. Rousseau, the "Prometheus of sentiment," cautioned continually that love made one totally dependent upon the beloved for the happiness of one's being.[16] Indeed, Saint Preux writes to Julie, "Do you not know that there is a time when no one's reason resists any longer, and that there is no man in the world whose good sense may then prevail? . . . I am no longer master of myself, I confess; my estranged soul is wholly absorbed in yours." Yet we know Rousseau's illusory empire of love is solidly built upon the inequality of the sexes in law that frames the social contract. For Wollstonecraft the danger of such sentimentality is that it corrupts women by encouraging them to sacrifice the self. Evidently, there are other lessons that Maria needs to learn through bitter experience before she can be free in mind and body.

In the prison Maria and Darnford eventually meet in person and exchange their stories. After learning from Jemima of her child's death, Maria gives the letters that were to teach her daughter independence to her fellow prisoner, letters that paint a vivid portrait of her sensibilities as well as reveal her romantic susceptibilities. Thus, she embarks on a romance she imagines will liberate her. Unfortunately Darnford, the Saint Preux substitute, does not embrace Maria with undying passion but with the fleeting desires of the moment. He offers sympathy for Maria's plight as an unhappy wife and boldly asserts that divorce should be more readily available. Echoing his experience in revolutionary America, he argues that marriage "can not bind minds governed by superior principles; and such beings were privileged to act above the dictates of laws they had no voice in framing." But his declarations of female independence from male tyranny disguise self-interest: "he appealed to her reason, but felt that he had some interest in her heart" (172). It is this interest in her heart that puts Darnford's intimate intentions into conflict with Maria's reason. When they meet again, "He adverted to her narrative, and spoke with warmth of the oppression she had endured.—His eyes, glowing with a lambent flame, told her how much he wished to restore her to liberty and to love" (172). Left alone in her cell, Darnford asks Maria to "'put it out of the power of fate to separate them.' As her husband she now received him, and he solemnly pledged himself her protector—and eternal friend" (173).

The story of Maria concludes by returning to the paradox of female power and powerlessness with which it began. The love that promises to open a new world for Maria instead entraps her in the very old world represented by the British judicial system. The scene shifts from the prison cell to the courtroom. The man who had pledged to protect her must turn to her for help in order to defend himself against the charge of seduction. The novel culminates in a courtroom scene in which Darnford is put on trial, accused of adultery by Maria's estranged husband, George Venables. Maria confronts a legal system that denied women freedom of body as well as of thought and expression. Unable to represent herself in court, she writes an account of her marriage to be read to the judge and jury. If the marriage contract, like the social contract, gains its legitimacy from the consent of the contracting parties, Maria argues that her marriage is invalid because she was too young to consent to marry Mr. Venables. "Married when scarcely able to distinguish the nature of the engagement, yet I submitted to the rigid laws which enslave women, and obeyed the man whom I could no longer love" (178). She repeats the brutal history of her marriage, telling of her escape, imprisonment, and grief upon hearing of the death of her infant daughter. Maria powerfully asserts that she had "deemed herself free" from her husband after the death of their child (180). More important, Maria claims that she was not seduced but freely chose to enter into a sexual relationship with Darnford. Jane Spencer asserts that "Wollstonecraft goes on to attack the ideal of feminine purity itself, and makes this novel the most radical of seduction tales by challenging the very term 'seduction.'"[17] Maria's statement to the court concludes with these revolutionary words: "I wish my country to approve of my conduct; but, if laws exist, made by the strong to oppress the weak, I appeal to my own sense of justice" (180).

This declaration of one woman's independence would have appeared particularly rebellious to a court composed of British antiJacobins. Wollstonecraft's final scene suggests her keen awareness that in the minds of many Englishmen the cause of women's rights had become conflated with the rhetoric of Robespierre and the violence of the Terror. Gary Kelly has argued that the English Jacobins, the early champions of the French Revolution, "had allowed their cause to become too closely identified with the fate of France.... The execution of Louis XVI and the outbreak of war between France and England early in 1793 made sympathy with France virtual treason."[18] Indeed, in 1795 the conservative British response to the Terror in France was ratification of the Seditious Acts, under which friends of Wollstonecraft and Godwin such as the novelist Thomas Holcroft were tried for sedition.

Thus, Maria's appeal to her "own sense of justice" stands out because it embraced the language of individual liberty. Her words were judged by the court to be nothing less than a call for anarchy. The judge summarized the jury's verdict by alluding to the dangers of the passions let loose by democratic politics. "We did not want French principles in public or private life—and, if women were allowed to plead their feelings, as an excuse or palliation of infidelity, it was opening a flood-gate for immorality. What virtuous women thought of her feelings?" (181). The revolution in France had truly opened a floodgate, if not of immorality, at least of feeling. Wollstonecraft's courtroom scene was all the more dramatic because of the political implications of Maria's defense of her own adulterous desires. Rather than making her bow her head in shame, Maria's illicit love affair empowered her to publicly express her political views and her personal interests—much to the horror of the court.

Jane Spencer has written:

> *The Wrongs of Woman* turns all the assumptions of the seduction tale upside-down, and its keen analysis of women's imprisonment within patriarchy is an optimistic vision of liberation through the feeling that in most seduction tales leads to ruin. . . . Wollstonecraft reveals that contradiction at the heart of the sentimental idealization of womanhood . . . "Feeling", said to be woman's distinctive and most wonderful attribute, is only condoned when it leads to self-renunciation and a stifling of natural instinct.[19]

Spencer goes on to suggest that Wollstonecraft might have privileged feeling in this text because of her growing disappointment with the progress of the French Revolution.

> In *A Vindication of the Rights of Woman,* she had suppressed sensibility and seen reason as the ideal, with the result that her vision of liberation did not include any liberation of sexuality. . . . Her movement away from the position . . . reflects the loss of revolutionary optimism in the later 1790's—difficult years for the English radicals, when it no longer appeared that reasoning would lead to immediate reform.[20]

I must take issue with this interpretation of the denouement of the novel. Wollstonecraft may indeed have been frustrated by the inability of reason to achieve the goals of liberty, fraternity, and equality. But she was also bitterly conscious that the fundamental wrong of womanhood was the propensity to succumb to feeling rather than to struggle for the power of reason. Indeed the court acts to silence Maria because the judge interprets her words as a defense of passion and immorality, not a vindication of reason and virtue.

POLITICIZING THE FEMALE READER

> She took up a book on the powers of the human mind; but, her attention strayed from cold arguments on the nature of what she felt, while she was feeling, and she snapt the chain of theory to read Dryden's Guiscard and Sigismunda.
> —Mary Wollstonecraft, *The Wrongs of Woman, or Maria*

The Wrongs of Woman represented a particularly powerful example of one author's attempt to explore the discursive tensions between novel and polemic. I have argued that the conflicts between femininity and authority were a central theme in Wollstonecraft's work. In this section I discuss the politics of her last fiction, focusing on the relationship between the author and her readers. Wollstonecraft's choice of the novel represented a political decision on her part, a decision that enabled her to directly address the female reader and to engage this reader more fully in a discussion about the rights and duties of women.

Dale Spender has asserted that "*The Wrongs of Woman* is an unapologetic attempt to present the fictionalized version—the more personalized construction—of *A Vindication of the Rights of Woman*."[21] In the last decade of the eighteenth century the novel was considered a uniquely feminine literary form. But Wollstonecraft had previously condemned the novel in her *Rights of Woman* as a poor alternative to other forms of written discourse. The feminist author declared, "When, therefore, I advise my sex not to read such flimsy works, it is to induce them to read something superior." Wollstonecraft used the novel as an example of the poor training that women received because of sexually differentiated education in English society. "In fact the female mind has been so totally neglected, that knowledge was only to be acquired from this muddy source, till from reading novels some women of superiour talents learned to despise them." Thus, we must question why Wollstonecraft chose to use this "muddy source" to further inculcate the values of reason to the "female mind."²²

As we have seen, the education of women was a politically explosive issue by the middle of the 1790s. Mary Wollstonecraft was at the center of an intellectual circle who, within their works, repeatedly discussed the connection between political rights and education. In an era of democratic revolutions, this democracy of the pen raised questions about the constitutions that banned women from participating in the freedoms of citizenship. Yet, as Hazel Mews has written, it was the women novelists who were singled out for criticism within the conservative press.

> That arch-baiter of Radicals, the "Anti-Jacobin Review," referred to them as "philosophesses." Mary Wollstonecraft was the most famous of the group, the others were Mary Hays, Mrs Inchbald and Mrs Opie. The extent of their commitment to political Radicalism varied considerably and the perspective of history has brought them more closely together than they were during their lifetime, when their varying religious views divided them. In their books they all however pay serious attention to the new ideas about the rights of women and give them fair consideration instead of condemning them out of hand.²³

The contentious political environment gave a particularly polemical twist to women's fiction of this period. Mitzi Meyers has pointed out that even the writings of Hannah More, which are today often read as offering a conservative response to Wollstonecraft's work, were in fact radical for their time.²⁴ The revolution in France revealed cracks in the social fabric in England. As Jerry Beasley has commented, "even the genius and eloquence of an Edmund Burke could not forestall the fervor of the 1790s or obscure the effects of radical writers like Thomas Holcroft, William Godwin and Mary Wollstonecraft, whose essays and novels attacked all vestiges of tradition in English political, social and domestic life."²⁵

Wollstonecraft's writing in didactic novel and polemical tract reminds us of the central role that gender played in the democratic debates at the end of the Enlightenment. Certainly, Burke's valorization of the past sought to return his reader to a time in which sex roles were more clearly defined by a powerful church and a strong monarchy. The writings of the "philosophesses" disturbed the stability of sex roles. Self-educated women were writing to protest the lack of educational opportunities for their sisters and calling for political and economic reforms. Cora Kaplan has suggested that the public in the 1790s was aware of "a growing agenda around the 'rights of woman' or 'emancipation' where a medley of voices, male and female, may be heard. Imaginative literature was the traditional secular space where issues of gender relations and sexuality could be discussed."[26] *Mary, a Fiction* and *The Wrongs of Woman* both indicate the need to revise our understanding of the importance of the novel in the struggle for women's rights. Clearly, as Jane Spencer has argued, "women's writing is not the same thing as women's rights."[27] I contend that women's relationship to the novel as authors and readers in the eighteenth century signifies that the difference in genre can offer critical insights into the historical politics of sexual difference. Women's political writing is now, and was then, inherently related to the political rights of woman.

The proliferation of novels written by women complicated and questioned the meaning of domesticity, the relationship of the sexes, as well as the opposition of authority to femininity. Virginia Woolf in one of the twentieth century's most influential analyses of women and fiction, *A Room of One's Own,* commented on the "extreme activity of mind" that characterized women's writing at the end of the late eighteenth century: "Thus, towards the end of the eighteenth century a change came about which, if I were rewriting history, I should describe more fully and think of greater importance than the Crusades or the War of the Roses. The middle-class woman began to write."[28] Women authors wielded a new form of influence, as their writings educated female readers who were excluded by prejudice and practice from the formal institutions of learning. The novel broke the isolation of the female day, and through reading the obstacles to formal female education were weakened. This was a time of movement, an intellectual quickening that showed signs of new life of the self and new ways of being in the world. Women's words were shaping generations of females and created a debate about sex roles, education, and marriage, which extended beyond the men and women of the radical circles of London to include fathers, mothers, sons, and daughters throughout the English countryside.

Ruth Perry has written extensively on the ideological function of the novel in eighteenth-century Britain. "[N]ovels developed at a time when literate women—the sort that figured in such books—were disposed of all meaningful activity save marrying and breeding, and when even these activities were to be done only in socially acceptable patterns." Perry asserted that the pressures of a nascent capitalism increased the inequalities between men and women as the workplace became separated from the home.

In this changing society, novels embellished and perpetuated the myths of romantic love needed to strengthen the new economic imbalances between men and women and necessary to make the lives of the dispossessed seem fulfilled. Love-in-marriage was a sop that evolved for women as they lost their real power in the society. Protected from the economic realities of life, they accepted their avocation for love in lieu of real work. Instead of being realistically assessed as contributing members of their society, they were idealized, set apart, robbed of their complex human identities, diminished to ornaments or to symbolic figures of moral purity.[29]

Wollstonecraft wrote in her *Rights of Woman* that "sentiments become events" to women who were "restrained from entering into more important concerns by political and civil oppression . . . reflection deepens what it should have effaced, if the understanding had been allowed to take a wider range." How could women engage in the struggles of the world when marriage imprisoned women for life?[30]

Mary Wollstonecraft certainly had conflicting thoughts on the novel and its role in women's education. In *Rights of Woman* she condemned the novel for providing female readers with sentimental instead of rational models.[31] Wollstonecraft argued that the heroines of popular novels became the models of femininity to women denied a formal education. Her concern with the novel in her treatise on women's rights indicated that she well understood the political implications of the identification of women with the heroines of popular novels. She argued that given women's lack of formal education it was not surprising female readers imitated and emulated the sentimental and childish behavior of their fictional sisters. The lessons of most novels were problematic because they glorified romance and vanity in the place of reason and civic virtue.

> Confined to trifling employments, they naturally imbibe opinions which the only kind of reading calculated to interest an innocent frivolous mind, inspires. . . . Thus, are they necessarily dependent on the novelist for amusement. Yet, when I exclaim against novels, I mean when contrasted with those works which exercise the understanding and regulate the imagination.—For any kind of reading I think is better than leaving a blank still a blank, because the mind must receive a degree of enlargement and obtain a little strength by a slight exertion of its thinking powers; besides, even the productions that are only addressed to the imagination, raise the reader a little above the gross gratification of appetites, to which the mind has not given a shade of delicacy.[32]

The fictional females of *The Wrongs of Woman* provide alternative models of womanhood to the female reader and offer an education based upon the experience of sexual difference. In this text women's lives are portrayed as a collection of interconnected narratives, personal histories that detail the traumas and costs of sexual difference in a patriarchal society. These characters deeply reflect the substance of Wollstonecraft's theoretical examination of her society and herself. We are invited to share the stories of several women of different classes: ladies of privilege and impoverished laundresses; women who, given the social hierarchy of their age, would not otherwise have communicated freely with each other. Maria is comforted during her imprisonment by Jemima, the female guard in the asylum whose tale of life as a housemaid is one of physical and sexual abuse.

The child of seduction, Jemima enters the world marked by the departure of her wronged mother, who dies in a garret shortly after giving birth to her daughter. Her early years are characterized by the emotional and physical scars she receives first at the hands of her stepmother and then from her mistress, after she is placed into domestic service. However, the most brutal treatment Jemima experiences are the sexual advances of the master of the house. When her mistress finds that Jemima is pregnant with her husband's child she throws the young woman out on the streets. In these desperate circumstances Jemima ingests poison to induce an abortion. Without a reputation or a trade, she turns to prostitution in order to survive. Eventually she becomes the mistress of a dissipated libertine, in whose home she receives her first formal education and where she is introduced to the men and ideas of literary society. At his death her hopes of being readmitted into society are dashed as she is left penniless. In the years that follow, Jemima's tale is one of hardship increased by human indifference and social injustice. She works as a washerwoman until she is injured under the weight of her load. Unable to work she is thrown into a poorhouse. It is there that she meets the warden who sees her potential as a beast of burden and offers her a position as a guard in the asylum in which she meets Maria.

Jemima's story, though different from Maria's, also raises difficult questions about the prejudices of a society that rewards the rake while condemning his victim. Their stories clarify the central issues of Wollstonecraft's feminist theory by personifying the injustice of a political system that recognizes women solely in terms of their relations with men. Categorized as daughters, sister, wives, and mothers, females are all dependent on the mercy of males to provide their livelihood and to protect their persons. Without a father or a husband to protect her, a woman is likely to become the prey of a sexual predator. Class privilege affords women little protection as both Maria and Jemima are hunted like animals through the streets of London. Wollstonecraft makes it clear that women are imperiled in a society based upon sexual double standards codified in the laws of the nation. Her solution is to trust in the bond between mothers and daughters to safeguard females from harm rather than to rely on the dubious protection of a paternalistic legal code.

In a society where the status of women is derived from their relationship to men, *The Wrongs of Woman* explores the relationships between females without the mediation of males. The most intriguing aspect of this fictional account of woman's situation that surely would have appealed to an audience of female readers was the emphasis on the critical importance of the relationship between mothers and daughters. Wollstonecraft herself was pregnant with her second daughter for most of the year during which she wrote and revised *The Wrongs of Woman*. Throughout the fiction she developed a recurrent theme that the loss of the mother blights the budding life of the daughter. Over and again Wollstonecraft's characters recount how their lives were changed for the worse by the death of their mothers. In this respect Maria's life story was modeled after the author's own. An especially poignant passage, which detailed the passing of Maria's mother, mirrored the death of Wollstonecraft's own mother, Elizabeth

Dixon, right down to echoing her dying words "a little patience, and all will be over!" (132), and one of the notes that survives from Wollstonecraft's lying-in repeats this tragic phrase. Repeatedly the tales of female suffering begin with the separation of mother and child, a separation that not only deprived the daughter of maternal love and support but of a woman's guidance as she entered the world.

Maria is forcibly separated from her child by the wiles of a grasping husband eager to get his hands on her inheritance. From its opening paragraphs the novel describes the pressing nature of the maternal bond. Emerging from her drugged state, Maria becomes conscious of her child's absence by the throbbing of her breast, the result of her physical need to nurse her infant. She realizes quickly that this separation could mean the death of the baby. Even though a wet nurse could suckle the infant, Maria worries that the lessons learned in a mother's arms are as necessary to nourish the growth and development of a child as breastfeeding. Desperate for news of her daughter's fate, Maria reflects on Jemima's story. "Maria thought, and thought again. Jemima's humanity had rather been benumbed than killed, by the keen frost she had to brave at her entrance into life; an appeal then to her feelings, on this tender point, surely would not be fruitless; and Maria began to anticipate the delight it would afford her to gain intelligence of her child." As a result of her reflections, Maria decides to ask Jemima to find her child, with the promise that they will share the rights and duties of motherhood if the infant is still alive. "With your heart, and such dreadful experience, can you lend your aid to deprive my babe of a mother's tenderness, a mother's care? In the name of God, assist me to snatch her from destruction! Let me but give her an education—let me prepare her body and mind to encounter the ills which await her sex, and I will teach her to consider you as her second mother, and herself as the prop of your age" (120). These precious plans come to nothing because after scouring London for news of the infant Jemima sadly returns to the prison with word of the baby's death.

It is only after the reunion between mother and daughter fails that Maria begins her affair with Darnford. We can only speculate as to how Wollstonecraft would have ended *The Wrongs of Woman*. Would Darnford have protected Maria from the insulting actions of George Venables and the slurs of society? How would the relationship evolve between Maria and Jemima? Mary

Wollstonecraft's own death in childbirth left these questions unanswered. Godwin published her notes for a number of alternative endings to the novel, in which the most developed finds Maria contemplating suicide after being abandoned by Darnford. The plot now comes full circle as Maria regains consciousness after an overdose at the very moment Jemima reunites the mother with her daughter who is alive and well. The fragment concludes with these maternal words from Maria, "The conflict is over! I will live for my child."[33]

The story of Maria is at once a cautionary tale and a call for rebellion. The point of this novel is to teach the female reader *not* to mimic the actions of this brave heroine. The moral of the story is that women must rely upon themselves and upon each other for protection within a hostile society, and that reason is the only reliable source of independence, strength, and ultimately solace. Dale Spender has written of Wollstonecraft's final fragment:

> It is fiction about women and for women that she writes, and the novel had not been so determinedly bent in this political direction before. The author's aim is to strip away the myths of the dominant reality which would have women suitably served by marriage, and to expose the misery which is being masked. Never does she lose sight of her awareness that what happens to the individual woman is the result of the division of power in society—that the personal is political.[34]

The further development of Wollstonecraft's political theory of women's rights is evidenced by the characters and confrontations that define this novel. The feminist author vindicates women's lives by vividly portraying the crosscutting pressures of sex and class. She depicts the struggle of women to assert their own identities within divided households. Most important, Wollstonecraft brings together the rich strands of personal experience and social history to explain the decision of one woman in a moment of desire. Maria exchanges her independence for self-knowledge, and this new understanding of the situated self gives her the power of political expression.

William Godwin recounted in the *Memoirs* that Wollstonecraft had written *A Vindication of the Rights of Men* in a matter of days. *A Vindication of the Rights of Woman* went from pen to the press in six weeks. But the feminist author devoted over a year of her life to *The Wrongs of Woman*. "All her other works were produced with a rapidity, that did not give her powers time fully to expand. But this was written slowly and with mature considerations."³⁵ In this text Wollstonecraft returned to her analysis of the opposition of femininity and authority, but her theoretical exploration of this relationship differed from that found in her earlier rights tracts. The thinking woman was no longer willing to sacrifice passion to reason. This is not to say that the mind/body split that seems to exist within her treatise on the rights of women disappeared in her novel on the wrongs that plague her sex. Instead, Wollstonecraft created a novel in which women's sexuality was an expression of the mind as well as the body. She challenged the discourse of political theory to comprehend women as complex beings who embody reason and experience desire.

In this effort Wollstonecraft succeeded in creating a truly humanist and democratic political theory where other philosophers have failed. She certainly would have agreed with theorists from Aristotle to Rousseau that sexual desires and sexual acts could be politically explosive, destroying the ties of family and of community. But she theoretically distanced herself from these thinkers by arguing that sexuality was explosive for both men and women. In *Rights of Woman* she subverted the traditional discourse on the relations between the sexes by claiming that "all the causes of female weakness, as well as depravity[,] . . . branch out of one grand cause—want of chastity in men." She sketched a portrait of a poor widow who "forgets her sex," in order to perform her duties as a citizen and mother.³⁶ Social opinion and custom demanded that this young woman suppress the human feelings of desire that formed the bonds between herself and others. In *The Wrongs of Woman* Wollstonecraft dismissed this alienation of women from their bodies, and their subsequent isolation from others. She suggested that men and women who do not know the intimacy of the human touch were the most likely to exhibit the brutality of the tyrant or the lonely pathos of the misanthrope.

FEMINIST AUTHORITY AND POLITICAL THEORY

> The Wrongs of Woman, like the wrongs of the oppressed part of mankind, may be deemed necessary by their oppressors; but surely

there are a few, who will dare to advance before the improvement of the age, and grant that my sketches are not the abortion of a distempered fancy, or the strong delineations of a wounded heart.
—Mary Wollstonecraft, *The Wrongs of Woman, or Maria*

Wollstonecraft's final fragment represents the fullest exposition of her political theory of the thinking woman. In this text female subjectivity and citizenship were portrayed in new and transforming ways. The feminist author formed a narrative that reflected an inclusive theory addressing the issues of class, gender, and generation. She represented females at different points in the life cycle, of diverse social groups, and equipped with varying levels of education struggling against laws that treated women as a monolithic group and reduced adult women to the status of dependent children. Wollstonecraft analyzed the chains formed by the patriarchal principles of primogeniture and conjugal right, which bound woman tight in the bastille of the marriage plot. She attacked the distribution of property within British society, in an argument extending the charges against class privilege that had formed her earlier argument about the destructive force of the "demon property" in *A Vindication of the Rights of Men*.

The Wrongs of Woman was a significant challenge to the foundations of eighteenth-century political thought. Both republican theorists on the Continent and liberal philosophers in England had defined their conception of the good society by constructing a public sphere composed of citizen fathers and an opposing private sphere of patriotic mothers. Wollstonecraft disputed the symmetry of this political cosmos, claiming that the power relationships that structured the institutions and processes of government were coterminous with those existing within the family. The importance of this theoretical revision has not been lost on recent feminist political theorists. Carole Pateman has positioned her work on the "Sexual Contract" along an analytical continuum that begins with Wollstonecraft. "Since at least 1792 when Mary Wollstonecraft's *A Vindication of the Rights of Woman* appeared, feminists have persistently pointed to the complex interdependence between the two spheres, but, nearly two centuries later, 'civil' society is still usually treated as a realm that subsists independently."[37]

Wollstonecraft's refusal to confine her analysis within the theoretical lines of the separate sphere argument allowed her to boldly assert that the oppression of women within the home was the consequence of the workings of politics, not of the laws of nature. In *The Wrongs of Woman* Wollstonecraft charged that the British government was complicit in the abuse of women within their homes. Her argument points to the contradictions within social contract theory that provide the basis for sexual domination. Men consent to form a government to protect themselves from the brutalities of the state of nature, but this government does not protect women from the abuses of the home. The laws that are made to protect the weak from the brutality of the strong within civil society do not extend into the kitchen or parlor to arrest the fist of the family tyrant. Thus, to paraphrase Wollstonecraft, women become citizens without a country, or in Maria's words, the "outlaws of the world" (146).

It is possible to draw a direct line from Wollstonecraft's discussion of the crosscutting patriarchal ties that structure the relationship between the sexes in both the home and the state on one hand to the current debates in feminist political theory on the other. However, our focus on these contemporary connections to Wollstonecraft's analysis should not obscure the radical nature of her challenge to eighteenth-century British political thought, which in itself has important implications for modern political theory. It was within the revolutionary context of the 1790s that her argument for women's citizenship in *The Wrongs of Woman* becomes particularly rebellious.

In her final novel Wollstonecraft developed a two-pronged attack on social contract theory. First, she argued that women did not have a country. The partial laws that protected men and their property within the civil sphere did not recognize women as subjects nor did they offer women protection within the home. The theoretical separation of home and state did not reflect the daily experiences of women nor did it safeguard women from the actual struggles for power. Second, she asserted that women could not be said to consent to any laws they had no part in framing. She focused specifically on marriage law, the legal code that had the most impact on women's lives. Since women were excluded from all forms of economic and political power except marriage they could not be said to actually consent to marriage. She refuted the claim that women freely entered into marriage, noting that a woman was not at liberty to choose to marry if there were no other options available. This argument would be reiterated as an example of Hobson's dilemma in the nineteenth-century feminist classic *On the Subjection of Women* by John Stuart Mill. What can we learn about the world of politics by reading the books of Mary Wollstonecraft? The feminist author's writings introduced new subjects to the theoretical table and brought new voices into the canonical conversation, challenging the canonized forefathers to think again about the meaning of membership within the discourse of political theory as well as within our larger civic community. Her early attempts to create a thinking woman in fiction spoke to the conflicts encountered by thinking women in late-eighteenth-century London. Wollstonecraft's preoccupation with rationality tells us much about the promise of the Enlightenment, but her struggle to redefine femininity, in a manner not opposed to reason, revealed the gender limitations that impeded the progress of individual liberty and social equality at the center of the project of human perfectibility.

The Wrongs of Woman, or Maria can be read as an allegory about the fate of feminist theory and practice in the aftermath of the French Revolution. Darnford, the democrat, and Maria, the feminist, begin the story imprisoned by the intolerance of English society. They each represent dangerous ideologies, and what is worse they have both been jailed because their wild theories have led them to perform bold actions. As the plot progresses Darnford has embraced Maria and her feminism. But the story concludes with Darnford free to think as he will and do as he likes, for democratic thought is no longer considered as dangerous to society as feminism. The courtroom scene makes it plain that democratic leveling is not the lesson of the excesses of the French Revolution, nor the source of English society's fear in the aftermath of the Terror. The judge attacks "women arguing their feelings." It is the different fate of the rights of man and the rights of woman that is the moral of the story. Ultimately, even England could find a place for the outcast Darnford because as a man he could be invited back into the fraternal order. But Maria and her theory of the rights of woman cannot be reconciled with the patriarchy of the English past.

Perhaps we have not fully appreciated the importance of Mary Wollstonecraft's writings to the discourse of political theory because her texts have been subject to the types of misreading that Rousseau warned his readers to avoid. In our passion to add the writing of worthy women to the works of great men in political thought, have we been "bad readers" of Wollstonecraft?

My research has revealed the tendency of scholars to isolate *A Vindication of the Rights of Woman* from her other texts. I think it particularly telling that those who charge Wollstonecraft with mimicking the very authors she criticized within this text do not position her study of women within the context of her broad discussion of political rights. In exploring the corpus of her writing we can see the chronological development of her ideas and the theoretical unity of her political ideals. This union of theory and practice, life and work, is lost when one text is examined apart from the others. More significant, by distancing her vindications from each other or her treatises from her novels, it has been possible to deny the magnitude of this woman's contribution to the late-eighteenth-century discourse about politics and society.

Mary Wollstonecraft, the female reader turned feminist author, took part in the wide-ranging debates that formed the conversation of political thought in the 1790s. Her vindications of the political rights of both men and women were direct responses to the theorists whose texts shape our modern understanding of this century of competing ideas and ideals. Wollstonecraft's writings were widely recognized and commented upon by her contemporaries. Succeeding generations of political thinkers have largely dismissed or ignored her work because it challenged the genesis of political thought by demanding the birthright of woman as citizens. Mary Wollstonecraft is certainly not the only political philosopher to have been forgotten by history. But as a feminist author, she has been reinvented and her work read again and again by women yearning to understand their history and eager to create their future. In the truest sense, Mary Wollstonecraft's theoretical writings in conduct books, polemics, and novels have provided a book of woman to thinking women for over two hundred years.

CONCLUSION

Reading Wollstonecraft

> Those who are bold enough to advance before the age they live in, and to throw off, by the force of their own minds, the prejudices which the maturing reason of the world will in time disavow, must learn to brave censure. We ought not to be too anxious respecting the opinion of others.—I am not fond of vindications.—Those who know me will suppose that I acted from principle.—Nay, as we in general give others credit for worth, in proportion as we possess it—I am easy with regard to the opinions of the best part of mankind.—I rest on my own.
>
> —Mary Wollstonecraft in a letter to Mary Hays, summer 1797

Mary Wollstonecraft, who theorized the political subjectivity of women in her polemical tracts on rights and fictionalized the subject position of women in her novels, has been herself the subject of fiction in numerous biographies and novels over the past two centuries. At issue in many of these works is the relationship of Wollstonecraft's own sexuality to her feminism. William Godwin began this mode of interpretation by describing her "serpentine" sexuality in *Memoirs of the Author of the "Rights of Woman"* (1798), a grief-stricken kiss-and-tell that provided voyeuristic readers with scandalous details of her love life.[1] Frances Sherwood's recent best-selling novel, *Vindication*, follows a similar thematic structure, reducing Wollstonecraft's rebellion in theory and practice to chapters bearing the names of her lovers and leaving her feminism as a historical footnote.[2] Mary Wollstonecraft the sadomasochistic heroine of Sherwood's novel becomes the text herself. Thus, it is not surprising that the real Wollstonecraft's revolutionary attempts to read women into theory and to theorize the novel are largely lost among the sensational scenes of this modern fiction.

In Sherwood's *Vindication* Wollstonecraft is transformed into a feminist fetish, a woman of masculine mind speaking the desires of the female body. It is ironic that Sherwood's portrayal subverts Wollstonecraft's own deliberate political efforts at self-definition, efforts that denied sexual difference and rejected social distinctions based upon sex. A clear refutation of such ill-informed re-imaging of the fictionalized Wollstonecraft can be seen in the characterization of her heroines in the early work *Mary, a Fiction* and her final fragment, *The Wrongs of Woman, or Maria*. In the last chapter I explored how Wollstonecraft's mature writing on sexuality and marriage in *The Wrongs of Woman* did more than politicize the wrongs suffered by women in a patriarchal society. In this didactic fiction Wollstonecraft exposed the danger posed to the female reader by an overidentification with the heroines of romantic novels. I began this study by examining Wollstonecraft's argument in response to Rousseau's Sophie and Julie, that when a woman sees herself in the sentimental heroines of fiction she becomes complicit in her own seduction and subjugation. I conclude my analysis by focusing attention on the harm done to women's intellectual history by identifying Wollstonecraft with the fictional feminist as created in the books of both Godwin and Sherwood.

Mary Wollstonecraft's life and work raises intriguing questions about the intersections between philosophy and feminism. Her writings were marked by a tension between mind and body that is familiar to modern readers of canonical political thought. What may be unfamiliar is the oppositional discourse created by feminist authors such as Wollstonecraft in response to the gender blind spots of the canonical tradition. The canonized forefathers were unable to visualize women as political beings and, by hiding them within the home, absented women from the canonical stories of the good society. One reason Wollstonecraft's didactic novels and polemical rights tracts may be little known to readers today is that, as both woman and author, she refused to remain within the gender borders separating public and private spheres and refused also to respect the discursive boundaries between philosophy and fiction.

Throughout this study I have argued that the corpus of Wollstonecraft's writing, from her adolescent letters to her final fiction, provides us with a unique example of the transformation of a female reader into a feminist author at the end of a century of Enlightenment. Wollstonecraft, as female reader, was well aware that women were not present at the level of meaning in most philosophical tracts. Therefore, as feminist author, she rejected the traditional opposition between marriage and quest plots in patriarchal political thought, in which women were born only to "propagate and rot." In her efforts to form a feminist philosophy she believed she was the "first of a new genus." Indeed, in theorizing the subject position of women, she performed an act of political genesis, creating a woman with mind enough to shape her own destiny. In both her semi-autobiographical novels, the heroines Mary and Maria display unconventional morality and an open disdain for the opinions of the world. Wollstonecraft utilized different literary forms to further her larger political project: *the vindication of the political rights of woman*. Her two radical fictions aimed at politicizing female readers. Modern readers can use her writing to explore the creative intersections between philosophy, fiction, and feminism.

Yet even as we do so it is important to remember that Wollstonecraft was a lifelong critic of the novel. As a feminist author she noted the poverty of philosophy in telling the stories of women's lives. However, throughout her literary career she remained deeply ambivalent about the role of the novel in the daily life of a woman confined within the walls of her household. Wollstonecraft wrote in her first book, *Thoughts on the Education of Daughters*, that although parents should encourage their children to read, they must be mindful of the corrupting influence of romances upon innocent young girls. After reading *Emile* Wollstonecraft published *Mary, a Fiction*, in which she fashioned a new type of heroine whose "thinking powers" differentiated her from the famous characters of sentimental fiction.[3] The fictional Mary embodied the possibility and problems of the self-educated woman in an age when women's education was aimed at helping others. Wollstonecraft's heroine turns the table on the traditional role of husband's helpmate by using her powers outside the marriage bond to serve the needs of friends and neighbors. Ultimately, there is no place for a woman who chooses this path in life and the fiction ends with a nod to the future.

From this fictional context, then, it is not surprising that in *A Vindication of the Rights of Woman* Wollstonecraft instructed female readers to put aside the gothic romance and take up a volume of history or a tract on natural philosophy in order to strengthen their minds for the "warfare of life." In this rights tract she battled with the male authors of philosophical treatises and sentimental novels who portrayed women as "perpetual children unable to stand alone." Wollstonecraft argued that false notions of sexual difference limited the life choices of all women. Whereas Rousseau claimed in the *Social Contract* that democratic self-rule was a garland over the chains of government, she asserted that theories of women's natural weakness of mind and body enchained females from their birth.[4] At the time of her death Wollstonecraft tried to "break the chains of theory" by writing a novel that would "embody" both her political ideas and her personal sentiments concerning the subjection of her sex. In *The Wrongs of Woman, or Maria* the feminist author likened the condition of married women under English law to prisoners "bastilled for life" at the time of the French Revolution. Wollstonecraft's attempts to work out in a fictional format the public consequences of private behavior led her to plot a distinctly feminist philosophy, and to experiment with different literary genres so that her critique of patriarchal society would reach a female audience of novel readers. A critical examination of her writing, from conduct books and reviews to novels and polemical tracts, complicates our modern understanding of the discursive boundaries between fiction and philosophy by raising questions about the politics of gender and genre.

I have explored Wollstonecraft's literary strategies and the issue of genre to illustrate the politics of gender. While the issues of gender and genre have been well canvassed within the field of literature, literary criticism is no substitute for political analysis.[5] Yet political theorists have failed to recognize the extent to which our notion of genre—what distinguishes political tract from polemical novel—is critical to understanding the history of women's political writing. If we want to seriously examine women's contribution to political culture and the rights debates of the eighteenth century, we must turn to the novel.

Wollstonecraft used the novel in expressly political ways and she also approached political writing in a novel manner.[6] During her lifetime the novel was widely recognized as a female literary genre. Denied the authority to enter political discourse, women used the novel as a discursive space for their own social commentary. In many ways the novel democratized discourse by multiplying the messengers; conservative and liberal writers of both sexes used this literary form to reach a growing audience. Thus in the 1790s the novel alternately reinforced and subverted gender politics.

Wollstonecraft herself contributed to the controversy surrounding the novel both in her own experimental use of the genre and in her reviews of popular fiction. Historian G. J. Barker-Benfield has argued that the popularity of the sentimental novel evidenced the growing acceptance of the moral philosophies of Edmund Burke, David Hume, and Adam Smith.[7] In this cultural context the novel encouraged the wider dissemination of philosophical principles and often highlighted the role of the individual in the reformation of society. The female reader, herself the subject of intense theoretical scrutiny, was thrust to the center of a reformist social practice. The women who frequented circulating libraries were learning the language of reform, and a significant number of these female readers began to write themselves. Within the pages of fiction, women wrote about the sexes, the arts and sciences, society and politics. The political consequences of these literary transgressions were widely debated in the late eighteenth century as polemicists decried the revolutionary potential of the novel. Indeed, Edmund Burke claimed in his *Reflections on the Revolution in France* that the new philosophies of the rights of men were nothing more than fictions.[8] Thus, Mary Wollstonecraft engaged in a form of revolutionary politics by trying to fictionalize the wrongs that women suffered as a sex denied their birthright by the philosophers of the rights of man.

Wollstonecraft's transformation from female reader into feminist author has been described by scholars and pundits as a theoretical trespass. She "braved censure" for daring to respond to Edmund Burke in the form of a political polemic in *A Vindication of the Rights of Men*. Reviewers claimed that women who wielded the pen should champion the rights of the female sex. Rising to the challenge, she wrote *A Vindication of the Rights of Woman*, in which she attacked Jean-Jacques Rousseau's notion of a woman's place in society. In her private behavior too, she stepped outside the bounds of convention, creating a public scandal at the end of the eighteenth century. As the controversial author of two rights tracts Wollstonecraft traveled to revolutionary France and took an American lover, Gilbert Imlay, who fathered her first child. Eventually rejected by Imlay, she attempted suicide, journeyed through Scandinavia writing passionate prose (which would be published as *Letters Written during a Short Residence in Sweden, Denmark, and Norway*), and upon returning to London entered into an affair with anarchist philosopher William

Godwin. Soon after, she found herself pregnant again, and the two philosophers who had previously denounced marriage were wed in a church ceremony. Within months Wollstonecraft died of childbed fever, and Godwin published his *Memoirs* in a collection of her posthumous works, which included the novel *The Wrongs of Woman, or Maria*. In 1798 the reading public condemned the feminist author who had championed the rational mind, first in reply to Burke and later in response to Rousseau, for being guilty of giving in to the erotic desires of the female body. In death, Wollstonecraft had at last become the Mary of fiction.

The real damage caused by William Godwin in the *Memoirs* is that he began a process of historical revisionism that would shift attention away from Wollstonecraft's political theory toward her personal story. He argued that by uniting her revolutionary theory with a rebellious personal practice she was a model of virtue for other women. Instead, friends and foes alike condemned this interpretation of Wollstonecraft's life work, claiming that she personified the perils of the public woman by acting out a male model of virtue unsuited to her sex. In the eighteenth century the term *public woman* referred most commonly to the prostitute. Following the publication of the *Memoirs*, Wollstonecraft herself was likened to a whore in the press. The following stanza comes from the *Anti-Jacobin Review*:

> William hath penn'd a waggon-load of stuff,
> And Mary's life at last he needs must write,
> Thinking her whoredoms were not known enough,
> Till fairly printed off in black and white.[9]

Her theory of political rights for women became equated with a philosophy of free love. Her argument for women to experience civic virtue through participation in politics was ridiculed as opening the door to gender-bending and public promiscuity.

Godwin's attempt to vindicate his wife's actions horrified readers, and he quickly revised the first edition of the *Memoirs* in an effort to rehabilitate the author of the *Rights of Woman* by disavowing her theoretical legacy as a thinking woman and casting her in a more sex-appropriate role as a woman of feeling. In the end this strategy failed, because by divulging the intimate details of her love life and the sensational scenes of her death in childbed Godwin made a warning of Wollstonecraft for future generations.

While Godwin's *Memoirs* ruined Wollstonecraft's reputation after her death, a comment of hers, in a letter from Scandinavia, vividly demonstrates that she very well knew the personal cost of being a rebel. "All the world is a stage, thought I; and few are there in it who do not play the part they have learnt by rote; and those who do not, seem marks set up to be pelted at by fortune; or rather as sign-posts, which point out the road to others, whilst forced to stand still themselves amid the mud and the dust."[10]

PUBLIC PERSONA

> It has always appeared to me, that to give the public some account of the life of a person of eminent merit deceased, is a duty incumbent on the survivors. It seldom happens that such a person passes through life, without being the subject of thoughtless calumny, or malignant misrepresentation.
>
> —William Godwin, *Memoirs of the Author of the "Rights of Woman"*

In the months following the death of his wife, William Godwin coped with his grief by pouring his emotional energy into editing Wollstonecraft's novel *The Wrongs of Woman*, examining her papers (some of which he burned), and collecting her letters to Gilbert Imlay for posthumous publication by Joseph Johnson. He also turned to Johnson for detailed information about Wollstonecraft's career, which he could use in the biography he was in the midst of writing. Wollstonecraft's friend and publisher produced for Godwin a lengthy letter that he entitled "A Few Facts," which highlighted her early years as an author and her efforts as a daughter and sister to support her family through their numerous personal struggles and financial hardships. Johnson recounted that he and Wollstonecraft had spent "many of her afternoons and more of her evenings," together over his shop in Saint Paul's Churchyard. Of these encounters he concluded "she was incapable of disguise, whatever was the state of her mind it appeared when she entered."[11] Strange, then, that the portrait of Wollstonecraft that emerges from Godwin's pen is so at odds with the image of the author that comes alive within Johnson's "A Few Facts."

In the *Memoirs* William Godwin sought to do justice to the

memory of Mary Wollstonecraft. It seems that the public persona of the "amazonian" author of the *Rights of Woman* was very different from the private person whom he had come to love. "The justice that is done the illustrious dead, converts into the fairest source of animation and encouragement to those who would follow the same career. The human species at large is interested in this justice, as it teaches them to place their respect and affection, upon those qualities that best deserve to be esteemed and loved" (204). And who better for men and women to respect and esteem than the author of the *Rights of Woman?* In writing this text Godwin claimed that Wollstonecraft believed herself to be "standing forth in defense of one half of the human species, laboring under a yoke which, through all the records of time, had degraded them from the station of rational beings, and almost sunk them to the level of the brutes" (231). Yet his eulogy did more to dissuade than to encourage women from following in Wollstonecraft's footsteps. Godwin attempted to reconcile the author, considered a hyena in petticoats for daring to write about politics, to the human species by emphasizing her womanly nature. It would appear that she was not what she seemed:

> In the champion of her sex, who was described as endeavouring to invest them all with the rights of man, those whom curiosity prompted to seek the occasion of beholding her, expected to find a sturdy, muscular, raw-boned virago and they were not a little surprised, when, instead of all this, they found a woman, lovely in her person, and in the best and most engaging sense, feminine in her manners. (232)

Since Godwin equated her "best" qualities with her femininity, as opposed to her authority as a writer, it is no surprise that in the following paragraph he criticized the lack of "method and arrangement" in *A Vindication of the Rights of Woman.* Speaking in the voice of the canonized forefathers he stated, "When tried by the hoary and long-established laws of literary composition, it can scarcely maintain its claim to be placed in the first class of human productions." Once again, when writing about rights Wollstonecraft had been relegated to second-class status by her sex. It was for subsequent generations of readers emboldened by the rights of woman to reassess her worth as a writer. Godwin concluded she "will perhaps here-after be found to have performed more substantial service for the cause of her sex, than all the other writers, male or female, that ever felt themselves animated in the behalf of oppressed and injured beauty" (232).

This refashioning of the feminist is interesting in light of Wollstonecraft's own comments about her presence in *Rights of Woman*. She wrote to the Jacobite poet William Roscoe while sitting for a portrait he had commissioned of her that, if the painting did not provide an accurate image, she would soon provide him with a book that would reveal herself fully, "head and heart":

> Be it known to you, my dear Sir, that I am actually sitting for the picture and that it will be shortly forthcoming. I do not imagine that it will be a very striking likeness; but, if you do not find me in it, I will send you a more faithful sketch—a book that I am now writing, in which *I* myself, for I cannot yet attain to Homer's dignity, shall certainly appear, head and heart—but this is between ourselves—pray respect a woman's secret.[12]

Wollstonecraft's own sense of self and the value she placed upon her production are erased by Godwin's pen. What is worse, in his own efforts to "champion oppressed and injured beauty" in the person of his wife, he vilified her memory by revealing her most intimate secrets. Richard Holmes tells us that William Roscoe wrote the following in his copy of the *Memoirs:*

> Hard was thy fate in all the scenes of life
> As daughter, sister, mother, friend and wife;
> But harder still, thy fate in death we own,
> Thus mourn'd by Godwin with a heart of stone.[13]

In his pages William Godwin candidly recounted Wollstonecraft's relationships with the painter Henry Fuseli as well as with the ex-patriot Gilbert Imlay. Shifting the scene from London to Paris he found "it almost unnecessary to mention" that the author of the *Rights of Woman* "was personally acquainted with the majority of the leaders of the French revolution" (238–39). Instead he focused upon Wollstonecraft's affair with Imlay, which he described as "that species of connection for which her heart secretly panted and which had the effect of diffusing an immediate tranquility and cheerfulness over her manners" (239). What kind of creature would engage in such an illicit affair? As Godwin details this connection, Wollstonecraft disappears from view as the woman is lost in the man and her head is subsumed by her heart. Godwin replaces the public image of the author as a "manly virago" with the private image of a Mary as a "female Werter [sic]." In this biography the feminist author becomes more feminine by being likened to Goethe's suffering, young Werther beset by emotional storm and stress. Godwin wrote that she was caught up in the emotions of personal and political upheaval and that "her whole character seemed to change with a change of fortune." Quite a revolution indeed, as Wollstonecraft is transformed again this time into a metaphorical serpent. "She was like a serpent upon a rock, that casts its slough, and appears again with the brilliancy, the sleekness, and the elastic activity of its happiest age." Godwin reveals that in Wollstonecraft's own words her sexual awakening was "talking a new language to her" (242). "Now, for the first time in her life, she gave loose to all the sensibilities of her nature" (243). But in describing her expressions of sexuality, he is hampered by the old language of women's nature found within the works of the canonized forefathers. Like Burke, he identifies Wollstonecraft's experimentation in revolutionary Paris as a process of de-evolution. She goes from being a woman to an animal and to an animal of the lowest order, the proverbial snake who is the ancient enemy of female virtue. Following Rousseau, Godwin casts Wollstonecraft from the Garden of Eden by surmising that sexual knowledge outside of marriage makes her a man.

William Godwin toned down his account of Mary Wollstonecraft's love affair with Gilbert Imlay in the second edition of the *Memoirs*. Specifically, he dropped all reference to her "serpentine sexuality" and argued that Wollstonecraft's "mistake" in regard to Imlay was that she "did not give full play to her judgement in this most important choice of life. . . . The least that can be said of the connection that she now formed, is, that it was a very unequal one. In years the parties were a match for each other; in every other point they were ill fitted for so entire an intimacy" (243).

This lapse of judgment takes on new meaning when contrasted with another significant change to the second edition, a few paragraphs that Godwin added to the concluding chapter of the biography on sex and intellect. "A circumstance by which the two sexes are particularly distinguished from each other, is, that the one is accustomed more to the exercise of its reasoning powers, and the other of its feelings." Sounding just like the tutor Jean-Jacques, Godwin remarks that the size and shape of women's bodies make them "more delicate and susceptible of impression than men." Since women as a result of their nature (stature?) are given a "less intellectual education" than their male counterparts, they are "more unreservedly under the empire of feeling." The consequence of the imperial sway of feeling is that women often make errors of judgment in love and life. Men are subject to different errors of judgment, which arise from improper reasoning such as sophistry and skepticism. Godwin argues that the corrective for these gender troubles is the free association between men and women, so that each can monitor the other. He summarizes his gender analysis by stating unequivocally, "Mary and myself perhaps each carried farther than to its common extent the characteristics of the sexes to which we belonged" (276). The danger of Godwin's revisionist biography is that it reinscribes Rousseau's gender binary that men are born to think and women are born to feel and thus undermines the very premise of Wollstonecraft's political project—specifically, that in a democratic age reason should rule, and since women are rational beings they are capable of governing themselves. The reader is left to wonder who was Mary Wollstonecraft and what was the purpose of her revolutionary theory?

SEXUAL SUBJECTION

> In my work I am free, and more than that, I advocate a life I do not live. You see, Joseph, I am writing about the necessity of rationality for our sex. My sex. I turn around and betray myself. I am betraying all who read me. I am not the person I wish to become. I am not rational. I am not independent. I am a fraud.
> —Frances Sherwood, *Vindication*

Today, in reading Frances Sherwood's *Vindication*, we confront the political paradox that the very sexuality which obscured Mary Wollstonecraft's theory and made her life a cautionary tale for nineteenth-century feminists has made her a heroine uniquely suited to the sexual struggles that marked the end of the twentieth century. This revisionist story vindicates the masochistic behavior of a fictional Wollstonecraft, not the feminist author's intellectual contribution to the history of ideas. Sherwood claims that her innovative novel is "loosely based" on Wollstonecraft's life. Yet readers familiar with Wollstonecraft's writing may conclude that the heroine of this fiction—while not a Clarissa, Lady Grandison, or Sophie—is also not Mary Wollstonecraft.

How would Wollstonecraft, the female reader turned feminist author, have read and reacted to the heroine of *Vindication*? Would she recognize her own conflicted self in the pages of this novel, or would she agree with the author that the heroine is a fraud who has been betrayed by sexual desire into a life of dependence and irrationality? Sherwood writes in the "Author's Note" at the beginning of her work, "*Vindication* is a work of fiction." In this fiction "there are many deviations . . . from the actual history of Mary Wollstonecraft and her contemporaries. They were the inspiration thanks to which an imaginative world of its own came into being." Perhaps Frances Sherwood also imagines herself to be "the first of a new genus," for she, too, creates a heroine different from those "generally portrayed." The Wollstonecraft of Sherwood's invention differs from the woman of Godwin's biographical pen. She is also distant from the character crafted by Ralph Wardle in his *Critical Biography,* and from the woman portrayed in more recent scholarly treatments such as Claire Tomalin's *Life and Death of Mary Wollstonecraft* and Emily Sunstein's *A Different Face.*

Mary Wollstonecraft, as the novel feminist fashioned by Sherwood, is the product of severe physical and sexual abuse. She is formed by brutalizing experiences both inside and outside the home, violent violations that begin in childhood and continue after she becomes an adult. The beatings and sexual abuse leave an indelible mark on the tabula rasa of the heroine's mind. Sherwood emphasizes the depths of this psychic wound, identifying her heroine's state of mind in the story by a bizarre repetition compulsion that forms a troubled alphabet of self. Whenever the fictionalized Wollstonecraft is in physical danger or mental pain, she repeats the letters of a children's primer and their associations to calm her nerves and settle her mind. "A is for acorn that grows on an oak; B is for boy who delights in his book; C is for canister, holds Mamma's teas; D is a drum you may sound as you please."[14] Throughout Sherwood's *Vindication* the fictional Wollstonecraft is infantilized, as this children's grammar is substituted for the books that detail the historical feminist's mature understanding of ontology. The subject of Sherwood's fiction is objectified and sexualized in a manner that Mary Wollstonecraft in *Rights of Woman* associated with male writers propping up patriarchy. The newest Mary of fiction reflects a fractured vision of the feminist epistemology that the personal is political. Sherwood certainly does not do justice to Wollstonecraft's own account and analysis of the abuse she suffered or to the feminist theory she developed to politicize the victimization of girls and women.[15]

Indeed, the central feature of Sherwood's novel is the thematic presentation of Wollstonecraft's friends and lovers, each representing a distinct chapter in her life. But rather than treat these relationships as the source of self-knowledge and personal growth, Sherwood displays these bonds as the source of personal regression and sexual repression. This is particularly problematic because Godwin's "serpentine sexuality" was to Wollstonecraft a source of inner strength for women in climbing the tree of knowledge. The feminist author had enough experience of the world to know that love provides no Eden. But love did not always condemn women to the hell of Sherwood's story either.

For in *The Wrongs of Woman* Wollstonecraft vindicated women after their fall by claiming that females ate the forbidden fruit out of a desire for the experience and knowledge denied them by patriarchal institutions and sexual distinctions in society. To her mind passionate love had the power to transform men and women when the relationship was based on reciprocity and equality. This love could move a person beyond the "passionate precipice" into a new region of self-awareness and social understanding. Indeed, it could form the bonds of a revolutionary community that moved beyond the limitations of fraternity to the possibilities of civic friendship. The feminist author understood that women were brutalized by the mind-body split in philosophy. But she was also a critic of the novel, and she warned female readers not to be seduced by the portraits of sentimentality in the fictions of her day. Wollstonecraft warred against the male authors of tracts and novels who represented her sex as creatures of cunning born to feel rather than think.

The Wrongs of Woman brought this message home to female readers by challenging the sexual double standards of eighteenth-century English society, which rewarded men for rakish behavior while ostracizing the women victims of seduction or savagery. Wollstonecraft tells this tale not out of penis envy or from a desire to vent her sexual frustrations but, rather, to give voice to her anger at the hypocrisy and tyranny that chastise women for expressing their own desires. In creating Maria, a heroine who linked women's sexual liberation to the larger goals of political liberty, Wollstonecraft was a woman ahead of her time.

In the two centuries since her death Mary Wollstonecraft has been the subject of a memoir and several biographies and the heroine of a number of fictions. Yet each of these demonstrates that there are many perils in fictionalizing the philosopher of the *Rights of Woman,* dangers that center on the politics of subjectivity itself and that raise difficult questions about feminist efforts to politicize personal life. Many feminists identify with Mary Wollstonecraft, so much so that they conflate her life story with their own. Yet we can only know Wollstonecraft through her writings, her enduring legacy of critical thought and experimental practice. The feminist author left us numerous works on wide-ranging topics, which catalog many aspects of her personal experience of life in a revolutionary century. Indeed, she wrote that her reader would find a portrait of the author as a young woman by perusing her works. In the passionate prose she wrote on her journey through Sweden she acknowledged a fear losing of herself:

> I cannot bear to think of being no more—losing myself—though existence is often but a painful consciousness of misery; nay, it appears to me impossible that I should cease to exist, or that this active restless spirit, equally alive to joy and sorrow, should only be organized dust—ready to fly abroad the moment the spring snaps, or the spark goes out, which kept it together. Surely something resides in this heart that is not perishable—and life is more than a dream.[16]

This sentiment may indicate an ambivalence about the role of future interpretations of her work. It has been a curious phenomenon that in recent scholarly treatments she has been both honored and vilified, both praised and blamed, for not living up to the expectations of her modern feminist readers.[17] Yet in refashioning the historical Mary Wollstonecraft as a feminist for the twenty-first century, we would be wise to attend to her own criticisms of heroines. Sherwood's *Vindication* demonstrates that, in abandoning her theory, we make a novelty of Wollstonecraft's life.

READING WOLLSTONECRAFT

> For we are apt to forget, reading, as we tend to do, only the masterpieces of a bygone age, how great a power the body of literature possesses to impose itself: how it will not suffer itself to be read passively, but takes us and reads us; flouts our preconceptions; questions principles we had got in the habit of taking for granted, and in fact, splits us in two parts as we read, making us even as we enjoy, yield our ground or stick to our guns.
>
> —Virginia Woolf, *The Common Reader*

In her *Rights of Woman* Mary Wollstonecraft argued, "Absolute, uncontroverted authority, it seems, must subsist somewhere," but she questioned whether placing this authority universally in men was a "direct and exclusive appropriation of reason."[18] Male writers were authorized to speak and to act in the public domain by a civic virtue that was for women unobtainable. Jean-Jacques Rousseau on the title page of the *Social Contract* proudly proclaimed himself citizen of the city state of Geneva, while Edmund Burke relied upon his years of experience as a parliamentarian in the House of Commons to give credibility to his *Reflections on the Revolution in France*. In an era of democratic revolution, reason and the duties of citizenship replaced honor and rank in the discussion of political rights. Yet women were excluded by their sex from exercising the political rights that were their birthright as rational beings. Wollstonecraft recognized that political theory had created a "male aristocracy" incompatible with the rebirth of democracy:

> Rousseau would carry his male aristocracy still further, for he insinuates, that he should not blame those, who contend for leaving women in a state of the most profound ignorance, if it were not necessary in order to preserve her chastity and justify the man's choice, in the eyes of the world, to give her a little knowledge of men, and the customs produced by the human passions; else she might propagate at home without being rendered less voluptuous and innocent by the exercise of her understanding; excepting, indeed, during the first year of marriage, when she might employ it to dress like Sophia.[19]

Mary Wollstonecraft's ability to imagine women as political

subjects distinguished her writings from the works of other authors. Her heroines displayed "thinking powers" and her polemics demonstrated "more mind." Both were intended to empower her female readers by providing a much needed example of feminist authority. Wollstonecraft's challenge to political theory destabilized the categories of public man and private woman that support the philosophical structure of canonical political thought. The study of her writing requires us to explore how politics was engendered in the late eighteenth century.

In a century of enlightened thinking, Wollstonecraft found it necessary to employ multiple rhetorical strategies in order to claim the authority to address the critical issues of individual autonomy, political equality, and sexual difference. She contested gender boundaries by experimenting on the borders of genre, writing didactic works, thesis novels, and political tracts. The rhetorical strategies she used demand that we analyze the politics of authority and anonymity as well as the props of masquerade and sexual subterfuge. Her use of these literary devices, among others, suggest that for a woman to speak about the good society and the well-lived life she needed to mask or disguise her sexual identity. Indeed, Wollstonecraft's transgression of discursive borders led her to be identified by supporters and critics alike as a masculine woman. From our historical vantage point we may ask how a woman of masculine mind could articulate a feminist theory? What were the politics of Wollstonecraft's theoretical trespass? What lessons can we learn from her war of words with the canonized forefathers?

We gain new insights into the relationship of women to politics by reassessing our reading of the canon through the works of Mary Wollstonecraft. We can learn important lessons about liberty and property from a woman whose own undervalued labor as a lady's companion, seamstress, teacher, and governess led her to theorize the dependent nature of women's situation. Her groundbreaking work as an author answered the question of how a woman denied a classical education was authorized to write political theory.

If one was not authorized to write about politics by an elite education, then one must turn to experience as a legitimating force. Is it any wonder that Wollstonecraft's feminist political theory appears so new even today? Her writing is a touchstone for modern feminist political theorists. In her early works she modeled her writing after the productions of successful authors, using their form and structure as a template, but the ideas were her own, each sentence smudged by life. At the end of her career she eschewed models and experimented with new forms of political writing in an attempt to gain a female audience of novel readers unversed in political philosophy.

Her personal struggles as a woman and an author led her to articulate the dynamic connection between political writing and political rights, both of which she argued had been "confined to the male line since Adam downward." Her writing fundamentally challenged this male birthright, bringing to life a new form of political analysis born of a woman. Empowered by this act of political genesis we can imagine stories that have not been told by the fathers of the canon. Reading Wollstonecraft we begin to think about girls and women as political subjects themselves with their own unique contributions to make to the historical quest for the good society.

Notes

INTRODUCTION: AT WAR WITH THE WORDS

1. See Virginia Sapiro, *A Vindication of Political Virtue: The Political Theory of Mary Wollstonecraft* (Chicago: University of Chicago Press, 1992); Diane Coole, *Women in Political Theory* (Boulder: Lynne Reinner Publishers, 1993); Jane Roland Martin, *Reclaiming the Conversation: The Ideal of the Educated Woman* (New Haven: Yale University Press, 1985).
2. Mary Wollstonecraft, *A Vindication of the Rights of Men*, in *The Works of Mary Wollstonecraft*, vol. 5, ed. Marilyn Butler and Janet Todd (New York: New York University Press, 1989), 20.
3. Mary Wollstonecraft, *A Vindication of the Rights of Woman*, in ibid., 157.
4. Ibid., 215.
5. Mary Wollstonecraft, *Mary, a Fiction*, in *Works*, 1:5.
6. Anonymous review of *A Vindication of the Rights of Men* in *Gentleman's Magazine* 61 (February 1791): 151.
7. Mary Wollstonecraft, *The Wrongs of Woman, or Maria*, in *Works*, 1:94.
8. Sapiro, *Vindication*. Professor Sapiro and I catch a number of the same "thought fish" in our critical treatment of Wollstonecraft's political writing. My own research builds on Sapiro's historical analysis but our paths diverge over the issue of theorizing gender.
9. Gary Kelly's reading of Wollstonecraft reinforces the separation of men and women in the household and society. At the heart of the notion of the public and private split is the notion that a husband really can act in the interests of his wife, and Wollstonecraft never once supports this fundamental assumption. The other aspect of the patriarchal division of the spheres is the principle that a husband will protect a wife, and once more Wollstonecraft argues forcefully against this claim. These are the holes in Kelly's thesis about domestication. Gary Kelly, *Revolutionary Feminism: The Mind and Career of Mary Wollstonecraft* (New York: St. Martin's Press, 1992).
10. Wollstonecraft, *Rights of Woman*, 217.
11. See my interpretative essay and annotated bibliography, Wendy

Gunther-Canada, "The Same Subject Continued: Two Hundred Years of Wollstonecraft Scholarship," in *Feminist Interpretations of Mary Wollstonecraft*, ed. Maria Falco (University Park: Pennsylvania State University Press, 1996), 209–24.

12. Wendy Gunther-Canada, "Mary Wollstonecraft's 'Wild Wish': Confounding Sex in the Discourse on Political Rights," in Falco, *Feminist Interpretations*, 61–83; Susan Gubar, "Feminist Misogyny: Mary Wollstonecraft and the Paradox 'It Takes One to Know One,'" *Feminist Studies* 20, no. 3 (fall 1994): 453–73; Linda Kerber, *Women of the Republic: Intellect and Ideology in Revolutionary America* (New York: W. W. Norton, 1986); Joan Landes, *Women and the Public Sphere in the Age of the French Revolution* (Ithaca: Cornell University Press, 1988); Frances Sherwood, *Vindication* (New York: Farrar, Straus and Giroux, 1993); Lillian Faderman, "Who Hid Lesbian Theory?" in *Lesbian Studies*, ed. Margaret Cruikshank (Old Westbury, N.Y.: Feminist Press, 1982), 117; Cora Kaplan, *Sea Changes: Culture and Feminism* (London: Verso Press, 1986).

13. "But I war not with an individual when I contend for the rights of men and the liberty of reason." Wollstonecraft, *Rights of Men*, 7. Wollstonecraft made a similar statement in *Rights of Woman*, bringing Rousseau into the battle: "I war not with his ashes, but with his opinions. I war only with the sensibility that led him to degrade woman and make her a slave to love." *Rights of Woman*, 161.

14. Ibid., 166.
15. Ibid., 132.
16. Mary Wollstonecraft to Everina Wollstonecraft, November 7, 1787, in *The Collected Letters of Mary Wollstonecraft*, ed. Ralph Wardle (Ithaca: Cornell University Press, 1979), 164.

1: POLITICAL THEORY AND THE FEMALE READER

1. Jean-Jacques Rousseau, *Emile, or On Education*, ed. and trans. Allan Bloom (New York: Basic Books, 1979), 363.
2. Rousseau's gender theory continues to generate debate about sexual politics in the household and republic. See Joel Schwartz, *The Sexual Politics of Jean-Jacques Rousseau* (Chicago: University of Chicago Press, 1985); Penny Weiss, *Gendered Community* (New York: New York University Press, 1993).
3. See Wendy Brown, *Manhood and Politics* (Totowa, N.J.: Rowman and Littlefield, 1988); Anne Phillips, *Engendering Democracy* (University Park: Pennsylvania State University Press, 1991); Kathleen Jones, *Compassionate Authority* (London: Routledge, 1993); Linda Zerilli, *Signifying Woman: Culture and Chaos in Rousseau, Burke, and Mill*

Notes to Pages 15–21 ~ 175

(Ithaca: Cornell University Press, 1994).

4. Moira Gatens, *Feminism and Philosophy: Perspectives on Difference and Equality* (Bloomington: University of Indiana Press, 1991), 3 (emphasis in original).

5. Wollstonecraft, *Rights of Woman*, 76.

6. Rousseau, *Emile*, 391.

7. See Landes, *Women and the Public Sphere*. As Darnton put it, "[R]eading is a theme that appears everywhere in Rousseau's works. It obsessed him." Robert Darnton, *The Great Cat Massacre* (New York: Basic Books, 1984), 226. Nicola Watson, *Revolution and the Form of the British Novel, 1790–1825* (Oxford: Clarendon Press, 1994).

8. Rousseau, *Emile*, 387.

9. Ibid., 168.

10. Ibid., 184–85.

11. Weiss, *Gendered Community*.

12. Schwartz, *Sexual Politics*, 83.

13. Heilbrun argues that for women to achieve independence and for the sexes to be equal in society it is necessary for new stories to be invented, in which females leave the private spaces of the home to quest after an autonomous self in the public sphere. "Marriage, in fiction even more than in real life, has been the woman's adventure, the object of her quest, her journey's end." *Reinventing Womanhood* (New York: W. W. Norton, 1979), 171.

14. In Pateman's account, the patriarchal history of political philosophy subsumes the story of women as autonomous political subjects. The social contract is founded upon a preexisting sexual contract that subjugates all women to all men. Pateman argues that this sexual contract is a precondition of the egalitarian social contract that offers men equality and liberty at the cost of sexual subordination for women. Carole Pateman, *Sexual Contract* (Stanford: Stanford University Press, 1988). But whereas in political theory the story of female subjectivity seems to end with sexual segregation, in literature women's quest for independence has often been portrayed within the gothic novel. See Sandra Gilbert and Susan Gubar, *Madwoman in the Attic: The Woman Writer and the Nineteenth-Century Imagination* (New Haven: Yale University Press, 1979).

15. Rousseau, *Emile*, 386.

16. Ibid., 402.

17. Ibid., 368.

18. Ibid., 396.

19. Kaplan, *Sea Changes*, 60. Kaplan makes explicit the politics of reading in the eighteenth century and points to Wollstonecraft's contribution in democratizing discourse. "Late-eighteenth-century theories of reading, as they appeared in both aesthetic and political discourses, assumed a fairly direct relationship between reading and action, especially in the naive reader, the barely literate, uneducated working-class

person—and women. In this period of expanding literacy and political turmoil, the question of the ability to read is at the center both of progressive programs which sought to radicalize the mass of people, and conservative resistance to revolution." Ibid., 122.

20. Wollstonecraft, *Wrongs of Woman*, 96.
21. Rousseau, *Emile*, 390.
22. Wollstonecraft, *Rights of Woman*, 173, 187 (long quotation).
23. Kaplan, *Sea Changes*, 60; Wollstonecraft, *Rights of Woman*, 173.
24. G. J. Barker-Benfield, *The Culture of Sensibility: Sex and Society in Eighteenth-Century Britain* (Chicago: University of Chicago Press, 1992), 162–63.
25. Wollstonecraft, *Rights of Women*, 131.
26. Wollstonecraft cited in Barker-Benfield, *Culture of Sensibility*, 162.
27. Ibid.
28. Jean-Jacques Rousseau, *La Nouvelle Heloise*, ed. and trans. Judith McDowell (University Park: Pennsylvania State University Press, 1987), 68–69. References will be given parenthetically in the text.
29. Wollstonecraft, *Rights of Woman*, 46
30. Ibid., 95.
31. Ibid., 245.
32. Janet Todd, "The Biographies of Mary Wollstonecraft," *Signs* 1 (1976): 721–34.
33. Wollstonecraft, *Mary, a Fiction*, 12, 10, 11.
34. This scene is recounted in Claire Tomalin, *The Life and Death of Mary Wollstonecraft* (New York: New American Library, 1974), 57–63.
35. Wollstonecraft, *Rights of Woman*, 110 (emphasis in original).
36. Wollstonecraft, *Collected Letters*, 227.
37. William Godwin, *Memoirs of the Author of "The Rights of Woman,"* ed. Richard Holmes (New York: Penguin Books, 1987), 258.
38. Wollstonecraft writes of the taking of the Bastille: "Thus was the nation saved by the almost incredible exertion of an indignant people; who felt, for the first time, that they were sovereign, and that their power was commensurate to their will. This was certainly a splendid example, to prove, that nothing can resist a people determined to live free; and then it appeared clear, that the freedom of France did not depend on a few men, whatever might be their virtues or abilities, but alone on the will of the nation." Mary Wollstonecraft, *An Historical and Moral View of the French Revolution*, in *Works*, 6:100.
39. Wollstonecraft, *Wrongs of Woman*, 88.
40. I trace the development of this argument in Wollstonecraft's first *Vindication*, in "The Politics of Sense and Sensibility: Mary Wollstonecraft and Catharine Macaulay on Edmund Burke's *Reflections on the Revolution in France*," in *Women Writers and the Early Modern British Political Tradition*, ed. Hilda Smith (New York: Cambridge University Press, 1998), 126–47.

2: A VOICE FROM THE VOID

1. Wollstonecraft, *Rights of Woman*, 132.
2. Pateman, *Sexual Contract*, 221.
3. See Susan Moller Okin, *Women in Western Political Thought* (Princeton: Princeton University Press, 1979); Martin, *Reclaiming the Conversation*; Pateman, *Sexual Contract*; Coole, *Women in Political Theory*.
4. See Carol Gilligan, Nona Lyons, and Trudy Hammer, eds., *Making Connections: The Relational Worlds of Adolescent Girls at the Emma Willard School* (Cambridge: Harvard University Press, 1990); Luce Irigaray, *This Sex Which Is Not One*, trans. Catherine Porter (Ithaca: Cornell University Press, 1985); Jill McLean Taylor, Carol Gilligan, and Amy Sullivan, eds., *Between Voice and Silence: Women and Girls, Race, and Relationship* (Cambridge: Harvard University Press, 1995).
5. Carol Gilligan, "Teaching Shakespeare's Sisters: Notes from the Underground of Female Adolescence," in Gilligan, Lyons, and Hammer, *Making Connections*, 25.
6. "I should likewise beg pardon for not beginning sooner so agreeable a correspondence as that I promise myself yours will prove, but from a lady of your singular good nature I promise myself indulgence." Mary Wollstonecraft to Jane Arden, May 1–20, 1773, *Collected Letters*, 51–52.
7. Wollstonecraft to Arden, June 4–July 31, 1773. Ibid., 56.
8. Ibid., 57.
9. Wollstonecraft to Everina Wollstonecraft, January 1784. Ibid., 86.
10. Wollstonecraft to Arden, June 4, 1773–November 16, 1774. Ibid., 60.
11. Ibid., 60–61.
12. Wollstonecraft to Arden, May–June 1779. Ibid., 64.
13. Wollstonecraft to Arden, December 10, 1779–January 5, 1780. Ibid., 70–71.
14. Wollstonecraft to Arden, April–June 1780. Ibid., 72.
15. Ibid., 71–72.
16. Wollstonecraft to Arden, June–August 1780. Ibid., 75.
17. Wollstonecraft to Arden, April–June 1780. Ibid., 73.
18. Wollstonecraft to Arden, October 20, 1782–August 10, 1783. Ibid., 79.
19. Ibid. (my emphasis).
20. Ibid.
21. Wollstonecraft to her sister Everina, November 7, 1787. Ibid., 164.
22. Mary Wollstonecraft, *Thoughts on the Education of Daughters*, in *Works*, 4:5, 7. Page references will be given parenthetically in the text. See also Mary Poovey, *The Proper Lady and the Woman Writer* (Chicago: University of Chicago Press, 1984), 14.

23. Poovey, *Proper Lady*, 13.
24. Tomalin, *Life and Death*, 39.
25. See "Vulnerability by Marriage," in Susan Moller Okin, *Justice, Gender, and the Family* (New York: Basic Books, 1989).
26. Wollstonecraft, *Mary, a Fiction*, 5 (original emphasis). Page references will be given parenthetically in the text.
27. Wollstonecraft to Everina Wollstonecraft, March 22, 1797, *Collected Letters*, 385.
28. J. M. S. Tompkins, *The Popular Novel in England, 1770–1800* (Lincoln: University of Nebraska Press, 1961), 314.
29. Geoffrey Summerfield, *Fantasy and Reason* (Athens: University of Georgia Press, 1984), 229.
30. Mary Wollstonecraft, *Original Stories from Real Life; with Conversations, Calculated to Regulate the Affections, and Form the Mind to Truth and Goodness*, in *Works*, 4:361. Page references will be given parenthetically in the text.
31. Mary Wollstonecraft, *The Female Reader*, in *Works*, 4:55.
32. Zerilli, *Signifying Woman*. Zerilli's argument about woman as a signifier of the abyss or the unspeakable in political discourse demonstrates the canonical conventions that deny woman voice. However, her study of Rousseau, Burke, and Mill does not explore how historical women responded in their own writing to the representations of womanhood within the texts of the canonized forefathers.

3: THE REBEL WRITER AND THE RIGHTS OF MEN

1. Godwin, *Memoirs of the Author*, 229.
2. David Bromwich, "Wollstonecraft as a Critic of Burke," *Political Theory* 23, no. 4 (November 1995): 618.
3. Anonymous reviews of *A Vindication of the Rights of Men*, in *Critical Review* 70 (December 1790): 694–96; *Gentleman's Magazine* 61 (February 1791): 151–54; and *General Magazine or Impartial Review* 4 (January 1791): 26–27.
4. Ralph Wardle, *Mary Wollstonecraft: A Critical Biography* (Lincoln: University of Nebraska Press, 1966), 111, 117.
5. Ibid., 118.
6. "But what the reviewers said was unimportant; obviously all of them had approached Mary's essay with preconceived notions and merely wrote what their editors and readers demanded that they write of such an essay. What mattered was that they all said something, that they were not expected to ignore the work of this upstart young woman who had hitherto hardly presumed to trespass on the field of legitimate literature, much less the field of politics." Ibid., 121. Wardle's statement reiter-

ates Burke's gendered notions of authority and political discourse. I disagree with him about the importance of what the reviewers said about Wollstonecraft's first *Vindication*. Their responses would set the stage for her articulation of the rights of woman.

    7. Godwin, *Memoirs of the Author*, 235–36.

    8. Wollstonecraft, *Rights of Men*, 9. References will be given parenthetically in the text.

    9. Edmund Burke, *Reflections on the Revolution in France*, ed. John Pocock (Indianapolis: Hackett Publishers, 1989), 5. References will be given parenthetically in the text.

    10. Virginia Woolf claims, "Anonymous was a woman." *A Room of One's Own* (New York: Harcourt Brace Jovanovich, 1957), 51. For many Wollstonecraft scholars the anonymous first edition of *Rights of Men* has gone with little or no notice. Ralph Wardle comments in passing that several contemporary reviews of the controversial text remarked on the fact that the author was a female, when Wollstonecraft's identity was revealed with the publication of the second edition. Wardle, *Mary Wollstonecraft*, 120–21. Virginia Sapiro echoes the suggestion of the reviewer from the *Critical Review* that Wollstonecraft had "disguised herself as a man" within her work. Sapiro claims that the "disguise" is not a matter of anonymity but of a woman authoring political theory. Sapiro, *Vindication*, 24. Gary Kelly's skillful rhetorical analysis of Wollstonecraft's text curiously discounts her anonymity. He remarks that, for "tactical reasons," Wollstonecraft "uses masculine pronouns throughout, nowhere indicating that she is a woman or that the masculine gender assumed for humanity by such language is an issue for her." Kelly, *Revolutionary Feminism*, 90. But this logic seems to refute Kelly's own discussion of the limitations of gender and genre in political discourse. Indeed, Kelly notes that Wollstonecraft's name was not her only addition to the second edition of her reply to Burke. Wollstonecraft revised her concluding paragraph to include a sentence in which she again credits the rights of men to a benevolent God. Kelly writes, "As a 'mere' woman author writing on politics she had need to invoke divine validation" (100). Wollstonecraft, *Rights of Men*, 99–100.

    11. Wollstonecraft, *Rights of Woman*, 123.

    12. Godwin, *Memoirs of the Author*, 226. Poovey in *Proper Lady* examines the conflicts between ladylike behavior and literary authority in her study of the work of Mary Wollstonecraft, of her youngest daughter, Mary Shelley, and of Jane Austen.

    13. Wardle, *Mary Wollstonecraft*, 117–18; Poovey, *Proper Lady*, 57.

    14. Linda Zerilli discusses the implications of the exclusion of women from the discourse of political theory in "Machiavelli's Sisters: Women and 'the Conversation' of Political Theory," *Political Theory* 19, no. 2 (May 1991): 252–76. Wollstonecraft's writings suggest that women

were not entirely absent from the debates of their age. What is problematic is that the contributions of these "sisters" have not been included by the "brothers" in forming the canon that educates future generations.

15. Sapiro, *Vindication,* 187.

16. For many eighteenth-century authors, both men and women, anonymity provided the opportunity for publication without public knowledge of the author's identity. It has been frequently noted that anonymity was of greater importance for women authors because it protected them and their work from the ridicule that popularly greeted women writers. In the early part of her career, Mary Wollstonecraft often wrote anonymously. Moira Ferguson investigates the mystery man "Mr. Cresswick" whose name appears on the title page of Wollstonecraft's work *The Female Reader.* "Mary Wollstonecraft and Mr. Cresswick," *Philological Quarterly* 62, no. 4 (fall 1983): 459–75.

17. Vivien Jones, ed., *Women in the Eighteenth Century* (London: Routledge Press, 1990), 4. Wollstonecraft clearly articulates a vision of rational women formed for futurity in opposition to Burke's "lisping creatures" made only for love.

18. Tom Furniss, *Edmund Burke's Aesthetic Ideology* (New York: Cambridge University Press, 1993), 5.

19. Most modern readings of the *Reflections* tend to ignore the centrality of gender in Burke's analysis of the events in France. There have been a number of notable exceptions to this trend, which have led to exciting new work on Burke. Along with Tom Furniss, there is the work of feminist theorist Linda Zerilli who argues that Burke's conservative classic portrays the revolt in France as a sexual revolution. In *Signifying Woman,* Zerilli claims that woman acts as both sign and signifier of the boundaries of political discourse and the gendered borders of the public sphere. Zerilli's gender criticism seems to be at odds with more established interpretations of the *Reflections,* but it has much in common with the rhetorical analyses of two earlier critics of Burke, Mary Wollstonecraft and Catharine Macaulay Graham. Wollstonecraft scholar Virginia Sapiro in *Vindication,* her study of Wollstonecraft's political theory, also provides a feminist reading of the *Reflections.* My own interpretation of Wollstonecraft's reply to Burke in the next section highlights the differences between our understandings of the role that gender plays in her *Rights of Men.*

20. Zerilli, *Signifying Woman,* 63.

21. Terry Castle writes in her study of the masquerade, "At the deepest level the masquerade's work was that of deinstitutionalization. Eighteenth-century English culture was founded on a set of institutionalized oppositions: European and Oriental, masculine and feminine, human and animal, natural and supernatural. . . . At the masquerade, however, counterposed institutions everywhere collapsed into one another, as did ideological categories: masculinity into femininity, 'Englishness' into exoticism, humanity into bestiality. Without the principle of opposition, the

ordering principle of civilization itself, the classification of entities became impossible." *Masquerade and Civilization* (Stanford: Stanford University Press, 1986), 78.

22. Sapiro, *Vindication*, 189.

23. Wollstonecraft throws Burke's argument off its ideological axis by portraying the queen as vulgar. Gary Kelly correctly argues that both authors use gender as a template with which to measure the progress of a nation. "In both Burke and Wollstonecraft the condition of women represents the values of an entire society and culture." Kelly, *Revolutionary Feminism*, 95. In *Rights of Woman*, Wollstonecraft reveals the full extent of her philosophical differences with Burke by breaking the gender template in order to create new forms of citizenship that can embody women as political subjects.

24. Anonymous review of *A Vindication of the Rights of Men* in *Analytical Review* 8 (December 1790): 416. The other woman bold enough to respond to Burke was Catharine Macaulay Graham, who penned *Observations on the Reflections of the Right Honorable Edmund Burke* (London: Edward and Charles Dilly, 1790). I provide a comparative analysis of these bold replies in the essay "Politics of Sense and Sensibility," 126–47.

25. Tom Furniss writes that Wollstonecraft's "central strategy is to identify the feminine with the ancien régime and the masculine with bourgeois radicalism. She thus challenges conventional assumptions about the relation between gender characteristics and sexual anatomy by insisting that the 'manly' and the 'feminine' are, at best, unnatural exaggerations of physiological differences between the sexes." Furniss, *Edmund Burke's Aesthetic Ideology*, 191.

26. Sapiro has noted of this passage that Wollstonecraft contrasted "his nightmare women with his dream woman: the queen, whom he envisioned as immaculate beauty and domesticity. . . . Where Burke, in effect, employed the classic Eve and Mary ideals to illustrate different sectors of the moral world, Wollstonecraft drew them together in a common portrait of human life." Sapiro, *Vindication*, 203.

27. Ida Macalpine and Richard Hunter provide a fascinating study of madness and eighteenth-century medicine in *George III and the Mad-Business* (London: Pimlico, 1993).

28. In the discursive context of the late twentieth century, Wollstonecraft's rhetorical ploy raises critical questions about democratic thought and feminist theory. A number of feminist scholars have argued that Wollstonecraft's appropriation of the language of the rights debates suggests a fear of women's abuse of language. See Kaplan, *Sea Changes;* Landes, *Women and the Public Sphere.* Both of these studies focus on Wollstonecraft's later treatise, *A Vindication of the Rights of Woman,* and do not explore the lessons she may have learned about authority and audience from the publication of her reply to Burke.

29. "Perhaps with an implicit reference to the difference in their power, she acknowledged that even if she wrote more, she would in effect be silenced anyway." Sapiro, *Vindication,* 205.

30. Godwin, *Memoirs of the Author,* 230.

31. Anonymous review of *A Vindication of the Rights of Men,* in *Gentleman's Magazine* 61 (February 1791): 151. I am fascinated by the threat of the "horse-laugh." Wollstonecraft asserts in the opening paragraph of the her reply to Burke, "Reverencing the rights of humanity, I shall dare to assert them; not intimidated by the horse laugh that you have raised." Wollstonecraft, *Rights of Men,* 7. The reviewer apologizes for laughing at a lady but is overcome by the joke of a woman claiming to defend the rights of gentlemen like himself. It appears that laughter has often ended discussions about women's role within the political community. Plato tells us in book 5 of the *Republic* that Socrates heard the roar of laughter when he proposed that both women and men be educated for leadership of the just republic. Allan Bloom who, in his bestselling book *The Closing of the American Mind* dismissed feminist teachings within academe as a farce, also wrote that "Book V [of Plato's *Republic*] is preposterous, and Socrates expects it to be ridiculed. It provokes both laughter and rage in its contempt for convention and nature, in its wounding of all the dearest sensibilities of masculine pride and shame, the family, and statesmanship and the city." *The Republic of Plato* (New York: Basic Books, 1968), 380. Bloom's linkage of laughter and rage suggests that, for women to share in the good society, men will have to sacrifice much of what they value of the well-lived life. Feminist scholars know only too well that there is nothing funny about the historical struggle of women for an independent and equitable civil existence.

32. Joanna Russ, *How to Suppress Women's Writing* (Austin: University of Texas Press, 1983), 20.

33. Anonymous review of *A Vindication of the Rights of Men,* in *Gentleman's Magazine* 61 (February): 154.

34. Abigail Adams echoed Wollstonecraft when she too denounced the "stale and shameful" tricks of revolutionary men who denied women their individual freedoms in the newly constituted American democracy. Abigail Adams to John Adams, March 31, 1776, in *Feminism: The Essential Historical Writings,* ed. Miriam Schneir (New York: Vintage Press, 1972).

35. George Stead Veitch, *The Genesis of Parliamentary Reform* (Hamden, Conn.: Archon Books, 1965), 167.

36. Sapiro, *Vindication,* 201. I agree with Professor Sapiro that any discussion of Wollstonecraft's reply to Burke demands a critical examination of the language politics of the late eighteenth century. However, my own interpretation of the *Rights of Men* represents a fundamental departure from Sapiro's work in that I seek to understand the role of gender in Wollstonecraft's argument as well as in the reception of her pamphlet.

Sapiro discounts the influence of gender on the style and substance of the *Rights of Men*: "Whether there is strong evidence that gender accounts for differences in Wollstonecraft's and Burke's displays of emotion (I would be very surprised if there were), it is probably easier for reader's eyes to see natural and explicable emotion in a woman's than [in] a man's text." *Vindication*, 206. Surprise aside, the evidence suggests that, whereas Burke's display of emotion made him widely popular with readers (including "the Ladies"), Wollstonecraft's own emotional reply to Burke was dismissed as unfair and sensational because she was a woman. While I certainly do not claim that Wollstonecraft had a fully developed theory of gender at the time she wrote her defense of the rights of man, I do believe that her personal and political experience as a woman writing in response to Burke led her to vindicate, in a subsequent text, the rights of her sex.

37. Dr. Richard Price to Miss Wollstonecraft, December 17, 1790, in Pforzheimer Collection, reel 7.

38. Wollstonecraft wrote to her sister Everina that she had attended a masquerade ball in Dublin while she was a governess within the household of the Lord and Lady Kingsborough. She accompanied Lady Kingsborough and an acquaintance to the ball dressed in a domino. Castle notes that the domino was a full-body covering, which when worn with a mask entirely disguised the sex of the partygoer. Castle, *Masquerade and Civilization*. This incident is especially intriguing because Wollstonecraft claimed to act as an "interpreter" for the other young woman of the party, who, in taking on the garb of a woodland sprite, could not converse with others outside the state of nature. Wollstonecraft to Everina Wollstonecraft, March 14, 1787, *Collected Letters*, 143.

39. It is interesting to note that once the question of whether Mrs. W. was a "real or fictitious lady" was resolved, perhaps by the publication the following year of the *Rights of Woman*, Wollstonecraft's work was no longer examined critically within the pages of the *Gentleman's Review*.

40. Rousseau, *Emile*, 367.
41. Godwin, *Memoirs of the Author*, 230.
42. Wollstonecraft, *Rights of Woman*, 157.

4: THE FEMINIST AUTHOR AND WOMEN'S RIGHTS

1. Wollstonecraft, *Rights of Woman*, 75. References will be given parenthetically in the text for this chapter.

2. Poovey, *Proper Lady*.
3. Rousseau, *Emile*, 363.
4. "A greater variety of absurd stories have been related concerning the hyaena than any other quadruped. The antients gravely tell us, that

the hyaena is alternately male and female; that, when it brings forth, suckles, and rears its young, it continues to be female during the whole year; but that, the following year, it resumes the functions of the male, and makes its companion submit to the lot of the female. This story, it is apparent, has no other foundation than the fissure under the tail which is common to the male as well as the female, independent of the organs of generation peculiar to both sexes, which, in the hyaena, are similar to those of all other quadrupeds." Walpole's identification of Wollstonecraft as a hyena in petticoats takes on a particular distinction in light of the following sentence in Buffon's history: "The hyaena has been said to imitate the human voice, to remember the names of shepherds, to call upon, to fascinate, and to deprive them of the power of motion; and, at the same time, to terrify the shepherdesses, to make them run from and neglect their flocks, to render them frantic with love &c.—All this might happen without the hyaena! And I here stop, lest I should, with Pliny, incure the censure of delighting in compiling and relating ridiculous fables." George-Louis Leclerc, comte de Buffon, "The Natural History of the Hyaena," in *Natural History: General and Particular,* vol. 5, ed. and trans. William Smellie (London: Strahan and Cadell, 1781), 235–37.

5. Carol Blum, *Rousseau and the Republic of Virtue* (Ithaca: Cornell University Press, 1986); Sara Melzer and Leslie Rabine, eds., *Rebel Daughters: Women and the French Revolution* (New York: Oxford University Press, 1992); Harriet Applewhite and Darline Levy, eds., *Women and Politics in the Age of the Democratic Revolution* (Ann Arbor: University of Michigan Press, 1993).

6. Rousseau, *Emile,* 357.

7. In a chapter entitled, "New Girls for Old," Robert Palfrey Utter and Gwendolyn Bridges Needham discuss the innovations of Wollstonecraft's rational pedagogy for women as well as her criticisms of the portraits of femininity within the works of the most respected men of her era. "Mary Wollstonecraft may be said to have begun it when, in 1792, in her *Vindication of the Rights of Woman,* she sailed over the entrenched positions of her opponents, dropped high explosives, and mapped enough territory to keep her followers busy for a century and a half. She made direct hits on the Lass with the Delicate Air, the prude, the innocence-ignorance theory, on Rousseau, on Dr. Fordyce; she mopped up a lot of liquid sorrow; she advocated athletics; she heralded emancipation." *Pamela's Daughters* (New York: Macmillan, 1936), 385.

8. For Hazel Mews, this quotation indicates that Wollstonecraft assumed her readers were familiar with the writings of Gregory, Fordyce, and Rousseau: "Her detailed and incensed analysis of the views expressed by Gregory, Fordyce and even Rousseau, in her section called 'Animadversions of some of the Writers who have rendered Women Objects of Pity, bordering on Contempt' in *A Vindication of the Rights of Woman,* is an indication of how widespread she believes the influence of

these writers to be." This is an important point. Hazel Mews, *Frail Vessels: Women's Role in Women's Novels from Fanny Burney to George Elliot* (London: University of London Athlone Press, 1969), 13.

9. Landes, *Women and the Public Sphere*, 65.

10. According to Utter and Bridges, Wollstonecraft disputed Rousseau's connection of ignorance and chastity. "She urges upon all women to subordinate every duty to that of improving their minds. She does not believe that female morons can guard the priceless pearl of chastity by the density of their ignorance and the protection of heaven." *Pamela's Daughters*, 387.

11. Jean-Jacques Rousseau, *Discourse on the Origin and the Foundations of Inequality Among Men*, trans. Victor Gourevitch (New York: Perennial Library, 1986), 139.

12. Coole, *Women in Political Theory*, 82.

13. Rousseau, *Emile*, 365.

14. In this analysis Wollstonecraft prefigures Pateman's argument that a sexual contract, in which all men rule over all women, is the foundation of modern social contract theory, in which all men are equal by law. Pateman, *Sexual Contract*.

15. Sapiro, *Vindication*, 262–63.

16. Mary Hays, *Female Biography: or, Memoirs of Illustrious and Celebrated Women, of all Ages and Countries* (London: Richard Phillips, 1802).

17. Bathsua Makin, *An Essay to Review the Antient Education of Gentlewomen, in Religion, Manners, Arts & Tongues. With An Answer to the Objections against this Way of Education* (London: J.D. to be sold by the Parkhurst, at the Bible and Crown, 1673), 3, 3–4, 10, 10.

18. Mary Astell, *A Serious Proposal to the Ladies, for the Advancement of their True and Greatest Interest* (London: J. Wilken, 1695), 70.

19. Ibid., 68.

20. Dr. John Gregory, *A Father's Legacy to His Daughters* (Edinburgh: A. Strahan and T. Cadell, 1788), 122.

21. Dr. James Fordyce, *Sermons to Young Women* (Philadelphia: Carey and Riley of New York, 1809), 138.

22. Catharine Macaulay, *Letters on Education* (London: Charles Dilly, 1790).

23. Sarah Trimmer, *Reflections on the Education of Children* (London: 1792. Printed for T. Longman, Paternoster-Row; and J. and F. Rivington, St. Paul's Church-Yard).

24. Utter and Bridges, *Pamela's Daughters*, 389.

25. Wollstonecraft echoes Abigail Adams in bringing forth the threatening specter of disenfranchised women. Adams a decade earlier had warned her husband, John Adams, to remember "the ladies" when writing the American Constitution: "If particular care and attention is not paid to the ladies, we are determined to foment a rebellion, and will not hold

ourselves bound by any laws in which we have no voice or representation." Abigail Adams to John Adams, March 31, 1776, in Schneir, *Feminism*, 3.

26. See Christine Bolt, *The Women's Movement in the United States and Britain from the 1790s to the 1920s* (Amherst: University of Massachusetts Press, 1993); Linda Kerber, *Toward an Intellectual History of Women* (Chapel Hill: University of North Carolina Press, 1997).

27. For a discussion of the implications of this argument for classroom teaching, see my article "Teaching Mary Wollstonecraft: Women and the Canonical Conversation of Political Thought," *Feminist Teacher* 11, no. 1 (spring/summer 1997): 20–29.

28. Marilyn Butler, "Introductory Essay," in *Burke, Paine, Godwin, and the Revolution Controversy*, ed. Marilyn Butler (Cambridge: Cambridge University Press, 1984), 5 (original emphasis).

29. Martin treats the *Rights of Woman* in her study *Reclaiming a Conversation* and notes the absence of treatises on women's education by philosophers of education. She attempts to "reclaim a conversation" on the ideal of the educated woman by returning to the works of Plato, Rousseau, Wollstonecraft, Beecher, and Gilman. Martin's call for education for women focuses on women's "reproductive" acts, which she distinguishes from men's "productive" acts as citizens and workers. I find this false dualism very problematic. Martin's argument does little to address the political consequences of the sexually differentiated education she advocates.

30. Rousseau, *Emile*, 362, 363.

31. Utter and Bridges, *Pamela's Daughters*, 388. Utter and Bridges argue that contemporary British women writers who addressed the subject of women's education might have found Wollstonecraft's *Rights of Woman* too revolutionary. However, they suggest that Wollstonecraft's second vindication led to educational gains for girls and women in New England in the early nineteenth century.

32. The passage continues, "so that while physical love enervates man, as being his favorite recreation, he will endeavour to enslave woman:—and, who can tell, how many generations may be necessary to give vigour to the virtue and talents of the freed posterity of abject slaves?" *Rights of Woman*, 145.

33. In this declaration Wollstonecraft echoes her statement to Burke in the preface to *Rights of Men*: "But I war not with an individual when I contend for the rights of men and the liberty of reason. You see I do not condescend to cull my words to avoid the invidious phrase, nor shall I be prevented from giving a manly definition of it, by the flimsy ridicule which a lively fancy has interwoven with the present acceptation of the term." Wollstonecraft, *Rights of Men*, 7.

34. Her efforts to redefine motherhood are not entirely successful within the *Rights of Woman*. In the following chapter I discuss her notion of mothers' rights and duties in Wollstonecraft, *Wrongs of Woman*.

35. Rousseau, *Emile*, 361.
36. Anonymous review of *A Vindication of the Rights of Woman*, in *Analytical Review* 12, no. 3 (March 1792): 248.
37. Landes, *Women and the Public Sphere*, 131.
38. Ibid., 135.
39. Ibid., 65.

5: WRITING THE WRONGS OF POLITICS

1. Wollstonecraft, *Rights of Woman*, 70.
2. Wollstonecraft, *Wrongs of Woman*, 83. References will be given parenthetically in the text.
3. Moore, "Promises, Promises: The Fictional Philosophy in Mary Wollstonecraft's *Vindication of the Rights of Woman*," in *The Feminist Reader: Essays in Gender and the Politics of Literary Criticism*, ed. Catherine Belsey and Jane Moore (London: Basil Blackwell, 1989), 169.
4. Wollstonecraft, *Rights of Woman*, 215 (my emphasis).
5. Blackstone cited in Pateman, *Sexual Contract*, 91.
6. The play on words in the two titles is significant. It suggests that Wollstonecraft sought to attract new readers to this novel by reminding them of the controversial earlier treatise. I argue that many of these new readers would be women.
7. Virginia Woolf, *Three Guineas* (New York: Harcourt Brace Jovanovich, 1984), 58.
8. Wollstonecraft, *Historical and Moral View*, 100.
9. Lynn Hunt offers an intriguing study of the gender discourse of pre- and postrevolutionary France in *The Family Romance of the French Revolution* (Berkeley and Los Angeles: University of California Press, 1993).
10. Wollstonecraft's arguments concerning the political importance of motherhood differ considerably from Rousseau's, the century's most famous advocate of this gender ideology. See my article "Jean-Jacques Rousseau and Mary Wollstonecraft on the Sexual Politics of Republican Motherhood," *Southeastern Political Review* 27, no. 3 (September 1999): 469–90.
11. On September 20, 1792, the French National Assembly authorized divorce in an attempt to undermine the authority of the church and to establish secular power over "rituals of birth, death and marriage." Georges Lefebvre, *The French Revolution from Its Origins to 1793*, vol. 1, trans. Elizabeth Moss Evanson (New York: Columbia University Press, 1962), 244. Until 1843 in England divorce was impossible without a decree of parliament.

12. Elaine Showalter, *The Female Malady: Women, Madness, and English Culture, 1830–1980* (New York: Penguin Books, 1985), 1.

13. Jane Spencer, *The Rise of the Woman Novelist: From Aphra Behn to Jane Austen* (London: Basil Blackwell, 1986), 200, 133 (quotation).

14. In her second vindication, Wollstonecraft warns readers that "Novels, music, poetry, and gallantry, all tend to make women the creatures of sensation. . . . This overstretched sensibility naturally relaxes the other powers of the mind, and prevents intellect from attaining that sovereignty which it ought to attain to render a rational creature useful to others, and content with its own station: for the exercise of the understanding, as life advances, is the only method pointed out by nature to calm the passions" *Rights of Woman*, 130.

15. Certainly Maria was not the only woman who transposed Saint Preux's sentiments to a mortal demigod. Rousseau himself tells us in his *Confessions* that he credited the popularity of his novel with women to their propensity to see the author in the fictional lover. "What won me the women's favor was their belief that I had written my own story, and that I was myself the hero of my novel." Jean-Jacques Rousseau, *The Confessions*, trans. J. M. Cohen (New York: Penguin Books, 1953), 506.

16. Rousseau, *La Nouvelle Heloise*, 83.

17. Spencer, *Rise of the Woman Novelist*, 134.

18. He continues, "In Robespierre's Paris even Mary Wollstonecraft was in danger, and Tom Paine barely escaped the guillotine." Gary Kelly, *The English Jacobin Novel, 1780–1805* (Oxford: Clarendon Press, 1976), 10.

19. Spencer, *Rise of the Woman Novelist*, 135–36.

20. Ibid., 133.

21. Dale Spender, *Mothers of the Novel* (London: Pandora Press, 1986), 257.

22. Wollstonecraft, *Rights of Woman*, 257–58.

23. Mews, *Frail Vessels*, 27.

24. Mitzi Meyers, "Reform or Ruin: A Revolution in Female Manners," in *Studies in Eighteenth-Century Culture* (Madison: University of Wisconsin Press, 1982), 211.

25. Jerry C. Beasley, "Life's Episodes: Story and Its Form in the Eighteenth Century," in *The Idea of the Novel in the Eighteenth Century*, ed. Robert W. Uphaus (East Lansing, Mich.: Colleagues Press, 1988), 23.

26. Kaplan, *Sea Changes*, 10.

27. Spencer, *Rise of the Woman Novelist*, xi.

28. Woolf, *Room of One's Own*, 68. There is a problem with Woolf's analysis of the middle-class woman as author. Jane Spencer points out that women of all classes, but especially middle-class women, wrote in the eighteenth century to earn money to support themselves and their families. The restrictions on women's work in custom and

kind limited the economic opportunities of all women. For middle-class women, writing was seen as less objectionable than employment within the trades. Yet, as many women's narratives attest, making one's living with the pen in the eighteenth century was an unreliable and difficult enterprise.

29. Ruth Perry, *Women, Letters, and the Novel* (New York: AMS Press, 1980), x–xi.

30. Wollstonecraft, *Rights of Woman*, 256. For a discussion of the consequences of women's "imprisonment" within the canonical categories of political thought, see Virginia Sapiro, "Wollstonecraft, Feminism, and Democracy: 'Being Bastilled,'" in Falco, *Feminist Interpretations*, 33–45.

31. See Kaplan, *Sea Changes*, 60.

32. Wollstonecraft, *Rights of Woman*, 257.

33. Mary Wollstonecraft's literary legacy, however, was the birth of her second daughter, Mary Wollstonecraft Godwin Shelley, whose gothic novel *Frankenstein* carried the subtitle, *The Modern Prometheus*.

34. Spender, *Mothers of the Novel*, 256.

35. Godwin, *Memoirs of the Author*, 264.

36. Wollstonecraft, *Rights of Woman*, 208, 119.

37. Pateman, *Sexual Contract*, 12–13.

CONCLUSION: READING WOLLSTONECRAFT

1. Godwin, *Memoirs of the Author*, 242. References will be given parenthetically in the text.

2. Frances Sherwood, *Vindication* (New York: Farrar, Straus, and Giroux, 1993).

3. Wollstonecraft, *Mary, a Fiction*, 5.

4. Jean-Jacques Rousseau, *The Social Contract*, ed. Roger Masters, trans. Judith Masters (New York: St. Martin's Press, 1978), 46.

5. See Nancy Armstrong, *Desire and Domestic Fiction* (New York: Oxford University Press, 1987); Janet Todd, *The Sign of Angellica* (London: Virago Press, 1989); Patricia Meyers Spacks, *Desire and Truth* (Chicago: University of Chicago Press, 1990); Watson, *British Novel;* Claudia Johnson, *Equivocal Beings* (Chicago: University of Chicago Press, 1995).

6. The political novel was a family trademark. Godwin distinguished himself as the author of numerous polemical fictions, as did their daughter, Mary Wollstonecraft Godwin Shelley, famous author of the anti-Enlightenment *Frankenstein*.

7. Barker-Benfield, *Culture of Sensibility*, 225–28.

8. Burke, *Reflections*, 97.

9. Anonymous, "The Vision of Liberty: written in the Manner of Spencer," *Anti-Jacobin Review and Magazine* (April–August 1801), 518.

10. Mary Wollstonecraft, *Letters Written during a Short Residence in Sweden, Denmark, and Norway*, ed. Richard Holmes (New York: Penguin Books, 1987), 186.

11. Joseph Johnson, "A Few Facts," undated, Pforzheimer Collection, reel 9, Abinger Microfilm.

12. Wollstonecraft to William Roscoe, October 6, 1791, in *Collected Letters*, 202–3 (emphasis in original).

13. Roscoe cited in "Introductory Essay," in Mary Wollstonecraft and William Godwin, *Letters Written during a Short Residence in Sweden, Denmark, and Norway, and Memoirs of the Author of "The Rights of Woman,"* ed. Richard Holmes (New York: Penguin Books, 1987), 44–45.

14. Sherwood, *Vindication*, 27.

15. Carol Poston has argued that Wollstonecraft may indeed have been the victim of childhood sexual abuse, possibly incest. Poston's analysis draws from psychoanalytical theory and posits that the feminist author's ambivalence about the female body is a reflection of her own tortured experience of self. Carol Poston, "Mary Wollstonecraft and 'The Body Politic,'" in Falco, *Feminist Interpretations*, 85–104.

16. Wollstonecraft, *A Short Residence*, 112.

17. See Gunther-Canada, "The Same Subject Continued," 209–24.

18. Wollstonecraft, *Rights of Woman*, 157.

19. Ibid.

Bibliography

Anonymous. 1790. Review of *A Vindication of the Rights of Men*. *Analytical Review* 8 (December): 416–19.
Anonymous. 1790. Review of *A Vindication of the Rights of Men*. *Critical Review* 70 (December): 694–96.
Anonymous. 1791. Review of *A Vindication of the Rights of Men*. *General Magazine or Impartial Review* 4 (January): 26–27.
Anonymous. 1791. Review of *A Vindication of the Rights of Men*. *Gentleman's Magazine* 61 (February): 151–54.
Anonymous. 1792. Review of *A Vindication of the Rights of Woman*. *Analytical Review* 12, no. 3 (March): 241–48.
Anonymous. 1801. "The Vision of Liberty: written in the Manner of Spencer." *Anti-Jacobin Review and Magazine* (April–August): 518.
Applewhite, Harriet, and Darline Levy, eds. 1993. *Women and Politics in the Age of the Democratic Revolution*. Ann Arbor: University of Michigan Press.
Armstrong, Nancy. 1987. *Desire and Domestic Fiction*. New York: Oxford University Press.
Astell, Mary. 1695. *A Serious Proposal to the Ladies*. London: J. Wilken.
Barker-Benfield, G. J. 1992. *The Culture of Sensibility: Sex and Society in Eighteenth-Century Britain*. Chicago: University of Chicago Press.
Beasley, Jerry. 1988. "Life's Episodes: Story and Its Form in the Eighteenth Century." In *The Idea of the Novel in the Eighteenth Century*, ed. Robert W. Uphaus. East Lansing, Mich.: Colleagues Press.
Bloom, Allan. 1968. "Interpretive Essay." In *The Republic of Plato*. New York: Basic Books.
Blum, Carol. 1986. *Rousseau and the Republic of Virtue*. Ithaca: Cornell University Press.
Bolt, Christine. 1993. *The Women's Movement in the United States and Britain from the 1790s to the 1920s*. Amherst: University of Massachusetts Press.
Bromwich, David. 1995. "Wollstonecraft as a Critic of Burke." *Political Theory* 23, no. 4 (November): 617–34.
Brown, Wendy. 1988. *Manhood and Politics*. Totowa, N.J.: Rowman and Littlefield.
Buffon, George-Louis Leclerc, comte de. 1781. "The Natural History of the Hyaena." In *Natural History: General and Particular*, vol. 5, ed. and trans. William Smellie. London: Strahan and Cadell.

Burke, Edmund. [1757] 1812. *A Philosophical Enquiry into the Origin of our Ideas of the Sublime and the Beautiful.* London: F. C. and J. Rivington.
———. [1790] 1989. *Reflections on the Revolution in France.* Edited by John Pocock. Indianapolis: Hackett Publishers.
Butler, Marilyn, ed. 1984. *Burke, Paine, Godwin, and the Revolution Controversy.* Cambridge: Cambridge University Press.
Castle, Terry. 1986. *Masquerade and Civilization.* Stanford: Stanford University Press.
Coole, Diane. 1993. *Women in Political Theory.* Boulder: Lynne Reinner Publishers.
Darnton, Robert. 1984. *The Great Cat Massacre.* New York: Basic Books.
Faderman, Lillian. 1982. "Who Hid Lesbian Theory?" In *Lesbian Studies,* ed. Margaret Cruikshank. Old Westbury, N.Y.: Feminist Press.
Ferguson, Moira. 1983. "Mary Wollstonecraft and Mr. Cresswick." *Philological Quarterly* 62, no. 4 (fall): 459–75.
Fordyce, James. 1809. *Sermons to Young Women.* Philadelphia: Carey and Riley of New York.
Furniss, Tom. 1993. *Edmund Burke's Aesthetic Ideology.* New York: Cambridge University Press.
Gatens, Moira. 1991. *Feminism and Philosophy: Perspectives on Difference and Equality.* Bloomington: University of Indiana Press.
Gilbert, Sandra, and Susan Gubar. 1979. *Madwoman in the Attic: The Woman Writer and the Nineteenth-Century Imagination.* New Haven: Yale University Press.
Gilligan, Carol. 1990. "Teaching Shakespeare's Sisters: Notes from the Underground of Female Adolescence." In *Making Connections: The Relational Worlds of Adolescent Girls at the Emma Willard School,* ed. Carol Gilligan, Nona Lyons, and Trudy Hammer. Cambridge: Harvard University Press, 1990.
Godwin, William. [1798] 1987. *Memoirs of the Author of "The Rights of Woman."* Edited by Richard Holmes. New York: Penguin Books.
Gregory, John. 1788. *A Father's Legacy to His Daughters.* Edinburgh: A. Strahan and T. Cadell.
Gubar, Susan. 1994. "Feminist Misogyny: Mary Wollstonecraft and the Paradox 'It Takes One to Know One.'" *Feminist Studies* 20, no. 3 (fall): 453–73.
Gunther-Canada, Wendy. 1996. "Mary Wollstonecraft's 'Wild Wish': Confounding Sex in the Discourse on Political Rights." In *Feminist Interpretations of Mary Wollstonecraft,* ed. Maria Falco, 61–83. University Park: Pennsylvania State University Press.
———. 1996. "The Same Subject Continued: Two Hundred Years of Wollstonecraft Scholarship." In *Feminist Interpretations of Mary Wollstonecraft,* ed. Maria Falco, 209–24. University Park: Pennsylvania State University Press.

———. 1997. "Teaching Mary Wollstonecraft: Women and the Canonical Conversation of Political Thought." *Feminist Teacher* 11, no. 1 (spring/summer): 20–29.

———. 1998. "The Politics of Sense and Sensibility: Mary Wollstonecraft and Catharine Macaulay on Edmund Burke's *Reflections on the Revolution in France*." In *Women Writers and the Early Modern British Political Tradition*, ed. Hilda Smith, 126–47. New York: Cambridge University Press.

———. 1999. "Jean-Jacques Rousseau and Mary Wollstonecraft on the Sexual Politics of Republican Motherhood." *Southeastern Political Review* 27, no. 3 (September): 469–90.

Hays, Mary. 1802. *Female Biography: or, Memoirs of Illustrious and Celebrated Women, of all Ages and Countries*. London: Richard Phillips.

Heilbrun, Carolyn. 1979. *Reinventing Womanhood*. New York: W. W. Norton.

Hunt, Lynn. 1993. *The Family Romance of the French Revolution*. Berkeley and Los Angeles: University of California Press.

Irigaray, Luce. 1985. *This Sex Which Is Not One*. Translated by Catherine Porter. Ithaca: Cornell University Press.

Jacobus, Mary. 1989. "A Difference of View." In *The Feminist Reader: Essays in Gender and the Politics of Literary Criticism*, ed. Catherine Belsey and Jane Moore, 49–62. London: Basil Blackwell.

Johnson, Claudia. 1995. *Equivocal Beings*. Chicago: University of Chicago Press.

Johnson, Joseph. "A Few Facts." Undated manuscript in the Carl Pforzheimer Collection of Shelley and His Circle. The New York Public Library.

Jones, Kathleen. 1993. *Compassionate Authority*. London: Routledge.

Jones, Vivien, ed. 1990. *Women in the Eighteenth Century*. London: Routledge Press.

Kaplan, Cora. 1986. *Sea Changes: Culture and Feminism*. London: Verso Press.

Kelly, Gary. 1976. *The English Jacobin Novel, 1780–1805*. Oxford: Clarendon Press.

———. 1992. *Revolutionary Feminism: The Mind and Career of Mary Wollstonecraft*. New York: St. Martin's Press.

Kerber, Linda. 1986. *Women of the Republic: Intellect and Ideology in Revolutionary America*. New York: W. W. Norton.

———. 1997. *Toward an Intellectual History of Women*. Chapel Hill: University of North Carolina Press.

Landes, Joan. 1988. *Women and the Public Sphere in the Age of the French Revolution*. Ithaca: Cornell University Press.

Lefebvre, Georges. 1962. *The French Revolution from Its Origins to 1793*, vol. 1. Translated by Elizabeth Moss Evanson. New York: Columbia University Press.

Macalpine, Ida, and Richard Hunter. 1993. *George III and the Mad-Business*. London: Pimlico.
Macaulay Graham, Catharine. 1790. *Letters on Education*. London: Charles Dilly.
———. 1790. *Observations on the Reflections of the Right Honorable Edmund Burke*. London: Edward and Charles Dilly.
Makin, Bathsua. 1673. *An Essay to Review the Antient Education of Gentlewomen*. London: J. D. to be sold by the Parkhurst, at the Bible and Crown.
Martin, Jane Roland. 1985. *Reclaiming the Conversation: The Ideal of the Educated Woman*. New Haven: Yale University Press.
Melzer, Sara, and Leslie Rabine, eds. 1992. *Rebel Daughters: Women and the French Revolution*. New York: Oxford University Press.
Mews, Hazel. 1969. *Frail Vessels: Women's Role in Women's Novels from Fanny Burney to George Elliot*. London: University of London Athlone Press.
Meyers, Mitzi. 1982. "Reform or Ruin: A Revolution in Female Manners." In *Studies in Eighteenth-Century Culture*. Madison: University of Wisconsin Press.
Moore, Jane. 1989. "Promises, Promises: The Fictional Philosophy in Mary Wollstonecraft's *Vindication of the Rights of Woman*." In *The Feminist Reader: Essays in Gender and the Politics of Literary Criticism*, ed. Catherine Belsey and Jane Moore, 155–73. London: Basil Blackwell.
Okin, Susan Moller. 1979. *Women in Western Political Thought*. Princeton: Princeton University Press.
———. 1989. *Justice, Gender, and the Family*. New York: Basic Books.
Pateman, Carole. 1988. *The Sexual Contract*. Stanford: Stanford University Press.
Perry, Ruth. 1980. *Women, Letters, and the Novel*. New York: AMS Press.
Phillips, Anne. 1991. *Engendering Democracy*. University Park: Pennsylvania State University Press.
Poovey, Mary. 1984. *The Proper Lady and the Woman Writer*. Chicago: University of Chicago Press.
Poston, Carol. 1996. "Mary Wollstonecraft and 'The Body Politic.'" In *Feminist Interpretations of Mary Wollstonecraft*, ed. Maria Falco, 85–104. University Park: Pennsylvania State University Press.
Price, Richard. 1790. Manuscripts of letter from Richard Price to Mary Wollstonecraft dated December 17, 1790, in the Carl Pforzheimer Collection of Shelley and His Circle. The New York Public Library.
Rousseau, Jean-Jacques. [1755] 1986. *Discourse on the Origin and Foundations of Inequality Among Men*. Translated by Victor Gourevitch. New York: Perennial Library.
———. [1761] 1987. *La Nouvelle Heloise*. Edited and translated by Judith McDowell. University Park: Pennsylvania State University Press.
———. [1762] 1979. *Emile, or On Education*. Edited and translated by

Allan Bloom. New York: Basic Books.
———. [1762] 1978. *The Social Contract*. Edited by Roger Masters, translated by Judith Masters. New York: St. Martin's Press.
———. [1782] 1953. *The Confessions*. Translated by J. M. Cohen. New York: Penguin Books.
Russ, Joanna. 1983. *How to Suppress Women's Writing*. Austin: University of Texas Press.
Sapiro, Virginia. 1992. *A Vindication of Political Virtue: The Political Theory of Mary Wollstonecraft*. Chicago: University of Chicago Press.
———. 1996. "Wollstonecraft, Feminism, and Democracy: 'Being Bastilled.'" In *Feminist Interpretations of Mary Wollstonecraft*, ed. Maria Falco, 33–45. University Park: Pennsylvania State University Press.
Schneir, Miriam, ed. 1972. *Feminism: The Essential Historical Writings*. New York: Vintage Press.
Schwartz, Joel. 1985. *The Sexual Politics of Jean-Jacques Rousseau*. Chicago: University of Chicago Press.
Sherwood, Frances. 1993. *Vindication*. New York: Farrar, Straus and Giroux.
Showalter, Elaine. 1985. *The Female Malady: Women, Madness, and English Culture, 1830–1980*. New York: Penguin Books.
Spacks, Patricia Meyers. 1990. *Desire and Truth*. Chicago: University of Chicago Press.
Spencer, Jane. 1986. *The Rise of the Woman Novelist: From Aphra Behn to Jane Austen*. London: Basil Blackwell.
Spender, Dale. 1986. *Mothers of the Novel*. London: Pandora Press.
Summerfield, Geoffrey. 1984. *Fantasy and Reason*. Athens: University of Georgia Press.
Taylor, Jill McLean, Carol Gilligan, and Amy Sullivan, eds. 1995. *Between Voice and Silence: Women and Girls, Race, and Relationship*. Cambridge: Harvard University Press.
Todd, Janet. 1976. "The Biographies of Mary Wollstonecraft." *Signs* 1:721–34.
———. 1989. *The Sign of Angellica*. London: Virago Press.
Tomalin, Claire. 1974. *The Life and Death of Mary Wollstonecraft*. New York: New American Library.
Tompkins, J. M. S. 1961. *The Popular Novel in England, 1770–1800*. Lincoln: University of Nebraska Press.
Trimmer, Sarah. 1792. *Reflections on the Education of Children*. London: Printed for T. Longman, Paternoster-Row; and J. and F. Rivington, St. Paul's Church-Yard.
Utter, Robert Palfrey, and Gwendolyn Bridges Needham. 1936. *Pamela's Daughters*. New York: Macmillan.
Veitch, George Stead. [1913] 1965. *The Genesis of Parliamentary Reform*. Hamden, Conn.: Archon Books.

Wardle, Ralph. [1951] 1966. *Mary Wollstonecraft: A Critical Biography*. Lincoln: University of Nebraska Press.
Watson, Nicola. 1994. *Revolution and the Form of the British Novel, 1790–1825*. Oxford: Clarendon Press.
Weiss, Penny. 1993. *Gendered Community*. New York: New York University Press.
Wollstonecraft, Mary. [1787] 1989. *Thoughts on the Education of Daughters*. In *The Works of Mary Wollstonecraft*, vol. 4, ed. Marilyn Butler and Janet Todd. New York: New York University Press.
———. [1788] 1989. *Mary, a Fiction*. In *The Works of Mary Wollstonecraft*, vol. 1, ed. Marilyn Butler and Janet Todd. New York: New York University Press.
———. [1788] 1989. *Original Stories from Real Life; with Conversations, Calculated to Regulate the Affections, and Form the Mind to Truth and Goodness*. In *The Works of Mary Wollstonecraft*, vol. 4, ed. Marilyn Butler and Janet Todd. New York: New York University Press.
———. [1789] 1989. *The Female Reader*. In *The Works of Mary Wollstonecraft*, vol. 4, ed. Marilyn Butler and Janet Todd. New York: New York University Press.
———. [1790] 1989. *A Vindication of the Rights of Men*. In *The Works of Mary Wollstonecraft*, vol. 5, ed. Marilyn Butler and Janet Todd. New York: New York University Press.
———. [1792] 1989. *A Vindication of the Rights of Woman*. In *The Works of Mary Wollstonecraft*, vol. 5, ed. Marilyn Butler and Janet Todd. New York: New York University Press.
———. [1794] 1989. *An Historical and Moral View of the French Revolution*. In *The Works of Mary Wollstonecraft*, vol. 6, ed. Marilyn Butler and Janet Todd. New York: New York University Press.
———. [1796] 1987. *Letters Written during a Short Residence in Sweden, Denmark, and Norway*. Edited by Richard Holmes. New York: Penguin Books.
———. [1798] 1989. *The Wrongs of Woman, or Maria*. In *The Works of Mary Wollstonecraft*, vol. 1, ed. Marilyn Butler and Janet Todd. New York: New York University Press.
———. 1979. *The Collected Letters of Mary Wollstonecraft*. Edited by Ralph Wardle. Ithaca: Cornell University Press.
Woolf, Virginia. [1929] 1957. *A Room of One's Own*. New York: Harcourt Brace Jovanovich.
———. [1938] 1984. *Three Guineas*. New York: Harcourt Brace Jovanovich.
Zerilli, Linda. 1991. "Machiavelli's Sisters: Women and 'the Conversation' of Political Theory." *Political Theory* 19, no. 2 (May): 252–76.
———. 1994. *Signifying Woman: Culture and Chaos in Rousseau, Burke, and Mill*. Ithaca: Cornell University Press.

Index

Abelard and Heloise, 24–25, 119
abuse: domestic, 132, 135, 152; sexual, 146, 190n
American Revolution, 81, 88, 139
Analytical Review, 35, 73, 122
animals, 52, 64–65, 100; cruelty to, 32, 66
Anti-Jacobin Review, 143, 160
Arden, Jane, 33, 43–45, 48, 50
Aristotle, 14, 150
Astell, Mary, 9, 110–12
Augustine, Saint, 14–15
Austen, Jane, 45
authority, 4–6, 75, 91, 95; abuse of, 128; and anonymity, 75–76, 99, 179n, 180n; and femininity, 5, 9, 16, 77–78, 101–2, 124–25, 142, 144, 150, 162; parental, 15, 27. *See also* family; government

Barbauld, Anna Laetitia, 10, 52
Barker-Benfield, G. J., 23, 159
Behn, Aphra, 9
birthright, 39, 50, 96, 102, 159
Bishop, Meredith, 33, 49
Blackstone, Sir William, 132
Blake, William, 62, 65
Blood, Fanny, 33–34, 47, 49, 58
Bromwich, David, 58
Buffon, George-Louis Leclerc, comte de, 101, 184n
Burgh, James, 49
Burke, Edmund, 3, 11, 33, 69, 74, 76, 82, 84, 90, 98–99, 101, 143, 159, 160, 164; *Reflections on the Revolution in France*, 5–6, 11, 35, 53, 70–72, 74–75, 78, 98, 100, 159, 169
Butler, Marilyn, 116

Cambon, Madame de, 73
Chapone, Hester, 10, 110
charity, 63
Charlotte (queen of England), 87
children: relationship of, to adults, 43, 63. *See also* education; family; fathers and fatherhood; mothers and motherhood
chivalry, 5, 81, 83–84, 87, 95, 119
Christie, Thomas, 35, 73
citizenship, 85, 108, 113; birthright and, 39, 50, 96, 102, 159; and democracy, 36; and duty, 120, 169; and gender, 131; women and, 4, 5, 7, 10, 13–16, 42, 109, 122, 127–29, 133, 151, 154. *See also* government; republicanism; women
Clare, Rev., 47
class, 7, 11–12, 66, 91, 112; aristocratic, 78, 81, 85; and differences between women, 146, 149, 151; and education, 116; and hereditary wealth, 78–79; middle, 85. *See also* property
commerce, 63, 67
Coole, Diana, 106
corruption, 30, 68, 95; of society, 63

Darnton, Robert, 17

democracy, 10, 68, 79, 85, 141; and citizenship, 36, 143. *See* government

dependence, 4, 79, 103, 107, 119, 127; and women, 7, 11, 47, 170. *See also* independence

divorce, 136, 138–39. *See also* marriage

duty, 10; civic, 29, 109; gender and, 13, 42; and rights, 10; women and, 101, 120. *See also* citizenship; rights

education, 108, 130; in boarding schools, 57; and class, 23, 116; civic, 113, 115; coeducational, 109, 112; of females, 5–6, 8–11, 23, 26, 51–54, 57, 109, 116, 127, 133, 143, 147; of gentlewomen, 10, 57; methods of, 63, 66, 112; purpose of, 118; and sexual difference, 6, 102, 104, 107, 142; and women's rights, 113. *See also* women

emotion. *See* reason; sensibility

Enfield, William, 69

Enlightenment, 8, 9–10, 41, 74, 78; and human perfectibility, 9, 68, 113; and humanism, 8, 95, 121; philosophers of, 83, 91; philosophical traditions of, 14, 98; reason and, 8, 80; and women, 4, 8–9, 59. *See also* French Revolution

equality: civic, 12; political, 4, 12, 14, 99, 170. *See also* education; government; rights

family, 11, 103, 127; marriage and, 54; status of women in, 134. *See also* fathers and fatherhood; marriage; mothers and motherhood; parents and parenthood

fathers and fatherhood, 80, 106; duties of, 13. *See also* family; mothers and motherhood; parents and parenthood

femininity, 14, 77, 82, 99, 118; and authority, 9; definitions of, 21; models of, 145–46; and passivity, 84, 104; and rationality, 100, 107, 109, 127, 153; as sensibility, 20–24; and virginity, 26. *See also* human nature; masculinity

feminism, 121, 151; history of, 9–10; and philosophy, 156–57, 168

feminist theory, 68–69, 79, 94, 98, 128, 152–53; development of, 3–4, 9–12, 16, 41–42, 56, 69, 129; and women's rights, 15. *See also* political theory; Wollstonecraft, Mary; women

Fénelon, François de Salignac de La Mothe, 17–20, 39, 119, 138

Filmer, Sir Robert, 84

Fordyce, James, 51, 104, 112

French Revolution, 5, 10, 35–36, 68, 74, 76, 78, 81, 84–85, 97–98, 101, 113–14, 127, 134, 141, 153, 158, 163; and Robespierre, 140; and the Terror, 62. *See also* Enlightenment

friendship: civic, 95, 167; between women, 43–44, 46. *See also* love

Fuller, Margaret, 110

Furness, Tom, 82, 181n

Fuseli, Henry, 163

Gabell, Rev. Henry, 59

Gatens, Moira, 15

gender, 20, 78–79, 102, 131; and genre, 4–6, 12, 92–93, 122, 125, 158, 170. *See also* femininity; masculinity; men; women

Genlis, Madame Stepanie Felicite Brulart de, 69

Gentleman's Magazine, 5, 91–92, 94, 123

George III (king of England), 47,

87, 92

God, 9, 10, 64, 104; and duty, 10. *See also* religion

Godwin, William, 10, 38, 69, 72–73, 77, 96, 135, 140, 143, 159, 166; as editor of Wollstonecraft, 39, 149, 161. Works: *Caleb Williams*, 61; *Enquiry Concerning Political Justice*, 38, 61; *Memoirs of the Author of "The Rights of Woman,"* 12, 39, 71, 90, 123, 149–50, 155–56, 160–64, 167

government, 75–76; foundation of, 106; function of, 85; and family, 7, 13, 151–52; representatives of, 127; self-rule and, 30; tyranny and, 101, 114; women and, 102–3, 115. *See also* authority; citizenship; equality; family; republicanism

Gregory, John, 51, 107, 112

Hays, Mary, 10, 110, 143, 155
Heilbrun, Carolyn, 19, 175n
Hobbes, Thomas, 15, 106, 129
Holcroft, Thomas, 10, 140, 143
Holmes, Richard, 143
Hume, David, 5, 77, 159

Imlay, Gilbert, 36–38, 159, 161, 163–64
Inchbald, Elizabeth, 143
independence, 7, 42, 44, 80, 104, 120; of the female mind, 4, 6, 52; women and, 4, 108, 140. *See also* dependence
Irigaray, Luce, 42

Johnson, Joseph, 35–36, 38, 58, 72–73, 75, 78, 90, 91, 94, 98, 161
Jones, Vivien, 82
justice, 66, 140–41, 162. *See also* equality; government

Kaplan, Cora, 21–22, 144, 175–76n
Keegan-Paul, Charles, 37
Kelly, Gary, 7, 140, 173n, 179n
Kilmer, Dorothy, 52
Kingsborough, Lord and Lady, 34–35

Landes, Joan, 17, 105, 124
law, common, 80; illegitimacy and, 37; status of women in, 34, 44, 126–32, 134, 147, 151–52, 158. *See also* government; marriage
liberalism, 128, 151. *See also* political theory
liberty, 50, 76, 85; defined, 92; individual, 12, 141; women's sexual, 168. *See also* government; property
Locke, John, 5–6, 15, 56, 63, 72, 77, 85, 106, 129
Louis XVI (king of France), 36, 140
love, 46; and passion, 118. *See also* friendship; marriage

Macaulay, Catharine (Graham), 9, 10, 110, 113
Machiavelli, Niccolò, 5, 15, 77
madness, 87, 136; and women, 19, 29, 49, 137
Makin, Bathsua, 9, 110–12
manners, 100; and morals, 109. *See also* morals
Marie Antoinette (queen of France), 6, 11, 84, 86–87, 99
marriage, 29, 54, 61, 63, 109, 112, 127–28, 131, 135, 151–52; adultery in, 140; children and, 40; and coverture, 80, 132; as a contract, 39, 49, 56, 129, 140; and divorce, 136, 138–39; early, 56–57; economic dependence of women in, 23, 55, 60, 133, 135; legal status of women in, 12, 14, 34, 38, 59; in political theory, 19; women

and, 12, 40, 57–58, 60. See also abuse; divorce; family; parents and parenthood; women
masculinity, 14, 64, 77, 82, 100, 118, 124. See also femininity
men. See fathers and fatherhood; masculinity
Mews, Hazel, 143, 184–85n
Mill, John Stuart, 12, 69, 110, 115, 153
Milton, John, 53
monarchy and monarchical politics, 11, 83, 134; court culture of, 83, 85, 95
Moore, Jane, 130
More, Hannah, 113, 143
mothers and motherhood, 14, 121, 127, 132, 137–38, 147; duties of, 13, 120, 148; postpartum depression and, 49; republican, 135. See also family; fathers and fatherhood; parents and parenthood; women

nature: and culture, 14; female, 100, 102–5, 107, 162, 164; human, 10, 13, 57; state of, 101, 106, 107, 152. See also femininity; masculinity
Necker, Jacques, 73
novels, 7, 21, 61–62, 98, 145; epistolary, 25, 130; and women's rights, 144. See also Wollstonecraft, Mary

Opie, Amelia, 10, 143
oppression, 129; of women, 145, 152

Paine, Thomas, 10, 73–74, 113, 116
parents and parenthood, 51, 63, 109; and education, 64. See also fathers and fatherhood; mothers and motherhood

passion, 9, 56, 61; and knowledge, 29
Pateman, Carole, 19, 41, 129, 151, 175n
patriarchy: and politics, 9, 13, 18, 21, 23, 54, 60, 85, 92, 96, 106, 135; and society, 79, 81, 102, 108, 136, 146, 158. See also family; fathers and fatherhood; government; mothers and motherhood; political theory; women
Perry, Ruth, 145
Pizan, Christine de, 110
Plato, 5, 77; *The Republic*, 14, 26, 30, 40, 102, 117–18; Socrates and, 40, 102
Plutarch, 26
political theory, 41, 68, 69; and the canon, 3, 6, 8, 10–12, 15, 68–69, 110, 156; and the female reader, 13–39; feminist theory and, 8–12, 116; gender and, 5, 11, 16, 30; images of women in, 11, 13–16, 21, 27, 30, 69, 132, 156; and the marriage plot, 11, 17, 19–20, 27, 30–31, 134, 157; and the quest plot, 11, 17, 19, 27, 30–31, 157; and patriarchy, 9, 80; and Wollstonecraft, 3, 6, 8, 10–12, 16, 21, 97, 130–31, 151–54, 169–71; women and, 5–6, 9–11, 15, 25–26, 42, 68, 170. See also feminist theory; liberalism; republicanism
Poovey, Mary, 51, 54, 77
Poston, Carol, 190n
poverty. See class; property
pregnancy and childbirth, 34, 132, 146; and abortion, 146. See also family; mothers and motherhood; parents and parenthood; women
Price, Rev. Richard, 34, 36, 72, 75, 87, 93–94

property, 11, 76, 78–79, 85, 91–92, 112, 151; and inheritance, 59, 78–79, 148; primogeniture and, 23, 32, 67, 79, 92, 151; women and, 59, 62, 126, 132, 138. *See also* class; family; government; liberty prostitution, 135, 146; and marriage, 48. *See also* sexuality public and private spheres, 4, 7–8, 13, 19–31, 38, 69–70, 99, 101–2, 112, 114, 118, 124, 127–28, 131–32, 135, 141, 152, 156, 170. *See also* men; political theory; women

reason, 58, 60–61, 76, 79, 95, 98, 102, 108, 141; independence and, 149; and passion, 10, 22, 56, 150; and rationality, 137; and rights, 169; and virtue, 24; women and, 56, 99. *See also* education; Enlightenment; sensibility religion, 81, 83; and the Bible, 69 republicanism, 85, 114, 128, 151; and women, 31. *See also* government; mothers and motherhood; political theory; revolution revolution, 4. *See also* American Revolution; French Revolution Revolution Society, 75–76 Richardson, Samuel, 5 rights, 109; human, 95; natural, 38; of men, 87, 91, 153; property, 7; reason and, 136; of women, 11, 91, 153. *See also* birthright; citizenship; duty; marriage; women Roscoe, William, 163 Rousseau, Jean-Jacques, 3, 6, 12–13, 16, 18, 20, 33, 38, 63, 69, 72, 77, 88, 100–101, 104–5, 107, 117, 129, 150, 160, 164; on childhood development, 64; on marriage, 15, 28, 30; and naturalist fallacy, 106; and sexual difference, 13–14, 16–17, 19–20, 22, 28–29, 121, 159; on sexually differentiated education, 6, 17–18, 20, 114, 117. *See also* republicanism. Works: *Discourse on the Origin and Foundations of Inequality Among Men*, 105; *Emile*, 5–6, 11, 13–14, 17–23, 30, 39, 56, 59, 64–65, 100, 103, 118, 121, 153, 157; *La Nouvelle Heloise*, 11, 13–14, 21–30, 39, 53, 61, 103, 121, 138; *The Social Contract*, 13, 16, 30, 61, 106, 139, 158, 169; *Les Solitaires*, 20 Russ, Joanna, 92

Salzmann, Christian Gotthilf, 73 Sapiro, Virginia, 6–7, 79, 84, 90, 93, 109, 110, 179n, 181n, 182–83n Schwartz, Joel, 18 sensibility, 6, 21, 39, 86, 88–90, 99, 115, 127, 133, 141; reason and, 68. *See also* femininity; reason separate spheres. *See* public and private spheres sexuality, 8, 141, 144, 150; and corruption, 30; heterosexuality, 15; homosexuality, 8. *See* prostitution Shakespeare, William, 53, 69 Sherwood, Frances, 12, 155–56, 165–66, 168 slavery, 48, 89; African, 120; and education of slaves, 112; and ignorance, 120; marriage likened to, 61 Smith, Adam, 159 Smith, Charlotte, 69 social contract, 4, 13, 18–19, 80, 85, 88, 101, 129, 131, 140, 152; status of women in, 19, 29. *See also* citizenship; government; marriage

Spencer, Jane, 137, 140–41, 144
Spender, Dale, 142, 149
Stael, Germaine de, 110
Summerfield, Geoffrey, 62
Sunstein, Emily, 166

Talleyrand, Charles Maurice de, 97, 102, 114
Todd, Janet, 31
Tomalin, Claire, 166
Tompkin, J. M. S., 61
Trimmer, Sarah, 62, 110, 113

Veitch, George Stead, 92–93
virtue, 6, 26, 61, 63–66, 91, 100, 108, 115; civic, 79, 81, 109, 145, 160, 169; in men, 19, 64, 164; models of, 20; moral, 82; political, 95; and sexual character, 101; and sexual difference, 28; vicarious, 19, 28, 31, 36; and vice, 64, 89, 127; and virginity, 26–28; in women, 19–20, 105, 141, 164. *See also* Enlightenment; femininity; government; masculinity
Voltaire, 69

Walpole, Horace, 101, 124
Wardle, Ralph, 43, 72, 74, 77, 79, 166, 178–79n
Watson, Nicola, 17
wealth. *See* class; property
Weiss, Penny, 18
Williams, Helen Maria, 10
Wollstonecraft, Edward (father), 32, 44
Wollstonecraft, Eliza (sister), 33, 34, 49
Wollstonecraft, Elizabeth Dixon (mother), 32, 148
Wollstonecraft, Everina (sister), 49, 59
Wollstonecraft, Mary: as author, 3–9, 14, 39–40, 42–43, 50, 58, 63, 77, 89, 97, 99, 124, 161; and authority, 4, 10, 32, 36, 90, 94, 169–70; biography of, 31–39, 41, 43, 45, 72, 155, 161, 166, 168; and the canon, 3–12, 41, 97, 101–2, 153, 156, 170–71; death of, 39, 41, 149, 160; and education, 12, 16, 21–22, 31, 43, 68; education of, 33, 51, 68, 105; employment of, 45, 47, 58; and the female reader, 21–22; and feminism, 3, 4, 7, 9–12, 16, 21, 30, 39, 41, 48, 70, 79, 94, 98, 113, 121, 127–28, 135, 147, 151, 153, 155, 158, 167; friendships of, 43–44, 46–47; and the marriage plot, 11, 20, 22–24, 29, 30, 32, 36, 38, 49–50, 60, 151, 157; on marriage, 4, 43, 48–50, 55–56, 135; on motherhood, 49; and the novel, 21–22, 130, 142, 145–46, 157, 167; and parents, 4, 32–33, 49, 68, 147–48; and political theory, 3–6, 14, 16, 21, 40–41, 62, 93, 100, 110, 120, 123, 125, 150, 166, 169, 170; and pregnancy and childbirth, 9, 37, 39, 41, 49–50, 147, 160; and the quest plot, 11, 23–24, 38, 60, 157; and religion, 9, 55; and sexual equality, 14, 99; and sexuality, 8, 164–68; and siblings, 32–33, 43–44, 49; suicide attempts of, 37–38, 159; and vice, 63; and virtue, 8, 16, 24, 31, 160; and women's rights, 4, 10, 16, 31, 109, 113–14, 126, 142, 152. Works: *Letters Written during a Short Residence in Sweden, Denmark, and Norway*, 37, 159, 168; *The Female Reader*, 69, 73; *Mary, a Fiction*, 5, 11, 32, 35, 43, 55, 58–61, 66, 121,

144, 156–57; *Original Stories from Real Life*, 11, 43, 52, 62–65, 67, 73; *Thoughts on the Education of Daughters*, 5, 11, 21, 34, 43, 51, 53, 56, 58–59, 63, 66–67, 69, 109, 125, 157; *A Vindication of the Rights of Men*, 5, 11, 35, 71–73, 75, 101, 113–14, 122–24, 136, 149, 151, 159; *A Vindication of the Rights of Woman*, 5–6, 11, 31, 36, 38–39, 51, 53, 61, 75, 90, 142, 149, 151, 154, 157–59, 162–63, 167, 169; *The Wrongs of Woman*, 6, 12, 38–39, 121, 156, 160–61

Wollstonecraft, Ned (brother), 32, 33, 44

women: and citizenship, 4, 5, 10, 16, 42, 58, 80; and duty, 42, 101; education of, 110, 120; intellectual history of, 9, 11, 156; legal status of, 44, 76, 79, 92, 106; literacy of, 18–19, 23; and professions, 7, 133, 136; as readers, 6, 8–9, 12, 158, 168; and reason, 58, 59; rights of, 10, 11, 102; and weakness, 57, 82, 98; as writers, 7, 10, 61, 69, 83, 102, 109–10, 125, 143–44, 154, 158–59. *See also* femininity; feminism; feminist theory; novels; political theory; Wollstonecraft, Mary

Woolf, Virginia, 71, 133, 144, 169

Zerilli, Linda, 69, 83, 84, 178n, 179n, 180n